The Meaning of Language

The Meaning of Language

Robert M. Martin

A Bradford Book
The MIT Press
Cambridge, Massachusetts
London, England

Second printing, 1988
© 1987 Massachusetts Institute of Technology

This book was set in Palatino by Achorn Graphic Services and printed and bound by Halliday Lithograph in the United States of America.

Library of Congress Cataloging-in-Publication Data

Martin, Robert M.
  The meaning of language.

  "A Bradford book."
  Bibliography: p.
  Includes index.
  1. Languages—Philosophy.   2. Semantics (Philosophy)
1. Title.
P106.M354   1987   415   86-27575
ISBN 0-262-13224-9
ISBN 0-262-63108-3 (pbk.)

To George and Ethel Martin, my parents, who taught me to love language, and to Joanna and Erica Martin, my children, who learned it from me.

Contents

Acknowledgments

I warmly acknowledge invaluable help and encouragement from David Braybrooke (Dalhousie, Nova Scotia), Sheldon Wein (Otago, New Zealand), James Brown (Toronto), and James Kelly (Miami, Ohio), who read and criticized earlier drafts of this book. I also wish to thank my students in two philosophy of language classes at Dalhousie, who were victimized by having to read earlier versions, who helped me to recognize and fix some of the more unintelligible parts, and who convinced me that instruction in the philosophy of language is useful and possible. Also subjected to readings of some of the chapters were graduate students and colleagues at Dalhousie and at the University of Nebraska, who responded with helpful criticisms and suggestions.

And most of all, I thank my friend and colleague Terrance Tomkow. Terry's work on many of the issues treated here is some of the most original and powerful philosophy being done now. When his book on philosophy of psychology and language (*Against Representation*, Cambridge University Press) appears, it will revolutionize the field. My discussions with Terry about problems in philosophy of language in general and about my work while writing this have influenced this book profoundly. More than anything else, his arguments and encouragement have made this book possible.

The Meaning of Language

Introduction

Language is the most pervasive feature of our everyday experience. Almost all our activities are full of talking and listening to talk, reading and writing. The central feature of bits of language—what makes them *language*—is that they have meaning; so linguistic meaning is something you encounter more often and are more familiar with than just about anything else. It is remarkable, then, that it is so difficult to explain exactly what linguistic meaning is.

Here is a sample linguistic object:

The cat is on the mat.

To get a hint of these difficulties, ask yourself exactly what it is for this string of black marks on paper to have meaning. This string is a physical thing, and so is your left shoe and Cleveland, Ohio, and the planet Jupiter; but unlike those other physical objects, this one *means something*. But when we say that this string means something, what are we saying about it? What is it that makes these marks, and certain other marks and certain noises we make, mean something? Why don't other physical objects mean something? This book is devoted to examining philosophers' answers to these questions.

Philosophy of language has always been a central area of philosophical concern, but it has achieved even more prominence during the current century. The questions in this field are difficult, and because this century's philosophers have made so much progress in answering them, today's journal articles and books are usually quite technical, presupposing knowledge of a large stock of philosophical jargon, distinctions, positions, and arguments. The philosophy of language is therefore one of the hardest areas for the beginning student. This book attempts to solve this problem.

It is written for newcomers and presupposes absolutely no background in philosophy of language, or in philosophy in general. My aim is to provide a comprehensible and reasonably thorough introduction to the field; the readings listed throughout are basic and clear enough for readers to manage profitably. I avoid philosophical jargon, except when it has become so standard that readers can expect to find it, unexplained, in the literature and thus should know what it means; when this is the case, I define jargon terms at their first use.

The book is divided into two parts. The first, chapters 1 through 10, is concerned with a variety of miscellaneous matters, more or less centered around the question about what language is *for*—what meaning has to do with individual ideas and intentions and with social communication; chapters 8 and 9 introduce a powerful and influential family of ways of understanding meaning on the basis of the social place and function of language. The rest of the book (except for the last chapter) builds on and considers problems with the second major contemporary theoretical approach to meaning, which concentrates on the connection between bits of language and the bits of the world each is *about*. Many recent books and academic classes in the philosophy of language concentrate on the issues and approaches dealt with in the first or second parts of this book. One of my central aims has been to make both available and to connect them; realizing, however, that teachers and students may continue to wish to concentrate on one or the other, I have constructed things so that either part can be read independently. Readers who want only the bare basics can ignore chapters 3, 7, 10, 22, or 23 without damaging their comprehension of the rest. Chapters 1 through 10 can each stand more or less on their own, so dabblers can read these selectively and in any order without missing too much. Chapters 12 through 21, on the other hand, proceed linearly and cannot be understood unless the previous chapter has been read; so readers who do not wish to go through all of them should omit from the end, not the middle, of this part.

Beginners in philosophy should realize that philosophy is controversy and argument. In many other fields but not here, one begins by mastering accepted truths and reaches the disputed ground much later. Everywhere in this book, then, I give arguments for *and* against controversial positions. Sometimes it is clear what my own views are; readers should not, however, take these matters as settled but should approach all views critically and take opposing arguments seriously. Students should not be discouraged by this apparent indecisiveness; nor should they worry if their instructor disagrees with several important interpretations or arguments in this book. Controversy is what makes philosophy exciting; and it does not imply that there is no philosophical progress or truth or that one opinion is just as good as any other. On the contrary, it is my hope that the reader will finish this book with philosophical convictions, with appreciation of what some of humanity's best minds have accomplished, and with the knowledge that the philosophical enterprise is progressive and worthwhile.

Special Conventions

1. Language shows up in both spoken and written form. Throughout this text I refer to what people say or write, hear or read. In order to avoid tedious repetition, I simply mention spoken and heard language, but you should understand that I mean written and read language as well.

2. Following a fairly widespread convention of philosophical writing, I use double quote marks (" ") for direct quotations of what someone actually said (for example, Fred said, "The cat is on the mat") and as scare quotes (for example, the "language" of the bees); I use single quote marks (' ') around words mentioned, not used (for example, the word 'procrastinate'). The mention/use distinction is discussed in chapter 15.

3. In the section called Suggested Readings at the end of almost every chapter I list sources quoted in that chapter and appropriate further readings. Original bibliographical sources for each work are cited there. Because many of these works are conveniently reprinted or excerpted in widely available anthologies, I have listed these anthologies at the back of the book and refer to them by number inside square brackets.

I
Language and Minds

1

The Structure of Language

Infinity and Novelty

One fact about language that any account of meaning has to deal with is its enormous size. During the time that any major language has existed, a huge number of words and sentences has been spoken. How many? It is of course impossible to estimate the number of words that people have spoken since English began, but we can take a stab at the number of *different* words, at least in contemporary English: One estimate is about 50,000 (Kučera 1969). The "how many" question is ambiguous: How many words are there in the sentence 'The cat is on the mat'? There are six actual words, but there are five different words, because 'the' occurs twice. To eliminate this potential ambiguity, philosophers use the technical terms *word type* and *word token*. There are six word tokens in that sentence and five word types. Similarly, we can speak of *sentence types* and *sentence tokens*. The following list contains three sentence tokens but only two sentence types:

> The cat is on the mat.
> The dog is on the log.
> The cat is on the mat.

How many sentence types are there in English? The answer is not some large number. There is an *infinite* number of well-put-together, meaningful sentence types in English. To see why, note that 'I have one kumquat' is a meaningful sentence and so is 'I have two kumquats' and so is 'I have three kumquats'. This series could be continued literally infinitely, producing meaningful sentences at each step.

Again, a general rule is that, if you take any two meaningful sentences and join them together with 'and', you get a third meaningful sentence: Thus 'He drove like mad and he drove like mad' is meaningful and so is 'He drove like mad and he drove like mad and he drove like mad' (although nobody is likely to say it, because it can be said more economically). Thus we can produce more and more sentences just by adding 'and he drove like mad' to the previous member of the series. A sentence consisting of 'He drove like mad' followed by a string of 2,498,503,448 'and he drove like mad's would be very strange indeed, and certainly nobody would ever say it (or understand it if it were said), but it *seems,* strictly, to be meaningful. (Why did I say "seems"? It might be argued that, because nobody could understand such a long sentence or produce it to express something they wanted to say, it is meaningless. But on the other hand, having understood the rules of the language, we could, at least in theory, figure out what it means.) This again shows that the number of possible sentences is literally infinite. There are different sentence types with the same meaning, but it seems that there is an infinite number of different meanings as well. Perhaps adding an additional 'and he drove like mad' to a long sentence of the type discussed does not change its meaning, but raising the number of kumquats does.

A language consists, loosely, of a pairing of meanings with sentences; when we know a language, what we know is what meaning is paired with each sentence. One might be tempted to think that what we have inside us, when we know a language, is a sort of "code book" in which each sentence of the language is paired with its meaning. But this picture cannot be right, for there is an infinite number of sentence types in any *natural language,* so this code book would have to be infinitely long. (*Natural languages* are languages that evolve as cultural artifacts, such as English, Swahili, and Latin, as contrasted with *artificial languages,* which are invented, such as secret codes, symbolic logic, and Esperanto.) It would be impossible, not just difficult, to learn or to store in our minds an infinite number of pairings of meanings and sentences, one at a time.

The same thing is shown by another, related feature of natural languages. It is always possible that you might encounter a sentence that you have never heard before, no matter how extensive your previous experience with the language. Children are able to understand and produce sentences that they have never heard before: Having been taught to understand 'Give me the ball' and 'Give me the book' and 'Give me the toy', a child who already understands the word 'dish' might very well understand the sentence 'Give me the dish' the first time she hears it. In fact, it is possible to construct a sentence that has never been uttered by anyone in the entire history of the language. Here is an example:

My third cousin enjoys carving symbolist poetry stanzas on watermelon rind.

We cannot be sure, but it is likely that this book contains the first appearance in history of a token of this sentence type. This shows again that our mastery of language cannot consist of an internalization of a code book giving the meaning, one by one, of each sentence type. Presumably, this code book would have to be learned; but you are somehow able to understand and to produce meaningful sentences that you have never encountered—that nobody has ever encountered—before.

The two properties of language just remarked on are its *infinity* and its capacity for *novelty*. These are not exactly the same property; it is possible for a language to have the novelty property but not the infinity property. We can imagine a language with a large but finite number of sentence types; it has the novelty property, because people can construct and understand sentences that they have never encountered before or that have never been produced, but the number of sentence types in it is not infinite. Linguists believe, however, that natural languages have both properties.

Phrase Structure Grammar

It is easy to see how we can explain, in basic outline anyway, the infinity and novelty properties of language. Imagine, by analogy, that we are constructing a secret code. In order to invent one capable of encoding an infinite number of messages, we do not need to write and learn a code book containing an infinite number of pairs of code sentences and meanings. What would do the trick is a large but finite number of code words plus a large but finite number of ways that they can legally be put together into code sentences, each way having a peculiar kind of effect on the meaning of the sentence thus composed. Under certain conditions this could produce an infinity of possible sentences.

Contemporary linguists think that natural languages have such a structure. They see their job as providing a theory of language that represents the ways in which sentences are put together. The following is a simplified, brief, and superficial look at the beginnings of such a theory of English. (You will probably notice all sorts of ways in which this needs to be modified and expanded.)

Compared to many other natural languages, English has a large vocabulary but nevertheless—perhaps—a finite one. I do not mean *fixed over time*—clearly the invention of new words continuously expands the vocabulary of the language. But is the vocabulary of English finite at any one time? Perhaps there are rules for combining and mutating words so that an infinite number of words can be generated, each of which we can understand without needing a definition. If so, then the vocabulary is infinite. Examine even a small dictionary and you will see that many of the words in English are rarely used; out of the rest we are able to produce an infinite number of different sentences to express what we need to in every conceivable situation. This richness is a result of the fact that words can be combined in a large number of ways to produce an infinite number of sentence types.

To illustrate this, consider. the following. A linguist writes that twenty-five speakers will almost certainly come up with twenty-five different sentences to describe the situation portrayed in the same simple drawing and that computer analysis shows that the vocabulary used in a sample set of twenty-five such sentences could be used to produce almost 20 billion different sentences, all describing the same situation (Ohmann 1969). Why, by the way, only a mere 20 billion? Couldn't we use the 'and' rule, as in the 'and he drove like mad' example, to create an infinite number of sentences?

This book, containing about 78,000 word tokens, contains only about 4,800 different word types. Over 25 percent of the word tokens are of the nine most common word types ('the', 'of', 'is', 'that', 'to', 'a', 'and', 'is', 'this'). A small portion of the list of word types in this book is instructive:

> maybe me mean meaning meaningful meaningfully meaningless meaninglessness meanings means meant mechanism mechanistic meet meeting meets member members membership men mental mentalese mentalistic mentality mention mentioned mentioning mentions menu mere merely mergle merits mess messages met metal metalanguage metaphor metaphorical metaphorically metaphors metaphysical metaphysically method Michigan microchip microchips microphone middle midga midnight might migrate.

The sample shows that there is probably a larger proportion of different word types than is found in most everyday talk, because this book contains many philosophical jargon words ('mentalistic'), proper names ('Michigan'), and made-up words and abbreviations ('mergle'). One would expect that ordinary talk and simpleminded writing (for example, in a bad newspaper), rely on even a smaller number of word types. And, of course, many of the words are grammatically derived from others. Thus, once one knows what 'mention' means, one can use and understand 'mentioned', 'mentions', and 'mentioning'. The infinity of sentences in English, then, is largely the result of grammatical variations on words and of different word combinations into sentences.

The study of the ways in which English combines words into sentences begins with the observation that words come in grammatical categories. Here is a list of some of these categories (with abbreviations and examples):

noun (N) → turtle, book, nose
verb (V) → throw, sneeze, help
adjective (Adj) → funny, green, vague
pronoun (Pro) → she, it, they
preposition (P) → in, under, at
article (Art) → a, the

A complete list of the words of English with the grammatical categorization of each is called the *lexicon* of English.

Words can be put together in certain ways into phrases. A noun phrase (NP) can be, for example, the subject of a sentence or the object of a verb or preposition and may be composed of, for example, an article followed by a noun ('the turtle'), a pronoun ('she'), or an article followed by an adjective followed by a noun ('the stupid book'). We can abbreviate these rules for construction of noun phrases as follows:

(1.1)   NP → Art N
(1.2)   NP → Pro
(1.3)   NP → Art Adj N

Formula (1.1) means that a noun phrase *may be* constructed by an article followed by a noun, although there are other ways of constructing a noun phrase, but that *every* article followed by a noun makes a noun phrase. Similarly, expression (1.2) means that any pronoun constitutes, by itself, a noun phrase.

A *tree diagram* can be drawn showing how phrases are constructed from their parts. Thus, for example, the following tree diagram demonstrates the structure of the NP 'the stupid book':

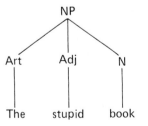

One way to construct a prepositional phrase (PP) is by a preposition followed by a noun phrase ('in the zoo', 'at her', 'on a nice day'):

(1.4) PP → P NP

A verb phrase (VP) can consist of a verb alone ('sneezed') or a verb plus a noun phrase ('kicked the cat') or of a verb followed by a prepositional phrase ('ran under the bridge'). Thus

(1.5) VP → V
(1.6) VP → V NP
(1.7) VP → V PP

A sentence (S) can consist of a noun phrase followed by a verb phrase ('She kicked the turtle', 'The stupid animal ran under the bridge'):

(1.8) S → NP VP

Here is the tree diagram for 'The stupid animal ran under the bridge':

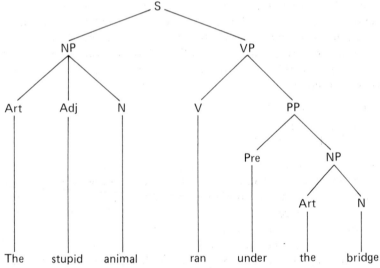

What has been presented so far is obviously a highly incomplete account of grammatical categories and of how phrases can be constructed. Let's look at just one simple way our beginnings of an account must be expanded.

Recursive Rules

One way our account of noun phrases is too limited is that a noun phrase may also be constituted of an article, more than one adjective, and the noun:

Art Adj Adj N

as in 'a short funny book'. In fact, three or more adjectives can be inserted between the article and the noun ('a short funny red book' and so on), although piling up ten adjectives results in stylistic disaster and stacking a million in practical incomprehensibility. We can take account of this fact by defining an *adjective phrase* (AP) as one or more adjectives in a row and by substituting for formula (1.3) the following:

(1.3')   NP → Art AP N

How can we, however, produce rules that will provide for an AP to be constructed of one *or more*, that is, *any*, number of adjectives? One way would be to produce an infinite number of rules:

(1.9')   AP → Adj
(1.10')   AP → Adj Adj
(1.11')   AP → Adj Adj Adj
(1.12')   AP → Adj Adj Adj Adj

and so on. This is not a good idea, however. First of all, a theory is not a good one if all of it cannot be stated; second, if in some sense knowing English is knowing its rules, then these formulas could not be its rules, because it seems to be impossible to learn or know an infinite number of rules. But the same facts about English can be stated much more neatly by a mere two rules:

(1.9)   AP → Adj
(1.10) AP → Adj AP

Formulas (1.9) and (1.10) work together to allow any number of adjectives in a row. 'Red' is an adjective, so, according to formula (1.9), 'red' constitutes an adjective phrase. Given this and because 'funny' is an adjective, it follows from formula (1.10) that 'funny red' is an adjective phrase. And given this and because 'short' is an adjective, it follows from formula (1.10) that 'short funny red' is an adjective phrase. And one can continue to use formula (1.10) over and over again to add any number of adjectives to the phrase. Formula (1.9) gets us started, but it is formula (1.10) that pulls the trick off. This sort of useful rule is called *recursive;* this means that successive uses of a rule can generate successive members of a series. (The primary meaning of the word 'recursion' is "return"; as a term in mathematics, 'recursion' came to mean "an expression giving successive terms of series, etc." (*Concise Oxford Dictionary*).) The recursive property of formula (1.10) comes from the fact that AP occurs on both sides of the arrow; thus it may be used on the product of its previous use, over and over again, each time generating a longer product.

Recursive rules occur widely in the grammar of English; and everywhere they do, they allow the possibility of indefinitely long sentences. Another sort of case involves the construction of long noun phrases involving the stringing together of prepositional phrases: 'the hat of the man in a store on the street in the city'. These can be generated by

(1.1) NP → Art N

and

(1.4) PP → P NP

and

(1.11) NP → Art N PP

Try to use these rules to generate 'the hat on the man in a store on the street in the city'. None of these three is a recursive rule (that is, none can be used over and over on its own previous product); formulas (1.4) and (1.11) are, however, called a *recursive pair*, because each includes to the right of the arrow what the other has on the left, and thus they make a repeated circle possible.

Depth Grammar

So far, what I have been describing is called a *phrase structure grammar*. The small sample I have included here does not begin to do justice to English, and a tremendous amount more has to be added to this grammar; this is one of the tasks of the science of linguistics. Nevertheless, on the basis even of this small sample of the elementary beginnings of phrase structure grammar I have given here, it is possible to see the limits of *any* phrase structure grammar, no matter how elaborate, in producing a full account of language. Here are two things a phrase structure grammar cannot do.

Examine this set of sentences:

Harry captured the castle.
The castle was captured by Harry.
What Harry captured was the castle.
It was the castle that Harry captured.

The words in each sentence differ somewhat, and analysis of the phrase structure of each will differ. For example, the noun phrases that constitute the subjects of the sentences are 'Harry', 'the castle', 'what Harry captured', and 'it'. A successful phrase structure grammar tells us that each of these sentences is properly constructed, and it tells us the grammatical form of each by breaking down each into its component phrases. But what a phrase structure grammar does not tell us is that all four are different grammatical variations of the same underlying structure. This shows that phrase structure grammar does not give an account of everything in the structure of the language. Linguists say that what phrase structure grammar gives is an account of the *surface structure* of language; the four sentences differ in surface structure. But the fact that we can on the basis of grammar construct any of the sentences from any other, results from their sharing the same *deep structure*. The way contemporary linguistics attempts to provide a scientific theory of deep structures is to give a list of rules for transforming a sentence with one surface structure into another with a different surface structure.

The following sentences are not equivalent (whereas those in the previous list were):

Tabitha ate a bug.
Tabitha didn't eat a bug.
Tabitha ate something.
What did Tabitha eat?
Tabitha, eat a bug!

Here, each sentence contains a core with the same deep structure: Grammar allows us to construct each sentence out of the core by incorporating that core into an assertion, a question, a denial, etc.

The details of transformational grammar are extremely complicated and controversial, and I am not able here even to touch the surface of elementary theory in this area. You can get a feeling for the difficulties faced by transformational grammar linguists by looking at just a few examples of the complexity of the way English works.

The transformation between

Harry captured the castle.

and

The castle was captured by Harry.

cannot be covered by any *simple* rule, for

Marvin resembles Seymour.

is grammatically correct, but

*Seymour is resembled by Marvin.

is not. (The asterisk is a linguist's symbol for an impossible sentence.)
Similarly, the word 'up' may be moved in the pair

> He looked the word up in the dictionary.
> He looked up the word in the dictionary.

but not in the pair

> He looked it up in the dictionary.
> *He looked up it in the dictionary.

Here is another peculiarity of grammar:

> Serve yourself.
> *Serve you.

but

> *Get Mary to serve yourself.
> Get Mary to serve you.

The *structural* features of language that phrase structure and transformational grammar attempt to systematize and explain are called
the language's *syntax*. Understanding the syntax of a sentence is necessary for understanding its meaning. 'She read the letter to the
editor' means different things, depending on how its syntax is taken.
Is it a letter to the editor that was read, or was a letter read to the
editor? The following tree diagrams illustrate these two syntactic interpretations:

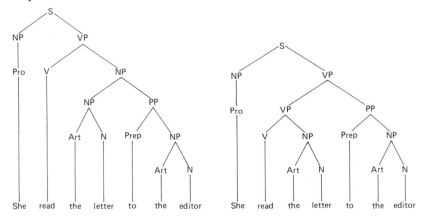

Syntax and Semantics

A language must consist of more than a lexicon and a syntax, for if
you knew everything about the lexicon and syntax of English but

nothing else about it, you would not be able to do much with it. You would be able to tell that certain sentences are genuine English ones and that other ones are impossible in the language, but you would not have the faintest idea what any of them mean. I can prove this to you by giving you a complete lexicon (of one-letter words) and a syntax for a tiny language I have invented:

Lexicon
N: a, b
V: f, g
Art: k, l

Phrase Structure Rules
NP → N
NP → Art NP
S → NP V

Transformation Rule
NP V = V NP

Now you know that these are sentences:

a f
f a
k b g
k k l l a f

and that these are not:

*f a k k
*a b

and that these two are transformational variations:

k b g
g k b

but you have no idea what any of the sentences means. Sentences of real language do not merely have structure (syntax)—they have meaning: *semantics*. The rest of this book deals in one way or another with what this thing called meaning might be.

Suggested Readings

Bach, Emmon. 1974. *Syntactic Theory.* New York: Holt, Rinehart & Winston.
    This book treats linguistic theory in depth.
Fromkin, Victoria, and Robert Rodman. 1978. *An Introduction to Language.* New York: Holt, Rinehart & Winston.

The authors give a long but still elementary account of contemporary linguistic theory.

Kučera, Henry. 1969. "Computers in language analysis in lexicography," in *The American Heritage Dictionary of the English Language*. New York: American Heritage, xxxvii–xl.

Ohmann, Richard, 1969. "Grammar and meaning," in *The American Heritage Dictionary of the English Language*. New York: American Heritage, xxxi–xxxiv.
A short article that gives a little more than the brief hint of contemporary linguistic theory offered in this chapter.

2

Meanings as Ideas

Speaker's Meaning and Sentence Meaning

Suppose that Sally wants to tell you that Fred has left, but she isn't a competent English speaker and hasn't gotten the meanings of 'arrived' and 'left' straight. She says, "Fred has arrived," but she really means that Fred has left. We might want to say, however, that the sentence she utters, despite her desires, does not mean that Fred has left—it really means that Fred has arrived. What we have here is a sort of ambiguity: In one sense what Sally said means that Fred has left and, in another sense, that Fred has arrived. More precisely, we can say that, what Sally meant by her sentence is that Fred has left, but what her sentence really means in English is that Fred has arrived.

This distinction between what a speaker means by a sentence and what that sentence really means is an important one that will come up in various places in this book. I distinguish these two sorts of meaning by calling the first *speaker's meaning* and the second *sentence meaning*.

These terms are somewhat misleading. Language can, of course, be used in speech or in writing, and if Sally wrote "Fred has arrived" with the intentions and the lack of full linguistic competence imagined already, then we could speak of the speaker's meaning here also, although nothing is spoken.

Another slight inaccuracy of these terms is that the term 'sentence meaning' is meant to apply not just to the meaning of whole sentences but to smaller (or larger) chunks of language as well. Thus we can speak of the sentence meaning of 'Fred has arrived' or of the word 'arrived'.

We do not usually have reason to distinguish sentence meaning from speaker's meaning, because the two normally coincide: People nearly always mean what they say. In the example discussed, however, speaker's meaning and sentence meaning are different, and we can imagine other cases in which the speaker does not mean what the spoken sentence means. A fully competent speaker can mean something different from what her uttered sentences mean when, for example, there is a slip of the tongue or she is mistaken about the name of the person she is talking about. Suppose that Sally thinks that the name of the person who has arrived is 'Fred' but his name really is 'Ferd'. We might want to say, then, that Sally means that *Ferd* has arrived, but the sentence she utters does not mean this. Also, in some sense, the speaker does not mean what she says when she is lying or practicing her lines in a play or speaking in her sleep or under the influence of drugs.

One of the central debates within philosophy of language is whether there really are these two kinds of meaning. Some philosophers think that there is only what I have been calling sentence meaning, and, whatever we might say regarding the speaker, this does not figure at all in linguistic meaning. Other philosophers think that speaker's meaning is the basic kind of linguistic meaning; although they admit the legitimacy of sentence meaning, they want to explain it on the basis of speaker's meaning, which they take to be primary. The various views on linguistic meaning I consider in this book concentrate on one or the other of these two sorts of meaning as basic.

The Idea Theory of Meaning

When we ask what is it for a speaker (or writer) to mean something by what she says, probably the first answer that comes to mind is that the words express the speaker's thoughts. The speaker encodes what she thinks into language, and the hearer decodes what he hears back into his thoughts. Successful communication occurs when the hearer's and speaker's thoughts are the same. This seems to be an obvious truth, but it has (as we will see) its difficulties.

Having noted the compositional structure of our natural languages, we might be disposed to think that the basic unit of meaning is the word and that, once we have learned the meanings of a sufficient number of words plus the significance of a sufficient number of ways that they can be put together into sentences, then we know the language. In the idea theory of speaker's meaning, then, each word we use means what it does for us because it is associated with a particular idea.

This has been a common philosophical view throughout history. Aristotle, for example, wrote, "Spoken words are the symbols of mental experience" (*De Interpretatione*, 16[a3]); and Locke wrote: "Words in their primary or immediate Signification, stand for nothing, but the Ideas in the Mind of him that uses them . . ." (1690, bk. 2, ch. 3).

There is something clearly right about this view; it seems evident that, when you say "cat," you have one idea and that, when you say "on," you have a different one, and that the meaning for you of these words as you use them has something centrally to do with what these ideas are. If the word 'pasquinade' means nothing to you, that is because you have no idea associated with it. If that word brings the idea to mind of a sort of sweet fruit drink, then that is what it means for you. (This is not its sentence meaning, however.) Someone not fully competent with the English language may say 'arrived' in association with the idea you associate with 'departed', so when Sally says "Fred has arrived" (assuming she has the other words right), you might take that to mean that Fred has arrived, but her (improper) association of the word with her idea entails that she means that Fred has departed.

But the first problem with this theory of meaning is that the notion of *idea* needs some clarification here. Do we have one idea for each word in a sentence that we understand or say? Are different tokens of the same word type associated with the same idea? When we are speaking rapidly about a subject with which we are quite familiar, it seems that we are conscious of hardly any ideas in our mind while speaking; at last, it does not seem plausible to say that there is a stream of events going through our mind at these times, one idea per word, exactly parallel to the stream of words spoken. This does not mean, however, that what we say means nothing to us. Are there ideas corresponding to each word but of which we are not conscious? We do not know how even to begin to answer these questions because we—so far, anyway—have so flimsy a notion of what an idea might be. Ideas are not discrete, identifiable, and reidentifiable little items that flit through our consciousness. To say that we know what we mean when we speak because we have an idea corresponding to each word does not really explain anything. It simply means that we know what we mean when we speak.

The Empiricist Theory of Ideas

The reason why the idea theory of speaker's meaning is so vague is that we have given the concept of idea so little content. Some philosophers, however, have tried to give more substance to this notion and to make it do philosophical work in a theory of meaning. One famous and influential theory of ideas and of meaning I look at is due to the British empiricists of the seventeenth and eighteenth centuries: Locke, Berkeley, and Hume. *Empiricism* is the doctrine that all our knowledge (with the possible exception of logic and mathematics) is derived from our sense experience. As idea theorists, Locke, Berkeley, and Hume thought that what gives words in our language meaning is their association with our ideas; and as empiricists, they tried to explain what our ideas are by connecting them to our sense experiences.

Suppose that you encounter a pork chop at dinner. It impinges on your senses in various ways: You see it, taste it, smell it, feel it on your tongue, and perhaps hear the sizzle. You have internal experiences of various sorts caused by the external pork chop and recognize it as a pork chop and give it that name on the basis of these internal experiences. (There are other ways: You may have read the name on the menu, or someone may have told you what it was.)

I assume that right now you are not having a pork chop dinner, but you are perfectly able to understand (or meaningfully say) the word 'pork chop', because the word calls to mind the sort of sense experiences that you have had when a pork chop was actually before you. You are able to picture in your mind's eye, in your imagination, the characteristic look of a pork chop, and you probably are able to remember other sense experiences associated with it (to "picture" its taste in the "mind's tongue"? its smell in the "mind's nose"?). The empiricists called the actual sense experiences *impressions* and claimed that we are able to call up in our mind comparatively dim and feeble *copies* of these impressions when we were not actually having those experiences; these copies are called *ideas*. Pork chop impressions are possible only in the presence of an actual pork chop, but the ideas that are copies of these impressions are carried around in one's mental baggage all the time. Of course, we do not always, comparatively rarely, "call up" the family of pork chop ideas; but these are what we are conscious of in our minds when we identify something as a pork chop, when we apply or use or hear the word. We learned the meaning of that word when we learned its association with that family of ideas, and it is the word's association with this family that gives it meaning to us.

Objections to Empiricist Theories

This fairly persuasive theory of ideas gives the notion of idea some content; now the idea theory of meaning has a bit more power. Unfortunately, it does not have enough power; and furthermore, this theory of ideas and the theory of meaning based on it both seem mistaken.

First, let's examine some arguments to the effect that both theories are mistaken. One thing that may be right about the copy-of-impressions theory of ideas is that there may be such things as mental images and that they may at least sometimes be something similar to faint sense impressions. Some psychologists believe that there is good reason to believe that mental images exist, that they are similar to dimly perceiving something, and that (at least sometimes) thinking about something is having a mental image of it.

Much more needs to be said and done scientifically to establish this conclusion, but right now I can give persuasive arguments to show that the dim-copy-of-impressions theory cannot be correct about *all* our ideas. Consider the sentence 'The cat is on the mat.' Each of these words is supposed to be associated with an idea, a dim copy of impressions, and perhaps you have some mental images associated with one or two of them, for example, with 'cat'; but do you have a mental image associated with 'the' or 'on'? Most people have no mental imagery associated with these words; thus the empiricist theory of ideas must conclude that they have no idea connected with them, and the empiricist theory of meaning must conclude that the words are meaningless to them. But this is absurd.

Whenever I hear or say the word 'Baltimore', I automatically call to mind the taste of those spicy hard-shell crabs I always eat when I am there. But this mental taste image has nothing to do with the meaning of the word 'Baltimore' (although we might want to say, somewhat metaphorically, that that taste is an important part of what 'Baltimore' means to me).

But there are more problems. I suppose that 'cat' is the most likely candidate in 'The cat is on the mat' for a word associated with mental imagery: If I try, I can get a visual image for this one. Now suppose that I get different visual images at different times. Does this mean that this word means different things to me on these different occasions? Well, maybe a staunch defender of the empiricist's theory of meaning would say yes and try to live with this peculiar consequence. Suppose that in my mind's eye I visualize a gray cat lying down when I hear or say the word 'cat'. How is it, then, that I can apply the name 'cat' to black cats or to cats that are standing up? Must I carry around with me a large number of different cat ideas, one gray, one black, one standing up, one lying down, etc.? But even this will not do, because I can correctly apply 'cat' to any of an indefinitely large number of different-looking cats, that is, when my impressions do not exactly match any one of however large a finite stock of ideas I might have. The problem is that sense impressions are always quite particular; so ideas that copy them must be particular also; but words can be general—can apply to things that do not resemble any particular idea.

The empiricists recognized this as a problem. Locke tried to explain how a mental image could stand for various different-looking particular things by supposing that the mind takes several particular quite specific sense impressions and "abstracts" from them; to get the general idea, for example, of *man*, people take the particular ideas of several people

> but only leave out of the complex idea they had of Peter and James, Mary and Jane, that which is peculiar to each, and retain only what is common to them all. (Locke 1690, bk. 3, ch. 3, sect. 7)

(Locke, of course, is using 'man' in the slightly old-fashioned way, to mean male or female person.) But it is implausible to think that we can have abstract mental images such as these. Our image corresponding to 'man' must be one picturing a person neither male nor female, neither short nor tall, neither standing nor sitting, facing neither right nor left nor straight ahead, and so on. If we imagine the mind blurring, so to speak, all the particular parts of this mental image, what is left?

Berkeley's response to the problems of general ideas rejects Locke's solution:

> . . . universality, so far as I can comprehend, not consisting in the absolute, positive nature or conception of anything, but in the relation it bears to the particulars signified or represented by it; by virtue whereof it is that things, names, or notions, being in their own nature particular, are rendered universal. Thus . . . the universal idea of a triangle . . . ought not to be understood as if I could frame an idea of a triangle which was neither equilateral, nor scalenon, nor equicrural; but only that the particular triangle I consider, whether of this or that sort it matters not, doth equally stand for and represent all rectilinear triangles whatsoever, and is in that sense universal. All which seems very plain and not to include any difficulty in it. (Berkeley 1710, Introduction, par. 15)

Beware when philosophers say things like that last sentence!

Berkeley's strategy here is to insist that our idea of a triangle is an image of a particular triangle but that we *use* this image to stand for any triangle whatever. The difficulty here is that, in order to recognize triangles, we must not only have this mental image but also know how to *use* it correctly: Some features of that image are to be used in recognizing triangles (three sides and angles, straight lines, etc.), and some are to be ignored (equilateral, one side horizontal, etc.). But if this is the case, then having an idea cannot consist merely in having a mental image; it must also consist in our knowing the right way to use it. In Berkeley's theory of the idea of 'triangle', for example, we have to know that the three-sidedness of the (say) right triangle image we have in mind is crucial to recognizing anything as a triangle, but the right angle on the mental triangle image is not. But if we know this, then why do we need a mental image at all? Just the knowledge that three-sidedness is crucially important for calling something a 'triangle' is sufficient all by itself, without any mental imagery. So having a mental image is never sufficient for knowing the meaning of a general word; and it appears that it is sometimes not even necessary.

This sort of objection holds regarding not only general words but also particular ones—words that name only one thing. Tokens of the name of a particular friend of yours mean something to you. Suppose that you have some mental images associated with the uses of that name, say, a visual image of her red hair and a sound image of her growly voice. Because she always has red hair and a growly voice, we do not get exactly the same problem we ran into with the general idea of a triangle. But it seems again that these images must be particular—of her hair from a certain angle or combed in a particular way and of her voice saying something in particular. But you recognize her (according to this theory) from these (and other) images even when she is seen from a different angle or when her hair is combed differently or when she is saying something else. Again you need to know rules for using the image—what to ignore in it and how to use the rest; and the same difficulty arises.

I admit that the mental image theory of ideas fares a bit better with some ideas than with others. Consider your idea of *blue:* it is hard to see how rules *alone* can suffice to constitute *blue;* here it seems we need a mental image to which we can compare impressions. But, again, a mental image alone is not sufficient, for a particular mental image, say of a royal blue colored circle, can be used to identify royal blue squares and cerulean blue circles, and so on.

Against Any Idea Theory

A good deal of the difficulty in making the idea theory of meaning work comes from problems that arise from the empiricist's theory of what an idea is. But we need not agree with the empiricists that copies of perceptions are the sorts of mental entity whose association with words gives them their meaning. It is difficult to see, however, what other sorts of mental item would do the trick, and I have no suggestions to consider here. (You might want to say that you have a *concept* for example, associated with each word; but saying that does not say anything more than that each word means something to you.)

I conclude this chapter with two general arguments against the possibility of any idea theory of meaning. The first argument is really a more general version of arguments already made, not linked to the image theory of ideas.

Any idea theory would have us suppose that there is some mental item—an idea, whatever that is—associated with each word and that it is this association that gives the word meaning to the language user. The idea theory is thus supposed to give us an account of what a speaker's language competence amounts to, and the presence of ideas in the speaker's mind is supposed to explain language competence.

The picture is this: Suppose that you say, "Bring me that blue thing." What I do to understand 'blue' is, first, find among my store of ideas the *right* idea—the one that corresponds to 'blue'. Then I am to look around me and see which of the things in the vicinity *corresponds* to this idea in the *right* way. Merely having some idea or other—even if it happens, say, to be an exact dim copy of the visual impression I would get when looking at that blue thing—would do me no good at all unless I were able to (1) bring it to mind when I hear 'blue' and (2) recognize that blue things fit this idea in the right way.

Merely having an idea, then, does not explain language competence: *Using* this idea *presupposes* competence at associating this idea, rather than any other, with the word and with things in the world. What is wrong with an idea theory of meaning, then, is that it does not answer any questions; it just shifts them. A question we started with was, What is it for 'blue' (for example) to have meaning to me? Clearly it means what it does to me because I judge that the word applies to some things and not to others. But what is there *in me* that permits me to do this? The answer is an *idea* corresponding to the word. But now we must ask, What is there in me that permits me to associate this idea with the word and with certain things? The same problem arises again, and it seems that no progress has been made at all by the introduction of the idea of *ideas* to answer questions about meaning. Wittgenstein put part of the current objection like this:

> Consider the order, "*imagine* a red patch." You are not tempted in this case to think that *before* obeying you must have imagined a red patch to serve you as a pattern for the red patch which you were ordered to imagine. (1958, p. 3)

My second general objection is of a different sort. The idea theory claims that each word in a sentence has meaning to me insofar as it corresponds to some one of my ideas. Now, it is not only words that mean something but also sentences. A sentence is a string of words, so how is the idea theorist to make sense of the meaning of a sentence? The obvious way is to see it as a string of ideas. But this will hardly do. Imagine (if you can) the idea you associate with the word 'the' and the idea you associate with the word 'cat', and similarly with the words 'on' and 'mat'. Now imagine those ideas coming to you one right after the other as you say, "The cat is on the mat." What you have is a succession of different ideas, but does this train add up to anything more than a succession of different ideas? Isn't there something significantly different from having a string of six ideas run through your head (two of them alike, for the repetition of 'the') and the idea that the cat is on the mat? If that sentence means something to you, this theory would claim that it is associated with a mental something, but surely that mental something is more than merely a train of ideas running one by one through your head. But what? Obviously, the same words strung together differently make a sentence with a different meaning (compare 'The cat is on the mat' and 'The mat is on the cat').

The idea theory thus cannot give an account of what language means merely by saying what words mean. Hume's answer to this problem is that, in addition to having ideas corresponding to each word, we have beliefs—perceptions of the connections between these ideas; thus the sentence 'Pigs oink' expresses the connection we make between our pig idea and our oink idea. But what is the nature of this connection?

In chapter 9 I present a theory of speaker's meaning that tries to explain the meaning of *sentences* by associating them with mental items, namely, beliefs and desires. The theory explained there, a modern one with a considerable amount of contemporary support, might roughly be classified as an "idea" theory insofar as it explains meaning by associating linguistic items with mental ones; but as we will see, it does this in a far different way.

Suggested Readings

Bennett, Jonathan. 1971. *Locke, Berkeley, Hume: Central Themes*. Oxford: Clarendon Press.
   An excellent critical examination of empiricist views.
Berkeley, George. 1710. *A Treatise Concerning the Principles of Human Knowledge*.
   Presentation of Berkeley's theories of ideas and of meaning. Available in a variety of editions.
Berkeley, George. 1713. *Three Dialogues Between Hylas and Philonous*.
   Berkeley's theories of ideas and of meaning. Available in a variety of editions.

3

Innateness

Arguments for Innateness

King James IV of Scotland (1473–1513) believed that Hebrew was the natural, original, innate language of humanity. His evidence was the Old Testament, but, deciding to put the matter to a scientific test, he arranged to have two newborn infants and a deaf-mute nursemaid placed in isolation. Several years later, the three were retrieved, and sure enough! the King reported that the children "spak very guid Ebrew" (Fromkin and Rodman 1978, p. 21).

We can imagine the reasoning that might make plausible the view that there is an innate language. We learn language from people who already know it, and languages evolve from other languages; but there has to be a starting point. Could the first language have been invented without the use of language? It seems that language could not have been developed by an early tribe unless they could already think and people cannot think unless they already have language.

An old (bad) joke: Adam returns home from a day of naming things and, pointing to a giraffe, tells Eve that he has named it 'giraffe'. "Why did you pick that name?" asks Eve. "Well," replies Adam, "it *looks* like a giraffe." In the joke Adam can think—indeed, talk—about giraffes even before he names them.

Thinkers used to "solve" this problem by postulating God's sudden creation of a whole language in humans. King James seems naive to us now in thinking that Hebrew must be the original language, but his belief that there is a natural, inborn language is, surprisingly, one that several well-respected contemporary philosophers and linguists also hold (although in a much more sophisticated version). In this section I look at what they suppose to be innate and at their reasons for thinking that it is.

Noam Chomsky, the best known proponent of the *innateness hypothesis*, argues that all natural languages studied so far share the same structures and transformations at the most basic level (that is, they share the same deep structure); given the possibility of running a language on many other types of structure, it would be too great a coincidence if this structure was not prewired genetically into our brains but just happened to develop the same way in each language.

Natural languages are enormously complex. We got a hint of this in chapter 1 when we took a brief look at the phrase structure and transformational grammar of English. Despite its sophistication, contemporary linguistics still falls short of describing the full structure of the language. The amazing thing, however, is that normal 10-year-old children already speak and understand the language with such sophistication that the most learned linguists cannot state the rules that their language operates under.

Children can use these enormously complicated rules at an early age, having had insufficient exposure to language by then to have learned the depth grammar of their language from experience. Anyway, a lot of what young children hear does not obey the rules, and a lot of the rest is consistent with structures other than the ones every child eventually does use. Chomsky has argued that our experience would be insufficient for us to learn language unless considerable parts of its structure were already "wired-in." He writes:

> The child must acquire a generative grammar of his language on the basis of a fairly restricted amount of evidence. To account for this achievement, we must postulate a sufficiently rich internal structure—a sufficiently restricted theory of universal grammar that constitutes his contribution to language acquisition. (Chomsky 1972, pp. 158–159)

> A consideration of the character of the grammar that is acquired, the degenerate quality and narrowly limited extent of the available data, the striking uniformity of the resulting grammars, and their independence of intelligence, motivation, and emotional state, over wide ranges of variation, leave little hope that much of the structure of the language can be learned by an organism initially uninformed as to its general character. (Chomsky 1965, p. 58)

(A former student of mine said that he is convinced that the innate language is Yiddish, because all his relatives speak it fluently and all of them are utterly out of contact with reality.)

Replies to These Arguments

Chomsky's claims are highly controversial, and many philosophers think that his arguments are faulty. Here are some criticisms.

1. The claim that all natural languages share the same deep structure is controversial and, at best, premature. That claim would be more believable if linguists had adequate accounts of the deep structure of every language; but they do not: Theories of the deep structures of even the most familiar and intensely studied languages are still incomplete.

2. Even if linguists eventually are able to construct adequate and similar deep structure theories for all, or a large number of, natural languages, this would not necessarily be evidence that these languages are in fact remarkably similar. It might be that each linguist is seeing in the language she studies the structure of her own language, because she is projecting onto the language being studied the deep structure of her own language. We do have the tendency to think that other languages are similar to our own: There is an old story of an anthropologist who, finding that some Indian tribe used the same color name for red and green things, rushed back to the scientific community with the news of a tribe of color-blind Indians. It turned out that the Indians could see the difference in color as well as anyone; they just used the same color word for red and green. Nobody is accusing contemporary linguists of silly mistakes such as this one, but they might be making an analogous mistake at a deeper level. Our native language is clearly a profoundly influential factor in how we think in general, and surely it must influence how we think about other languages.

3. But suppose that it really is the case that all natural languages share the same deep structure; would the *only possible* explanation for this be that this structure is prewired in the human brain by genetics? We know that the structure of English makes it a remarkably useful tool for communication. It just might be the case that this structure is the *best* way for humans to build a language and that any other way would make language impossible, or at least less useful. Thus languages with other structures would naturally not have developed; or if they did, they would have been replaced by better ones—ones sharing our structure. We do not know that this evolutionary explanation is the correct one, but its plausibility as an alternative to the innateness hypothesis removes some of the steam from Chomsky's arguments.

4. Anyway, it is possible that all natural languages evolved from a common ancestor; this might explain their similarities in structure.

5. Anyone who has tried to learn a foreign language as an adult knows that this is enormously difficult and time consuming. If the structure of all languages is innate, shouldn't learning a second language be easier?

6. When you calculate the huge amount of exposure children have to language and all the reinforcement and correction they experience, it adds up to an enormous amount—much more than college students get in language class, for example. If the basic structures of language were innate, we would expect that learning one's first language might be easier also. Given the huge amount of training we give our children before they can master our language, one does not need to suppose innate knowledge to start off with. Even low-IQ children learn language fairly well by the time they are 10, but ten years of intensive training is long enough to teach anybody anything.

This debate is ongoing and includes twists and complexities I cannot go into here. I let it hang inconclusively in the air and move on to an even more surprising extension of the innateness hypothesis.

Mentalese

The basic source for this extension is Jerry Fodor, another contemporary linguist and philosopher. He argues for the existence of innate knowledge not only of the syntactic categories and structures of language but even of internal *words*:

> Learning a language (including, of course, a first language) involves learning what the predicates of a language mean. Learning what the predicates of a language mean involves learning a determination of the extension of these predicates. Learning a determination of the extension of the predicates involves learning that they fall under certain rules . . . But one cannot learn that [predicate] P falls under [rule] R unless one has a language in which P and R can be represented. So one cannot learn a language unless one has a language. (Fodor 1975, p. 64)

(A *predicate* is roughly that part of a sentence that says something about the thing or things that sentence is about. Thus, in 'Fred is stupid', 'is stupid' is a predicate, and 'Fred is stupider than' is a predicate in the sentence 'Fred is stupider than Arnold', although this is not what is ordinarily called a predicate in grammar. Think of a predicate as an incomplete sentence that becomes a complete sentence when one adds a reference to some thing or things. The *extension* of a predicate is the set consisting of that thing or things of which a predicate is true. The set of green things is the extension of 'is green', and the *unit set* (the set consisting of one member) consisting only of the city Hobart is the extension of the predicate 'is the capital of Tasmania'.)

At first glance, Fodor's position seems entirely unbelievable. Is Fodor really saying that we are *born* with a language inside us in which there already is a word corresponding to *every* word we eventually learn to use in English? that a one-day-old baby is already equipped to talk to itself in its innate language (which we call *Mentalese*) about protons, philodendrons, and polygamy? Well, he need not go *quite* this far: Certain words we learn in English can be defined to us in simpler terms (for example, 'polygamy' means *the practice of having more than one spouse*) so we need not have Mentalese words for *each* English word. But because we do not (and cannot) learn all English words this way, if Fodor is right, there must be an enormous vocabulary in our innate language. Let's examine his argument.

Fodor's claim is that, when one learns to use a predicate, such as 'is a duck', in a natural language, one has to learn rules about what counts as a duck and what does not. He argues that you cannot have a rule internalized in your mind unless you have a way of internally representing that rule; thus you must be able to represent in your mind some rule to the effect that something counts as a duck if and only if it (say) waddles, quacks, and has feathers. But to have this rule in your mind, you must already be able to represent ducks in your mind. What represents ducks in your mind, which enables you to frame the rule about what counts as a duck, is the "word" in Mentalese for duck. (Remember the Adam joke.)

The rest of the argument follows easily: We cannot learn Mentalese, for to do that we would have to have some other representations in our mind in order to frame the rules for the concepts of Mentalese (not to mention the fact that Mentalese is never publicly "spoken," so it would be impossible for us to learn it). Thus we must conclude that this internal language is innate. Fodor takes all thought to involve internal representation; thus, although we may sometimes be said to think in our learned natural language, Mentalese is the primary "language of thought."

This account gives only a small and simplified part of Fodor's arguments. Basically his views are that, in order to learn language, we must already possess an internal mental information-processing system that is capable of representing externals and has a syntax—a structure that would, for example, permit infinity, novelty, and transformations; a system of this sort is exactly what is called a *language*. Fodor argues that there are other characteristics of thought which show that thought can be carried out only by an internal representational system that shares other characteristics of our external language.

One of Fodor's assumptions about which I raise questions is that learning a rule necessarily involves internal representation of that rule and of the things that rule is about. In order to deal with this assumption, we have to go into the notion of *rule* in some depth; this subject is dealt with in the next few chapters.

Suggested Readings

Chomsky, Noam. 1965. *Aspects of the Theory of Syntax*. Cambridge: MIT Press.
   Chomsky's position on the innateness hypothesis. See especially section 8 of chapter 1. Parts of this book are reprinted in [9].
Chomsky, Noam. 1972. "The formal nature of language," in his *Language and Mind*. New York: Harcourt Brace Jovanovich, 115–160.
   The innateness hypothesis according to Chomsky.
Chomsky, Noam, Hilary Putnam, and Nelson Goodman. 1967. "Symposium on innate ideas." *Boston Studies in the Philosophy of Science* 3:81–107.
   A symposium in which Chomsky summarizes his arguments and two noted critics attack them. Reprinted in [11].
Fodor, Jerry. 1975. *The Language of Thought*. New York: Crowell. Reprinted 1979 by the Harvard University Press.
   A source of Fodor's views.
Fromkin, Victoria, and Robert Rodman. 1978. *An Introduction to Language*. New York: Holt, Rinehart & Winston.

4

Going on in the Same Way

In this chapter I raise some issues that are connected with Fodor's argument for innateness. Connections between these issues and Fodor's arguments are drawn in the course of the discussion.

Here is a small puzzle I would like you to try to solve: Say what the next number in this series is:

$$1 \quad 4 \quad 9 \quad 16 \quad 25 \quad 36 \ldots$$

Probably you decided that the next number in the series is 49 (and the one after that is 64). Wrong! The next number in the series is 322 (and the one after that is 324).

The reason most people who make any sense out of this series think that the next number is 49 is that they notice that the first number in the given list is 1^2, the second is 2^2, the third is 3^2, and so on, so the seventh number must be 49 ($= 7^2$). They think that the rule that generated the first six members of this series and that will yield the seventh one, is the nth member of the series $= n^2$.

There is nothing particularly wrong with this reasoning; it would probably yield the answer that would be counted as correct in an arithmetic class. The reason that the next member of the series is not 49, however, is that this rule is not the one I had in mind. My rule is, for $n = 1, \ldots 6$, the nth member of the series is n^2; for $n = 7$, the nth member $= 322$; for $n = 8, \ldots$ the nth member is the $(n - 1)$th member plus 2.

You might think that my puzzle is a bit of a cheat. There is nothing wrong with my answer, however. The rule I had in mind produces the first six members of the series as presented, and it yields 322 as the seventh member and 324 as the eighth. There is an infinity of different rules I might have had in mind in producing these six numbers, each of which would have produced a different member of the series at some point. When I produce a finite sample of members of a series and ask you to produce the next member, I am asking you to "go on in the same way." In this case what counts as going on in the same way is going on according to the rule I have in mind. But there is no way you can tell from the presented series which of the infinite number of possible rules, each consistent with the sample, I have in mind.

You could have known what was in your arithmetic teacher's mind when she gave you this puzzle. Is the moral of this story merely that I am perverse and there is no telling what such a person has in mind? Not exactly.

The moral is that a series of examples does not *in itself* contain the information of what constitutes going on in the same way. The series itself is consistent with an infinite number of ways of going on, and the only thing that makes 322 the next member of this series, instead of 49 (or 3 or 8492.3 or anything else), is that *I*, the producer of this series, had a rule in mind when creating it. *If* this is what makes some answers right and wrong, then finding out the right answer consists in figuring out what its producer had in mind when creating it, not in merely examining the properties of the series itself.

Going on in Language

Let's apply this line of thinking to language. There appears to be a strong analogy between learning a language and figuring out the next member of the series of numbers I gave. When we learn a language, we are presented with a finite number of particular cases of language use, and we are expected to be able to go on in the same way—to produce, as it were, "the next member," that is, a language use that follows the rules governing the sample uses but applies them to some new instance. The rules, as we have seen, are syntactic and semantic ones. (We will encounter arguments that language is not exactly a matter of what we call *rules* and that going on in the same linguistic way is not a matter of mind reading; but I ignore these for the moment.)

The fact that we must go on to produce uses that are not in the sample is demonstrated by the novelty and infinity properties of language, discussed in chapter 1, but not only by this. We must go on to a new member of the series even when we produce a token of a sentence type already encountered in our finite sample. Imagine, for example, that you are an infant learning to use the one-word sentence, 'Duck!' You are at the duck pond, and whenever a duck waddles by, Mom says, "Duck!" Your learning to go on in the same way includes your exclaiming 'Duck!' in a new case: perhaps in response to a duck different from the ones already demonstrated by Mom or perhaps even to one of those same ducks. (More than the first and, of course, more than the second is needed to demonstrate mastery of 'Duck!'—you will, for example, be required to apply 'Duck!' to ducks from a different sample and of quite different sizes, shapes, colors, and even species, and to refrain from applying 'Duck!' to nonducks such as houses, trees, sparrows, and even swans.) In neither case are you required to produce a token of a previously unencountered sentence type, but both are instances of "novel" uses, because 'Duck!' is being exclaimed in response to a different duck or to one of the same ducks in a different position, looking a bit different, or at least at a different time.

Learning 'Duck!' is thus learning how to go on in a series of which you have been presented with only a finite number of members. But, on analogy with the arithmetic example, the series *itself* does not determine a single right way to go on. It is consistent with *any* sample pairings of 'Duck!' with particular things that a pairing of 'Duck!' with this *next* thing be correct or incorrect, even if this next thing is one of the original sample. (To see this, imagine, for example, that Mom is teaching you 'Hungry!' This is paired with a duck gobbling your bread cubes; but later, having stuffed itself with bread, that same duck is no longer correctly paired with 'Hungry!')

In the arithmetic series, you could have correctly supplied the next member if I had told you the rule for generating members of the series straight off. By analogy here, Mom might give you this rule for using 'Duck!': "Use that word for any of various wild or domesticated aquatic birds of the family Anatidae, characteristically having a broad, flat bill, short legs, and webbed feet, dear" (definition from *The Concise Oxford Dictionary*).

Sometimes we can learn how to go on to use bits of language this way—by being told the rules. But there are several reasons that show that this is not and cannot be the way we learn all or even most of language. One reason, conclusive all by itself, is that you already have to understand the words in the rule in order to learn 'Duck!' this way. In this 'Duck!' case it is entirely implausible that you, as an infant, could understand this "rule." But whether or not you could understand it, you could not learn *all* of your first language this way, because you could never begin; you would not understand any statement of a "rule" for the first word you learned. (Explanation and further discussion of this point is found in chapter 7.) It follows that at least some of language must be learned merely by learning how to go on from a finite sample.

To learn 'Duck!', you must, in effect, eliminate hypotheses. The first pairing of that word is with a duck in the water; but hypotheses having to do with water might be eliminated by the next member of the series: 'Duck!' is paired with something on the land, and so on. The problem here is that there is, to begin with, an infinite number of possible hypotheses about the correct use of 'Duck!'; many of these may be ruled out by successive sample pairings of word and object, but after any finite sample an infinite number of different hypotheses consistent with that sample remain (just as an infinite number of different next members are consistent with any finite sample of numbers in a series).

Now we can connect this discussion with Fodor's argument presented in the last chapter. To think of an infant considering hypotheses and gradually ruling some of them out, we must think of her as thinking—as *framing* hypotheses to herself and considering some as ruled out by examples. This is to think of the infant as having an internal system of representation rich enough to frame and rule out hypotheses and thus rich enough to be called an internal, unlearned, "language of thought."

But there is a further point to be made here, again in support of a sort of innateness hypothesis. The indisputable fact is that we, as adults, encounter remarkably little difference among the ways the members of our linguistic community "go on" in using language. We all continue to use 'Duck!' in much the same way. That is, we all have settled on (more or less) the same hypothesis about the way to use that word and the rest of our language. There is a fact about the right way to use 'Duck!', and we have all learned it. There is an infinite number of wrong hypotheses about how to go on using 'Duck!' that are fully consistent with any sample of duck-'Duck!' pairings we have encountered, and yet rarely do we encounter any evidence that anyone believes any of these. Because these hypotheses are fully consistent with all our experience, we could not have *learned* that they are false. We must therefore postulate some *innate* mechanism that rules these out.

This argument does not prove the existence of an innate concept of duckness or of a word in Mentalese that translates into English as 'Duck!' What it does seem to prove, however, is that there are some innate restrictions on ways of thinking about things and of using language.

There is an interesting example that can be used to illustrate this point. The example involves two predicates invented by Nelson Goodman; he used these examples in connection with a somewhat different philosophical point, but they serve us as well.

Consider the predicate 'x is *grue*'. Define 'grue' as follows:

> 'x is grue' is true if and only if (1) it is before time t and x is green, or (2) it is time t or later and x is blue.

and suppose that time t is still in the future, say, midnight, January 1, 2000. Now you know how to use the word 'grue'. The leaves on the tree outside your window (if it is now summer) are grue, because they are green and it is now before time t. You can imagine waking up on New Year's morning, 2000, and discovering that the clear sky is grue, even though it was not grue the day before. (This is not the effect of clouds or of your hangover.) On that morning you would judge that the needles on your Christmas tree are no longer grue, although they had been the previous day; in fact, they had turned *bleen*:

> 'x is bleen' is true if and only if (1) it is before time t and x is blue, or (2) it is time t or later and x is green.

Had you spent the minutes around midnight watching that Christmas tree instead of drinking and carrying on, you would have seen it turn from grue to bleen exactly at midnight.

The Paranoid Hypothesis

Now, let us indulge in a bit of science fiction: Imagine that everyone else in the English-speaking world right now actually means *grue* when they say 'green', and *bleen* when they say 'blue'; you are the only one who uses 'green' to mean *green* and 'blue' to mean *blue*. I call this the *paranoid hypothesis*. It is understandable that you were not aware of this until I told you. They always say that the needles of fresh Christmas trees are 'green' and that the clear daytime sky is 'blue': It is still earlier than time t; they really mean that the needles of fresh Christmas trees are grue and that the clear daytime sky is bleen. You and everyone else have been right so far, and there is no way you could have found out that their meaning is different.

Perhaps you might try asking others whether they expect Christmas tree needles still to be "green" after time t; but this would not help. Suppose that they say yes. After time t they would be surprised to find out that the needles had turned "blue" ($=bleen$); they would then all say things such as "Those needles turned blue overnight!" and "The sky is green now!" and you would *only then* find out that they had been using those words differently. Or suppose that they answer no. They expect the sky, Christmas tree needles, etc. to turn color at time *t*; but this may be a peculiar general expectation about color change at time *t*, and thus not evidence that they mean something different from you now by 'green' and 'blue'.

Have you any good reason to think that the paranoid hypothesis is false?

The reason why you think it is false may be the following. If it were true, then everyone else would have the color concepts of *grue* and *bleen*, instead of *green* and *blue*, and you are pretty sure that they do not. *Grue* and *bleen*, after all, seem to be fairly peculiar concepts. But what makes them peculiar? One answer you might be tempted to give is that they involve what time it is, and this makes them illegitimate as color concepts.

But this will not do to rule them out. Someone who is using these concepts would not have to check her watch to see what color something is; she might just automatically start counting blue things as fitting that concept at *t* without thinking that there had been a change. To see why it is impossible to show someone who is using the concepts of *grue* and *bleen* that they illegitimately include what time it is, imagine that you meet someone who uses the words 'grue' and 'bleen' to mean *grue* and *bleen* and that you try to convince her that the color concepts she is using are illegitimate. Here is the dialogue between you and her:

Scene 1: January 1, 1985

YOU: Your color concepts are screwy. At time *t* the sky will turn from bleen to grue, and Christmas tree needles will turn from grue to bleen. But things don't change colors.

SHE: Well, I don't think they will change.

Scene 2: January 1, 2000

YOU: There!

SHE: You're right, the sky and the pine needles changed colors. So what? You sometimes have said that things change colors. Every fall, in your language, maple leaves change from 'green' to 'yellow' or 'red'.

YOU: Yes, but the sky and the pine needles didn't really change.

SHE: Yes they did. I was watching that Christmas tree at midnight, and I *saw* it change from grue to bleen.

YOU: But it doesn't look like a different color now, does it?

SHE: It sure does. Yesterday it looked perfectly grue, but today it looks as bleen as can be.

YOU: But *grue* and *bleen* are illegitimate color concepts, because their definition includes mention of a particular time. Regular color concepts, such as the concept of *purple,* which we both agree on, have nothing to do with what time it is.

SHE: I agree that regular color concepts have nothing to do with what time it is. My concepts of *grue* and *bleen* have nothing to do with what time it is. In fact, that's just what's wrong with *your* color concepts, which *do* involve the mention of time.

YOU: No, yours do.

SHE: No, yours do. The definition of the defective concept of *green* is:

'*x* is green' is true if and only if (1) it is before time *t* and *x* is grue, or (2) it is time *t* or later and *x* is bleen

The definition of your defective concept *blue* is:

'*x* is blue' is true if and only if (1) it is before time *t* and *x* is bleen, or (2) it is time *t* or later and *x* is grue

(*General confusion; curtain.*)

The philosophical point of this miniplay is that there is nothing *demonstrably* perverse or wrong with the concepts of *grue* and *bleen.* The reasonable assumption that other people's concepts are not usually perverse or irrational, then, does not rule out the paranoid hypothesis.

But now consider different concepts, $grue_1$ and $bleen_1$, defined as before, except that the time mentioned is January 1, 1980. You have good reason now to think that before that date others were not using 'green' to mean $grue_1$, because after that date they still said that Christmas tree needles were 'green': Had their 'green' meant $grue_1$, after that date they would have started saying that Christmas tree needles were 'blue', but they did not. You similarly have good reason to think that they did not mean $grue_2$ and $bleen_2$ (the time for defining these is January 2, 1980) by 'green' and 'blue'. And so on, for an infinite number of concepts different from *green* and *blue*. In the case of each concept, before the date mentioned in defining it, everyone's experience is just as consistent with using 'green' to mean *green* as with using it to mean the grue concept mentioning that date. So it turns out that every instant of past time shows that people were not using some grue concept that was until then equally consistent with all language use as was the concept of *green.*

This extraordinary fact—that we did not disagree in ways that experience did not rule out—needs some explanation. As should be clear, the fact that we did not disagree cannot be explained by our learning to use 'green' by sample pairings of word and thing, because those samples are equally consistent with the formation of some gruesome concept. And, as we have shown, there is nothing demonstrably peculiar about $grue_1$, $grue_2$, and so on, that would explain why we have avoided them. The only other explanation seems to be that we are innately, naturally constituted to avoid them. (The irony here is that Goodman, the philosopher who invented 'grue', is a staunch opponent of the innateness hypothesis.)

But does this give us any evidence against the paranoid hypothesis? You might be tempted by the following argument: We now know that when speakers have been saying 'green', they did not mean $grue_1$, $grue_2$, etc. for an infinite number of different grue concepts whose time is now past. This suggests an innate predisposition against all those grue concepts. But grue itself (whose t is still future) is also a grue concept; so we have indirect evidence that there is a similar innate predisposition against grue.

This argument is of a familiar form. It is similar to arguing that the fact that all previously observed species of snakes lay eggs makes it probable that some newly discovered instance of the same kind, that is, another species of snake, lays eggs also. This *sort* of argument is perfectly acceptable.

In this case, however, the argument fails. In order for the facts cited about $grue_1$, $grue_2$, and so on to give evidence about grue, the concept of grue would have to be *of the same kind* as $grue_1$, $grue_2$, etc. You think that it is, because you think that grue, like $grue_1$, $grue_2$, etc., involves a particular time. But this is just what a grue thinker would deny: As the miniplay shows, someone who uses the concept of grue would think that green, not grue, involves a particular time, and thus that green, not grue, is of the same kind as them. This argument assumes just what it sets out to prove; it thus (as philosophers say) *begs the question* and is no good.

The strange conclusion we are left with, then, is that there is no disproving the paranoid hypothesis, at least until t arrives. This sort of skepticism about finding out what others really mean by what they say is discussed again in chapter 6.

We have been supposing that language is a sort of "rule-governed" behavior, involving right and wrong "ways of going on." This supposition will, in one way or another, be the subject of the next few chapters. In the number series example that began this chapter, the right way of going on was determined by the rule the creator of the series had in mind; similarly, we were tempted to say that the right way of going on when we imagined you learning 'Duck!' was the way

Mom had in mind. The notion that the right ways of going on that constitute language are determined by what some person (or people) has in mind is what is behind idea theories of meaning, such as the empiricists' theory discussed in chapter 2. This supposition, as we will see, is brought into question by the private language argument, the subject of the next chapter.

Suggested Readings

Blackburn, Simon. 1984. *Spreading the Word*. Oxford: Oxford University Press, ch. 3.
  A discussion of the implications of 'grue' for philosophy of language.
Goodman, Nelson. 1955. "The new riddle of induction," in his *Fact, Fiction, and Forecast*. Indianapolis: Bobbs-Merrill, ch. 3.
  The first presentation of 'grue', although it is discussed in connection with a different sort of philosophical problem.

5

The Private Language Argument

Ludwig Wittgenstein, one of the most influential and controversial philosophers of this century, is responsible for the *private language argument*, which some philosophers think mortally injures any idea theory of meaning or even the notion of speaker's meaning itself.

One of Wittgenstein's major works, *Philosophical Investigations*, is largely taken up with explaining and exploring the consequences of this argument on our view of language (and our view of mind and a good deal else); this is a succinct statement of that argument:

> Let us imagine the following case. I want to keep a diary about the recurrence of a certain sensation. To this end I associate it with the sign "S" and write this sign in a calendar for every day on which I have the sensation.—I will remark first of all that a definition of the sign cannot be formulated.—But still I can give myself a kind of ostensive definition.—How? Can I point to the sensation? Not in the ordinary sense. But I speak, or write the sign down, and at the same time I concentrate my attention on the sensation—and so, as it were, point to it inwardly.—But what is this ceremony for? for that is all it seems to be! A definition surely seems to establish the meaning of a sign.—Well, that is done precisely by the concentrating of my attention; for in this way I impress on myself the connexion between the sign and the sensation. But "I impress it on myself" can only mean: this process brings it about that I remember the connexion *right* in the future. But in the present case I have no criterion of correctness. One would like to say: whatever is going to seem right to me is right. And that only means here that we can't talk about 'right'. (Wittgenstein 1958, pt. I, sect. 258)

(One gives an *ostensive definition* of a word by pointing at what the word refers to, as when we define 'mauve' by pointing at mauve things or by producing a color sample. This is contrasted with a *verbal definition*, for example, 'A *dodecahedron* is a solid with twelve faces'.)

The great importance of this argument is matched by the great obscurity with which it (and the surrounding commentary) are stated and by the great number of differing ways philosophers have understood it. I give a fairly simple explanation of it, but you must realize that many philosophers can be found who disagree.

What Wittgenstein wants us to imagine is that someone—let's call her Sally—is trying to create a name for her own private sensation (a general name that will apply to all sensations of the same kind). The argument is that this cannot be done. Wittgenstein reasons: In order for 'S' really to be the name of that kind of sensation, there must be a rule for applying it. In order for there really to be a rule, there must be something that counts as following the rule correctly and something that counts as violating it—ways of going on that count as the same way or as different ways.

Now, in this private case, Sally could believe that she is applying the rule correctly or that she has misapplied it, but there is no way for her or anyone else to check whether these beliefs are in fact true or false. Anything she can do (for example, concentrating hard when she first names a sensation and trying hard to remember what the first one was like when she wants to judge if the next sensation is an S or not) merely produces more *appearances* of correctness (or incorrectness); nothing she can do constitutes a real test of genuine correctness. Because nothing counts and nothing could count as a test showing that Sally is really correct or incorrect, there is no distinction between *seeming to her* to be right and actually *being* right. But "that only means here that we can't talk about 'right' " (or 'wrong'). And because we cannot talk about right or wrong application of a rule, what this really means is that there is no real rule here. And because there is no real rule here, Sally has not succeeded in giving 'S' a meaning for herself.

One crucial feature of this argument is that it talks about naming an event that has traditionally been held to be "essentially private," that is, that can be directly observed by only one person. Thus only the person who feels a sensation can directly observe that sensation; similarly, only the person who has a desire or a thought or anything else can directly observe it. Of course, others can have *indirect* evidence that it is there—if Sally grimaces and holds her toe, that is evidence of a toe pain sensation. Similarly, she can inform someone else of her private mental events.

Why does this argument concentrate on naming private items? It might seem that the same sort of reasoning might be applied to any belief that anyone might have, not just about naming and not just about private items. If Sally believes, for example, that there are three buttons on the table, then what can she do to make sure? Look harder? Count again? Concentrate more on the experiences that taught her how to count and on what it is like for there to be *three* things? But all these "ceremonies" can do no more than produce additional appearances of correctness.

Wittgenstein believed that being surrounded by a *community* of judges sometimes (but not in the case of Sally and her private sensations) supplies the needed contrast between merely seeming to be correct and actually being correct. But we can wonder, What is so special about *this* case? How can a community supply this contrast for *any* judgment? Suppose that Sally believes that there are three buttons on the table and that she is in the company of all her friends and relations, all of whom agree. It is by no means clear why this provides the contrast between *seeming* and *being* correct any more than Sally's checking several times herself. Of course, both Sally's rechecking and corroboration by the rest of the community make Sally feel more sure. But still, how does this give us a difference between merely seeming to be and actually being right?

Realism and Antirealism

All of us believe that some things that seem true to people are in fact true and would be true whether or not they (or anyone) believed them. We believe, in other words, in *mind-independent facts*. But there are some sorts of judgment that do not seem to have this sort of correspondence to mind-independent facts, for example, the judgment expressed by 'this ice cream is delicious'. If the ice cream seems delicious to me but seems awful to you, there really is no truth of the matter to make one of us right and one of us wrong. Many people do not think, for example, that judgments of morality correspond to a mind-independent reality or that its categories (such as *evil*) are "out there" in the world. They think instead that these categories are merely invented by us and, as in the case of ice cream taste, that there are no facts of the matter. (This view of morality is quite philosophically controversial.) The position that some family of judgments and categories does correspond to a mind-independent reality is called *realism* about that family, and its contrary is called *antirealism*.

Let's assume realism about at least some ordinary facts, such as the fact that snow is white. This means that there is a fact of the matter and that this does not depend on how anything seems to anybody. This enables us to say that, if snow seems white to Sally, then *she is correct.* (What entitles us to say this is another matter: Realists can nevertheless wonder why we are entitled to think that the way things *seem* is ever the way they really are. This is one of the oldest and most puzzling philosophical questions, but it is not the question here.)

Wittgenstein is not arguing that we should believe in an antirealist view of *all* judgments but merely of the judgment that a private name is correctly applied to a private item. Why be an antirealist about this sort of case in particular?

Let's look at a different case in which antirealism seems at least plausible. Suppose that Sally tastes some ice cream and says, "This is delicious." Note that she is, in this case, applying a public-language word: 'Delicious' already exists in English. Let us assume that she is using this word correctly: Is her judgment that the ice cream is delicious correct? If someone else thinks it is not delicious, is he wrong? If Sally changes her mind and decides that the ice cream is not delicious, does that show that she was right one time and wrong the other? What I want to say here is that *seeming* delicious to someone is really all there is; there is no question about whether the ice cream really is delicious. There are no facts of the matter, nothing about the ice cream independent of tasters' reactions, that makes that ice cream really, in fact, mind-independently, delicious.

Public and Private Language Meanings

Now let's turn to beliefs about public language: Should we be realists or antirealists about meaning? Is the fact, for example, that in English 'Snow is white' means what is does, a real fact of the world, independent of mind and of the way things seem to users? Or is there only the way things seem (in which case one would not talk here about 'right')? Well, from one perspective there are real facts about the matter, but from another there are not. Let's examine each perspective separately.

No Real Facts about Public Language

Imagine that tomorrow the earth is showered by z-rays from outer space and that the peculiar result is that all speakers of English begin to think that the sentence 'Snow is white' means *Grass is green*— improbable, of course, but not in principle impossible. (Perhaps there would have to be changes in what meanings they assigned other sentences also; more on this in the next chapter.) English speakers would then have trouble understanding books written before the z-ray attack, but they would continue to understand each other as well as they do now. In fact, from that point on, 'Snow is white' would mean *Grass is green*, and this would be the case merely because it seemed that way to all English speakers. This amounts to saying that there is no *real*, mind-independent fact about what 'Snow is white' really means; it is only a matter of what it *seems* to mean to everyone, and one should not speak here of 'right'.

Compare this with another imaginary example: Suppose that those z-rays instead made everybody think that grass is orange. We assume here that the z-ray attack left language use unchanged, so when people expressed their belief about the color of grass they would say, "Grass is orange," and by this they would mean *Grass is orange*. I suppose that, because everyone thinks grass is orange, nobody would have any reason to doubt their views; but *they would all be wrong*. It is surely possible that everyone could be wrong about this and other things; at certain times everyone thought the world was flat. Grass really is green, despite what anybody or everybody happens to think. This is realism about color, in contrast to antirealism (of a sort) about meanings.

Real Facts about Public Language

Suppose now that those z-rays affected *only Sally*. Tomorrow, she begins to think that 'Snow is white' means *Grass is green*, but all other English speakers still think it means *Snow is white*. It seems to Sally that it means *Grass is green*, but she is wrong. There *is* still a fact of the matter, and that fact is that 'Snow is white' means *Snow is white*. What we should say about this imagined circumstance is that there is a difference between the way things seem to Sally and the real facts of the matter; thus one *should* speak of 'right' (and 'wrong'). Perhaps we have realism (of a sort) about meanings. Certainly, this sort of realism about meaning looks plausible for what we have been calling sentence meaning—what the sentence actually means.But it is hard to say whether this applies also to what we have been calling speaker's meaning. Even though Sally's sentence really means *Snow is white*, isn't what she means by it something different, namely, *Grass is green*? More about this later.

These considerations lead us to some important conclusions about meaning in public language. What we have here is an intermediary case between realism and antirealism. When it seems to a community of language users that some linguistic item has some meaning, when a belief about language *seems* right to a community of language users, there is no external fact of the matter to compare this to. What seems right to the community is all there is. This implies antirealism about public meanings—for the community. But this community acceptance does establish facts of the matter for an individual: An individual can be really correct or incorrect about meanings, depending on whether her understandings correspond to the views of the community. This implies realism about public meanings—for the individual.

But now let us return to an individual's own private language, as when Sally attempts to name her own sensation 'S'. Here we are not considering a public language but rather an *idiolect*. (An *idiolect* is a language or language variant spoken only by one person.) In this case there is no community view on meanings to set the standards; all there is is Sally's own feelings—the way things seem to her. And if this is all there is, then there is no sense in speaking of 'right' or 'wrong'. Unless there is a right and a wrong way to use a word, there is no language. So Sally cannot create a private language.

Notice that one feature of Wittgenstein's example seems irrelevant here, namely, that Sally is attempting to name a private item. Our current understanding of the argument works just as well when Sally attempts to name a public object, such as a color. Suppose that Sally decides to call a particular color before her 'C': Without public standards for the correct use of 'C', all there is is what seems to Sally to be a correct application of that word, and there is no question of right and wrong. What difference does it make whether Sally is trying to make up a name for a private or for a public object? Well, in this case, there is at least the possibility of creating a public standard. If other people observe the sorts of color that Sally calls 'C' and deny that they are 'C', eventually we might get a public standard that results from community use and thus have the possibility that Sally's uses are right or wrong. But if Sally is trying to name a private object, for example, her own sensation, then because nobody else can perceive these items, there is no possibility of a public standard. Thus we can conclude that a language of names of public objects is impossible when only one individual invents and uses those "words" before the development of a public standard; but a language of names of private objects is *altogether* impossible.

Privacy and Speaker's Meaning

Let us now step back from the details of this argument and see what it has to do with what we have discussed in previous sections.

Recall that we have been trying to make sense of speaker's meaning by understanding it as the association by the speaker of a certain word or sentence with an idea in the speaker's mind. We have had trouble in making the notion of idea useful in this explanation: The empiricists' theory will not do, but this appears not to make any difference if the private language argument is a good one. Whatever private item we take an idea to be, it appears that the attempt to establish a meaning by the association of a bit of language with that private item cannot work.

But perhaps the private language argument is not really all that destructive to the notion of speaker's meaning, explained by means of association of words with private ideas.

Consider first the possibility of speakers' meaning for words in a public language. After Sally alone was affected by z-rays, she got the meaning of a sentence wrong, but can't we talk about the way she got that meaning (and that it was wrong) and about the way any other individual got that meaning (and that it was right)? We might try to explain *sentence* meaning as equivalent to what is established by community standards, but this does not seem to rule out the idea of *speaker's* meaning, which may or may not match this and which has something to do with something inside the speaker.

But it might be the case that the private language argument does not destroy the notion of speaker's meaning of words in an idiolect, even one that names private objects. Let's accept Wittgenstein's claim that in this sort of case one cannot speak of right and wrong. Does that mean that there is no such thing as an idiolect? It does mean that a speaker cannot really be right or wrong about what meanings the words in such an idiolect have and that there are no real facts about what these meanings are, but does this imply that they have no meanings?

In a sense this is a moot question. If we decide to, we can take something to have a meaning only if there is a fact of the matter, and thus we can decide that Sally's idiolect is without real meaning. But why not simply say that it does have meaning—meaning for her, that is, although there are no real facts about her idiolect for her impressions of meaning to be right or wrong about?

We might want to say: When there are no real facts about meaning, there is no language; but this may amount to a *stipulative definition* of 'language'. (A stipulative definition is a definition of a new word or a new definition of an old word beyond or contrary to the common understanding of that word.) Let us all agree that Sally's idiolect lacks an important ingredient of public languages—a fact of the matter about meanings. Does this imply that it is not a language at all? We can decide to call this either a language lacking a usual ingredient or a nonlanguage, depending on how we stipulate a meaning for 'language'; and if we assume that calling something 'language' in ordinary use does not rule out one stipulation or another, the whole matter boils down to the way we prefer to apply that word and is totally uinteresting and without philosophical import. So let's not worry about merely how to apply the word 'language'; whatever we call Sally's idiolect, the important thing to note is that it lacks what is at least an important element of real language.

The same sort of point applies to Sally's speaker's meaning of words in English, understood as amounting to Sally's association of internal items with bits of English. Because we can say that, what Sally takes some bit of English to mean is right or wrong, it certainly seems to follow that there exists such a thing as what Sally takes that bit of English to mean, and this certainly seems to have something to do with Sally's mental furniture. Now, consider whatever it is that is established by the association in Sally of bits of English with her "ideas" (or whatever the appropriate sort of item in her mental life is). Can we say that these establish speaker's meanings or that it is a language ("Sally-English") that matches real English in some ways and not in others? Again, this seems to be a matter merely of stipulating meanings for 'meaning' and for 'language', and nothing is gained by doing this. Whether or not these associations are meanings and whether or not Sally-English is language, these associations certainly lack an important ingredient that real sentence meanings have, and Sally-English certainly lacks an important ingredient of public English. From this perspective, then, the conclusion is not that speaker's meaning is not meaning nor that a private language is not a language but just that there are important differences in each case. Perhaps this is the moral of the private language argument.

Suggested Readings

Jones, O. R., ed. 1971. *The Private Language Argument*. London: Macmillan.
    Wittgenstein's arguments are discussed by several experts.
Kripke, Saul. 1982. *Wittgenstein on Rules and Private Language*. Cambridge: Harvard University Press.
    A recent controversial interpretation and discussion of the private language argument. Parts of this book are reprinted in [5].
Wittgenstein, L. 1958. *Philosophical Investigations*. Oxford: Basil Blackwell.
    The private language argument is raised in several sections, including part I, section 258, and surrounding sections.

6
Radical Translation

How to Translate Tribish

Imagine that you have gone to live among an isolated, newly discovered tribe. You do not understand a single word of their language (which we call Tribish); your job is to try to make sense of what they say.

This task would be much easier if you had some kind of toehold on their language. If they spoke Italian, for example, you would be able to learn to translate their language comparatively quickly and easily, for Italian shares the Latin roots of English and a number of words in it and a good deal of its syntax resemble English fairly closely. You could also expect a number of behavioral similarities that would facilitate the job. Perhaps the native speakers would share our convention of pointing with extended index finger; thus you could start by pointing to familiar objects and trying to elicit their names for them. You could try out hypotheses you had formed by uttering the word you think names a kind of thing while pointing at it or holding it up; Italian speakers, fortunately, have a word that sounds similar enough to 'no' and a head-shaking gesture that is easily recognized as a denial; or perhaps they would smile to indicate that you had things right. (I was considerably unnerved, however, when I visited a country in which turning one's head from left to right is the convention for *agreement*.)

But we imagine that the language of your tribe has no apparent similarities with any language you already know and that you cannot count on *any* similarities in behavioral conventions. Translating a language of this sort, a *much* more difficult job of course, is an important philosophical thought experiment. This example and a discussion of its philosophical implications are due to the enormously influential twentieth-century philosopher W. V. O. Quine. Quine named this sort of task *radical translation*. It is convenient to look at radical translation as the job of writing a manual for translating Tribish into English.

Despite the obvious difficulties involved in radical translation, we know it can be done because it *has* been done. We now are confident that all major living languages have, in effect, such translation manuals, and some translations tasks must have been at some point fairly close to radical ones. Certain dead languages (for example, Etruscan) have not satisfactorily been translated, but this is because we cannot interact with its speakers and because so little written matter is now available. We assume for our imaginary case of radical translation that unlimited samples of Tribish are available to you and that you can interact with its speakers.

Let's try to imagine at least a small part of what you would do and, more important, what you would have to assume in order to produce a radical translation of Tribish. One obvious part of your task is to find out the general terms referring to ordinary objects; one way to begin doing this is to notice what sorts of words the native speakers use in the presence of objects when you think they perceive them—when they are *stimuli*. This starting point correlates native linguistic behavior with current environmental stimulation; these correlations yield hypotheses about what Quine calls the *stimulus meaning* of utterances. "A rabbit scurries by, the native says 'Gavagai', and the linguist notes down the sentence 'Rabbit' (or 'Lo, a rabbit') as tentative translation" (Quine 1960, p. 29).

Of course, single instances of such connections establish hardly anything. The native might "really" have been meaning any one of a number of things, including

> Lo, a fuzzy animal.
> Lo, an animal.
> Lo, an alligator. [The native is confused about animals]
> I saw that thing yesterday.
> Hand me my bow and arrows.
> I sure am hungry.
> Damn, I forgot to videorecord the Bugs Bunny Show this week.
> Taxi!

Repeated observations of linguistic behavior might make 'Lo, a rabbit' the most plausible translation of 'Gavagai' if you find that it is said only in conjunction with rabbits, not with other animals, with rabbits previously observed and unobserved, when the speaker is hungry and when he is not, and so on.

Mere observation of correlations would not be your only way of ruling out hypotheses; in addition, linguistic interaction would be essential. Suppose, for example, that wild rabbit sightings are rare and that the only uses of 'Gavagai' you manage to observe are in the presence of the speaker's own rabbit, which resides in a cage in back of his house. In order to discover whether 'Gavagai' should be translated as 'My rabbit' or even 'Lo, a cage', you would need to bring around someone else's rabbit outside a cage and show it to the native. But if the speaker looked puzzled on this occasion and did not say anything, this would not show you much. Perhaps he is just puzzled about why you brought around someone else's gavagai. What is needed here is a way to question speakers in their own language: You ask, "Gavagai?" when demonstrating this new animal and get an affirmation or denial from the speaker.

> Thus suppose that in asking 'Gavagai?' and the like, in the conspicuous presence of rabbits and the like, he has elicited the responses 'Evet' and 'Yok' often enough to surmise that they may correspond to 'Yes' and 'No', but has no notion which is which. Then he tries the experiment of echoing the native's own volunteered pronouncements. If thereby he pretty regularly elicits 'Evet' rather than 'Yok', he is encouraged to take 'Evet' as 'Yes'. Also he tries responding with 'Evet' and 'Yok' to the native's remarks; the one that is the more serene in its effect is the better candidate for 'Yes'. (Quine 1960, pp. 29–30)

Clearly, this is a long and complicated process, with the possibility of numerous blind alleys that will be difficult to avoid and out of which it will be difficult to backtrack. No doubt, professional field linguists know shortcuts and rules of thumb that make this process manageable. But our interest here is not in the practicalities of the matter but in its philosophical implications. Let us try to draw out some of these.

The Assumptions Necessary for Radical Translation

The first philosophical moral of our imaginary excursion into radical translation is that as the radical translator you cannot begin your investigations with a blank mind; you must make some initial assumptions. You must assume, for instance, that the natives are friendly and not characteristically interested in lying or putting you on. (This assumption is not always correct: Recent critics of the famous anthropologist Margaret Mead allege that her native informants regularly lied to her about the customs of their tribe.)

Another closely related assumption is that at least most of the beliefs the natives express are true. For example, if you suspect that 'geegle' means *snow*, and 'gleek' means *is white*, this hypothesis is shown false if the natives regularly deny 'Geegle gleek'—but only on the assumption that they *believe* that snow is white. Of course, it is possible that any group of people share some false belief; but in order to confirm the comparative adequacy of any theory—any translation manual of a lot of words—you have to assume that at least most of what the native speakers say using those words is (what you believe is) true. Otherwise, there is no way to understand them. If you allow the real possibility that a great deal of what they say is false, you have no way at all even to begin to rule out any translation manual whatever. That is, the very possibility of your arriving at a translation of what they say depends on your taking most of what they say to be true. Philosophers have called this rule of translation the *principle of charity*. This principle means that, everything else being equal, the best translation manual is the one that translates the largest number of the native speakers' sentences into true sentences in your language.

You must also assume that the natives are stimulated by features of their environment in somewhat the same way you are. This assumption need not always be true: Ways of perception are certainly to some extent learned and can vary across cultures.

Some basic initial assumptions about the natives' language are also necessary, for instance, that it has a compositional structure and a grammar with categories somewhat similar to ours. These assumptions are necessary for any progress whatever in radical translation; without them it would be literally impossible ever to begin to make a translation manual.

In the course of investigation, some (but only some) of these assumptions might be somewhat modified or even rejected, but the radical translator cannot do without them altogether or revise all of them. This need not, however, be a cause of despair to someone who hopes for a truly scientific procedure for radical translation. Recent philosophers of science have emphasized that *all* scientific discovery works this way; they say that the view that you may have learned in elementary science classes—of utterly open-minded scientists coming to the world completely free of prejudice and presupposition and allowing reality itself to be the only source of their beliefs—is and must be a mistaken one.

Holism and Underdetermination

Another philosophical moral of the radical translation story is that one does not and *cannot* learn meanings one by one. In the extremely oversimplified Tribish example, your learning what 'Gavagai' means depends on your learning what 'Evet' and 'Yok' mean, and vice versa. As radical translator, then, you must in a sense pull yourself up by your bootstraps, making a variety of assumptions only thinly supported by previous experience about the meanings of a number of words at once. Your experience and experiments do not confirm hypotheses about *single* meaning-utterance connections; rather, they confirm what should rather be called a *theory*—a *system* of hypotheses about meanings of various utterances (plus, as we have seen, a number of other assumptions). This view is *holism* about translation theory confirmation.

The word 'confirm' does not mean *show finally to be true*. The scientific procedure in radical translation as well as elsewhere (as Quine has been instrumental in convincing us) lends more credibility to some theories than to alternative ones and may show a particular theory to be so much better than others that it is adopted and alternative ones rejected by all sensible people. But there is no on/off switch that gets thrown here at some point to indicate that some theory is finally and irrevocably true.

Another point is that various alternative hypotheses can fit the observed data more or less well, but that is not the only consideration used in assessing their relative acceptability. One must consider, in addition, such factors as their internal simplicity, their connections with other theories, their coherence with certain general firmly rooted prior suppositions, and their general usefulness. These are general criteria of adequacy for all theories.

All these considerations lead to the real possibility that two alternative theories—ones that are incompatible with each other—might at a certain point (or even forever) be equally acceptable. Each theory is rated for adequacy in the various ways we have noted: It is their total score that matters, and there may be two different ones that are better than others but equally good.

Two incompatible theories might score equally well on the criterion of coherence with the observed facts:

> Who knows but what the objects to which ['gavagai'] applies are not rabbits after all, but mere stages, or brief temporal segments, of rabbits? In either event the stimulus situations that prompt assent to 'Gavagai' would be the same as for 'Rabbit'. Or perhaps the objects to which 'gavagai' applies are all and sundry undetached parts of rabbits; again the stimulus meaning would register no difference. When from the sameness of stimulus meanings of 'Gavagai' and 'Rabbit' the linguist leaps to the conclusion that a gavagai is a whole enduring rabbit, he is just taking for granted that the native is enough like us to have a brief general term for rabbits and no brief general term for rabbit stages or parts. (Quine 1960, pp. 51–52).

Quine goes on to point out a number of other ingenious alternative hypotheses. Thus his position is that observed facts may not determine that one theory is preferable to another; thus we have the *underdetermination* of theories by the facts.

Translating Your Own Language

A surprising and important consequence of Quine's arguments is that they apply not only to radical translation but also to application of meanings to the words of other people who use *your own* language. In a sense, when you hear other people's words, you think you understand them because you "translate" them into the language you speak. Usually, of course, you believe that others who make the same kinds of noises you do are speaking the same language: that someone else's word 'rabbit' should be "translated" into your word 'rabbit'. This is called the *identity translation*. But sometimes other theoretical considerations might show that the identity translation is not the best one. Imagine, for example, that someone went around saying things such as "The snow is blue" and "There are stars in the snow tonight" and "The sky fell several times this winter" and "I'll go skiing only if there is a lot of sky on the ground." The principle of charity, together with the identity translation of the other words in that sentence, plus all those other considerations for a good theory we have briefly surveyed might show that the best translation manual for this speaker's language translates his 'snow' as your 'sky' and vice versa.

Usually, however, the fact that a translation manual for someone who makes the same sounds as you do contains a large number of identity translations is a strong point in its favor. Perhaps, then, we have a reason to rule out the paranoid hypothesis of chapter 4: The identity translation (which translates other English speakers' 'green' into your 'green') is preferable, everything else being equal. The point here is that our understanding of the language we speak is just as much a theory and just as much subject to the general criteria of scientific theoretical adequacy as is any theory of radical translation. When you are trying to figure out what any term means as used by speakers of your own language, you pick the best theory.

Quinian Antirealism about Meanings

Quine's views on the way we understand language agree with one conclusion that can be drawn from the private language argument: Knowing what someone means is not knowing what speakers have in mind when they speak—not knowing what associations they make between words and private ideas. Knowing what someone means is having a good theory about a speaker's public language behavior. What determines the "right" translation is *not* that it matches Tribish utterances with what Tribish speakers have in mind when they say them; if two theories systematically translate Tribish into English equally well, then we cannot ask which is *really* the right one. The supposition that one is *really* right because it corresponds to what a speaker has in mind is disallowed. In this sense Quine agrees with Wittgenstein's antirealism about private meanings.

But Quine appears to go even further. He is a sort of antirealist even about *public* meanings. Realists about public meanings would claim that, if two different contradictory translation theories of Tribish into English fit the public behavior of their speakers equally well, both of them cannot be true; they would also claim that there is an independently existing external fact of the matter of public meanings and that a theory is true when it says what the case is in that external reality.

Quine, however, is almost an antirealist when it comes to radical translation. His claim is that it does not make sense to think that there is some real fact of the matter, what the natives *really* mean. The only thing we can do is to get a good theory, that is, a good translation manual. (Kripke's argument in his book on Wittgenstein on private language, is a good deal similar to this.) A *better* translation manual is a better theory not because it comes closer to the real facts about meaning but because it satisfies the criteria for an acceptable theory better than its competitors; and that is all there is to the matter. (Another philosophical joke—this one unintentional—from a past student of mine: The student offered this proof of God's existence. The Bible has been translated into hundreds of different languages, but in each language *it says exactly the same thing!* A miracle! There must be a God! In the light of Quine's arguments on translation, maybe it is a miracle after all.)

Compare this to the conclusions drawn from the discussion of the paranoid hypothesis about 'grue' (chapter 4). There could be no reason, so far, for a radical translator to choose a theory that translated a Tribish word as 'green' over one that translates it as 'grue'. If these two theories are equally good, that is the end of the matter. There is no real fact of the matter, at least not until time *t*, which makes one theory right and the other wrong.

These important points need to be stressed. The conclusion we are being led to is quite a radical one: Our discovery of what others mean is nothing but our putting together a translation manual that best fits available empirical facts and satisfies our requirements for a good theory. This theory tells what they mean, and there is nothing else there. We must abandon the idea that something is going on "inside" Tribish speakers' minds that constitutes what they "really" mean when they speak and that our best theory might get right or wrong. Of course, further empirical evidence or rearrangement of the theory might result in a better theory; but the best theory we have is what *constitutes* what they mean (at least, for us and for the time); *it is what they mean.* This amounts to a thorough rejection of the idea theory of meaning or of any view of meaning that sees meaning as something "in the heads" of speakers.

What Quine is rejecting is not only any idea theory of language but also the view that there are objective rules that constitute a language. If there were such rules, finding them out would be finding out their meanings. Quine's scientific linguist is constructing a theory about mere brute facts, not about rules. Wittgensteinians sometimes argue that the public rules of a language establish the real truth about meaning and that even in cases in which *all* observable language behavior is consistent with two incompatible hypotheses, one hypotheses is the right one because it fits the rule. Quine, on the other hand, does not think that there is any real fact of the matter in a case such as this. When behavior is consistent with going on in different ways, there is no answer to the question of which way is the right way, thus to what Quine calls the "indeterminacy of translation." Much more about rules is found in the next chapter.

We can sum up Quine's radical conclusion with this slogan (which possibly overstates things a bit): There is no such thing as *meaning;* there is only acceptable translation.

The Analytic/Synthetic Distinction

A further significant consequence of Quine's considerations concerns the traditional philosophical distinction between *analytic* and *synthetic* sentences and, in general, the notion that two words in one's language have the same meaning. In the traditional view a sentence is called analytic if its truth or falsity follows merely from the meanings of the words involved; it is true or false "by definition." 'Bachelors are unmarried' is thus analytic because 'bachelor' (in one sense of the word—never mind what that word means in 'bachelor of arts' or in 'bachelor buttons') means exactly the same thing as 'unmarried man'. A sentence is said to be synthetic if its truth or falsity does not follow merely from the meanings of the words involved. 'Ducks waddle' is a synthetic sentence; waddling is not part of the definition of 'duck', and so this sentence is not true by definition, is not analytic. (Similarly, 'Elephants fly' is false but not merely because of the definition of 'elephant'; thus it is synthetic also.) Quine and his followers have argued that the analytic/synthetic distinction and the notion of exact sameness of meaning are to be discarded.

Quinians come to this conclusion because of their views on linguistic holism. Understanding the words conventionally used in our own language is in the Quinian view a matter of choice of the best theory. Thus words are not understood one at a time. Hypotheses are accepted or rejected in large groups, and a change in one hypothesis will result in changing others; that is, words in our own language get their meanings not one at a time but from their relations with all the other words in the language, as connected by our best theory.

Quine has the following picture of our belief/meaning system. There are a number of sentences you accept (to which you assign the truth value *True*) and a number you deny (to which you assign the truth value *False*). These sentences are connected to one another in a complex network: If we decide that the sentence 'Turtles die if deprived of oxygen' is false, then we would have to make changes elsewhere, perhaps in a change of truth value accorded to 'Turtles are animals' or to 'Animals die if deprived of oxygen' or to some other sentence. A variety of different changes elsewhere would restore coherence to the system of accepted and denied sentences; we would decide to make one set of changes rather than another because of the same sorts of criteria of theoretical adequacy we have been looking at.

This system of accepted and denied sentences connects with our experience in complex ways. We count certain experiences as in accord with this system and others as in conflict with it. When experience is in conflict with our system, however, there is a variety of ways to change that system to fix it up. Thus we can see that individual sentences are not accepted or rejected *one at a time,* in consequence of their coherence or conflict with experience. Experience interacts with this system as a whole. *No* sentence is immune from revision because of conflict with experience.

Now, one consequence of linguistic holism is that there is no sharp contrast between analytic and synthetic sentences. We have instead a vast and blurry theory connecting various sentences that we count as true or false, and there is no distinguishing those sentences that are purely a matter of the meanings of the words from those that connect with experience.

Thus we cannot compartmentalize sentences into two sharp categories, those that are true (or false) merely because of the meanings of the words involved (analytic) and those that are true (or false) because of the facts, not merely the words (synthetic). Quine argues that *any* sentence we now count as true could be counted as false, given sufficient experience to alter the theory it is part of; thus no sentence is permanently true merely because of the meanings of the words involved. And insofar as our theory not only relates our beliefs about the world but also gives meaning to the words we use to talk about it, no sentence merely states the facts. All sentences (as they connect in a theory) to some extent give meanings to the words involved.

In the traditional view analytic sentences are thought to be *a priori*; that is, we can know that they are true or false independently of experience. It is clear why this is so: If 'bachelor' means *unmarried man*, then we can know independently of any sociological study that 'All bachelors are unmarried' is true (and that 'Some bachelor is married' is false). Synthetic sentences, such as 'Turtles die if deprived of oxygen', are not true or false *by definition*; so this route to knowing their truth or falsity is not available. We clearly need to look at turtles to determine the truth or falsity of that sentence; thus it is said to be *a posteriori*—known only after experience. (There has been, however, considerable philosophical controversy concerning the existence of the synthetic a priori, that is, about the question of whether or not any sentence not merely true or false by definition can nevertheless be knowable before experience. Traditional empiricists, as you might expect, characteristically deny the possibility of the synthetic a priori, believing that only analytic truths can be known independently of experience.)

As we have seen, a consequence of Quine's view is that the distinction between analytic and synthetic sentences is discarded. Quine does agree, however, that there is a distinction between sentences such as 'All bachelors are married' and 'Turtles die if deprived of oxygen': The first sentence is *comparatively* a priori, and the second *comparatively* a posteriori.

Quine argues, however, that there is no sharp dividing line between the two sorts of sentence. Both sentences count now as true; it is possible that experience could lead us to count *either* as false, when that experience is incompatible with the holistic theory we now believe. The difference between the two, however, is that 'All bachelors are married' is quite recalcitrant to change in truth value as the result of possible new experience. If would take a great deal of unexpected experience and a significant switching-around of sentence–truth value pairs in the language before we decided that this sentence is false. Seeing a few turtles remain alive after oxygen deprivation, however, would result in a change of truth value assigned to 'Turtles die if deprived of oxygen' and would be accommodated fairly simply into our general theory.

Some sentences, then, are comparatively a priori, that is, not easily overturned by experience, and some are comparatively a posteriori, that is, more easily overturned by experience, although possibly not by a single experience and not by experience *alone*; recall the other nonexperiential criteria for a good theory.

Quine and the Quinians argue that the analytic/synthetic distinction is worthless; but some philosophers respond to Quine's argument by admitting that there is no sharp line separating the analytic and the synthetic; but they argue that this difference surely does exist, perhaps not as rigidly as had been thought but to some degree. Some sentences have a far larger component of truth-because-of-meaning than others, which have a far larger component of truth-because-of-the-facts.

Suggested Readings

Grice, H. P., and Peter Strawson. 1956. "In defense of a dogma." *Philosophical Review* 65(2):141–158.

A reply to Quine's attack on the analytic/synthetic distinction. This article is reprinted in [5–9].

Quine, W. V. O. 1960. *Word and Object*. Cambridge: MIT Press.

A discussion of radical translation and its implications. See especially chapter 2, which is also reprinted in [7, 9].

Quine, W. V. O. 1961. "Two dogmas of empiricism," in the *From a Logical Point of View*. Cambridge: Harvard University Press, 20–46.

An attack on the analytic/synthetic distinction. This essay can also be found in [5–7, 9].

7

Rules

Some recent philosophers think that the notions of rule and of rule following are central to an account of what language is. John Searle, a champion of this view, asserts:

> Speaking a language is engaging in a (highly complex) rule-governed form of behavior. To learn and master a language is *inter alia* [among other things] to learn and to have mastered these rules. This is a familiar view in philosophy and linguistics. (1970, p. 12)

Familiar, yes, but not unanimous. Paul Ziff writes:

> Rules have virtually nothing to do with speaking or understanding a natural language. Philosophers are apt to have the following picture of language. Speaking a language is a matter of engaging in a certain activity, an activity in accordance with certain rules. If the rules of the language are violated . . . the aim of language, viz. communication, cannot save *per accidens* [by accident] be achieved. . . . Such a picture of language can produce, can be the product of, nothing but confusion. An appeal to rules in the course of discussing the regularities to be found in a natural language is as irrelevant as an appeal to the laws of Massachusetts while discussing the laws of motion. (1960, pp. 34–35)

The central distinction here is between regular behavior that has something to do with rules and behavior that does not. I call the first kind of behavior *rule-related behavior,* and the second *merely regular behavior.* Obviously, using a language is regular behavior; the question is whether it is rule related or not.

The reason this dispute is important is that some philosophers think that rule-related behavior cannot be understood unless we take account of the rules. Think of a Martian landing on earth and observing a football game. It could try to understand football in terms of peculiar regularities of behavior—alternating periods of clustering, running, kicking, pushing, throwing, catching, and so on—in terms of what we can call *brute facts* (pardon the pun). But unless the Martian found out the rules, it would not know that some of these activities constitute a touchdown or a fumble, etc. It would not know what the game is *about;* the game would make no sense, and the Martian would not understand it. It would not be able to play football, because any finite sample of football it observed would be consistent with going on in a variety of different ways, only some of which would be in accord with the rules. The Martian would have an incomplete description of what was going on.

Similarly, a brute-fact analysis of language would, these philosophers argue, leave out everything important; unless we take account of the rules of language, we would not know that some noise-making activities constitute informing, asking, promising, and so on. Some philosophers argue that the brute facts of past language behavior do not determine a *right* way of going on or what counts as going on in the same way. *Rules* are what determine this. Without taking account of the rules, we would be as much in the dark about language as the Martian would be about football.

It is a hotly debated question whether a theory that just speaks of regularities—brute facts—can do justice to a rule-related activity; but I cannot go any further into this general debate here. The prior question is whether language is in fact a rule-related activity.

In order to be able to judge the relative merits of the two sides of this question, we have to do a good deal of investigation into the idea of rule. What is a rule? When do regularities of action have something to do with rules?

The best way to approach this problem is to look at clear cases— *paradigms*—of rule-related and merely regular behavior in order to try to discover what makes them different. Here are two typical examples. Suppose that truck drivers by and large tend to behave regularly in two ways: They stop at red lights, and they rest their left arms on the ledge of the open window. The first is pretty clearly rule related in some sense, and the second is not. I consider a number of features of these paradigms and wonder whether these features constitute tests for the difference between the two kinds of behavior.

Inscriptions

We know that truck drivers' red-light-stopping is rule related because we know that a rule exists requiring them to stop at red lights; it can be found written among the official traffic laws. What brought this rule into existence is that it was written as part of an official ceremony by the appropriately empowered social authorities. Let's call the token sentence that establishes the existence of a rule the *inscription* of that rule.

There is, of course, no such official rule regarding where to rest one's left arm. Not just any written statement is sufficient to make it the case that a rule exists: I can write

> Truck drivers must rest their left arms on the ledge of the open window of their trucks.

but this does not suffice to create a rule. Many times it takes some sort of writing under particular ceremonial circumstances to create a legal rule. When *I* write

> Drivers must stop at red lights.

this token sentence is not an inscription of the rule. It is not the official written statement that creates the rule; it is merely a *report* of a rule that already exists because of its inscription.

The languages we ordinarily speak have no such rule inscriptions and were established by no such ceremonies; as Bertrand Russell says, "We can hardly suppose a parliament of hitherto speechless elders meeting together and agreeing to call a cow a cow and a wolf a wolf" (1921, p. 190).

Not all rules are official laws. We call rules that are not laws, *informal rules*. There do exist *some* informal written "rules" of language; examples are the rules of grammar one finds in textbooks and the rules of word meaning one finds in dictionaries. These, however, merely report correct language usage; they do not initially establish them; thus they are not inscriptions. The existence of these reports does not show that language is in any sense a system of rules, because they might be simply reports of mere regularities.

On the other hand, the nonexistence of inscriptions for language regularities does not show that language is not rule related. Many informal rules have no inscriptions. (Indeed, in countries with a common-law tradition, even certain laws have no inscriptions.)

Some of the regularities of language do not even have reports. It has already been mentioned that linguists have not yet discovered all the laws of grammar, and the meanings of all words are written nowhere. Where, for example, can we find the "rule" for the application of the adjective 'yellow'? Not in any dictionary. Here is an example of a dictionary entry under 'yellow':

> Of the colour between green and orange in the spectrum,
> coloured like buttercup or primrose or lemon or egg-yolk or gold.
> (*The Shorter Oxford English Dictionary*)

But this is not the rule for applying 'yellow'. The facts that this statement reports—that yellow things are the color of egg yolk, etc.—are
correct ones, but nobody ever uses these facts to judge whether or not
something is yellow. If buttercups and primroses turned a different
color and if we discovered that we had somehow been mistaken
about the place of yellow in the spectrum, we needn't change our use
of the word 'yellow'. If we have a "rule" for using 'yellow', it is not
reported in this, or any, dictionary.

Nor is the nonexistence of reports for some language regularities
conclusive proof that language is not rule related. Rules can exist
unreported. Imagine that your family follows the rule that Cousin
Billy, the black sheep of the family, should never be mentioned. This
rule can exist and can be understood and followed, even though
nobody has ever produced a verbalization of the rule. (Indeed, to
report the rule would be to violate it.) I call rules that have neither
inscriptions nor reports *tacit rules*.

Learning Rules

When one learns to drive, one is normally presented explicitly with
the rule that it is necessary to stop at red lights. Ziff argues:

> If there were "rules of language" then presumably such rules
> would be laid down in the course of teaching the language. This
> is another confusion: one is not taught one's native language,
> one learns it. In our culture a child is not taught to speak at
> school: he can speak before he goes to school. If he cannot, he is
> not likely to be taught much at school. If he can speak before he
> goes to school, who taught him to speak? The parent who
> teaches his child an occasional word may think he is teaching his
> child to speak. But a normal person during the early part of his
> life learns a thousand words a year, more than three words a day
> on the average. Who teaches him these words? . . . Children
> learn from one another; they rarely if ever teach one another.
> (1960, p. 35)

But this is not conclusive either. We can surely conceive of learning
what a genuine system of rules is without ever having been presented
with explicit presentations of those rules. One may learn football by
observing football games and trying to participate; this is how most

children in football-playing countries "learn the rules." Remember the argument that one cannot learn the rules merely by observing regularities, but perhaps one can learn by participating and being corrected when one breaks the rules. This suggests that a crucial feature of rule-guided systems is that there is a right and wrong way to do things.

Right and Wrong and Sanctions

Even though (we assume) truck drivers rest their left arms on their window ledges, nobody thinks it is wrong not to do so; but it is wrong to go through a red light. Rules tell you what you must, can, and cannot do. Thus they establish (within the system they are part of, anyway) right and wrong ways of doing things. Going through a red light may result in punishment (a *sanction*), but a truck driver may do whatever he likes with his arm with impunity. There are sanctions for doing things wrong. Ziff admits that there are some "rules" in language and some sanctions:

> There are so-called "rules of grammar" which children are taught at school. While at school an infringement of these rules carries with it the sanction of low grades. Apart from school matters such rules are associated with certain social taboos. . . . Generally speaking, such "rules of grammar" are laid down to inhibit the speakers of the language from speaking in a way they in fact speak. . . . Nothing (linguistically significant) follows. (1960, p. 36)

We can agree with Ziff that the rule that, for example, prohibits people from saying "He don't believe it" and the sanctions for corresponding misperformances, such as low grades or exclusion from the educated social class, are not a significant part of language. But surely there are more significant "rules," such as the rule that makes 'arrived' mean *arrived* and not *left* and thus prohibits people from saying "He left" when what they mean is *He arrived*, and the rule that prohibits people from saying "Is on at the," whatever they mean. We might be inclined to say that the sanction for violation here is non-communication. Ziff replies:

> A deviation from the regularities to be found in or in connection with a language may on occasion interfere with communication. But the importance of communication is usually exaggerated. (1960, p. 36)

Ziff points out that diplomatic speech, cocktail party chatter, and poetry are full of irregularity and noncommunication but meet with no sanctions and are not prohibited. This is not, however, an entirely convincing reply. In special contexts we of course permit noncomunication, just as when a chess game is not in progress, one may move chess pieces in any way one likes. But this does not mean that there are no rules or sanctions for moving chess pieces. One is excused from the rules of chess when it is understood that a game is not in progress, and one may say anything when it is understood that literal English is not being spoken. But when it is understood that English *is* being spoken, there are right and wrong ways of doing things. Breaking the rules typically does interfere with communication, and surely one does not exaggerate when one emphasizes the communicative function of language.

Nonetheless, it is not clear that the fact that we detect what we count as right and wrong ways of doing things is a good sign of the existence of rules. Someone who walks around with his finger touching the tip of his nose would be seen by most of us as doing something wrong—not morally wrong but just somehow peculiar or defective. This is a consequence of our inevitable conformist tendencies: We feel that anything extraordinary is "wrong." But this does not show that we operate under a rule such as "Don't walk around with your finger touching the tip of your nose." The face that so few of us act this way might be seen as a mere regularity, not the following of a rule; "violations" are felt to be wrong just because they are unusual. Or should we say, after all, that this is a tacit rule?

We must admit, however, that it is a bit strange to speak of sanctions in the case of breaking the rules of language. Breaking traffic law rules clearly does leave one liable to clear sanctions, but (aside from the cases Ziff mentions) there are usually no punishments for breaking language rules. When we discover that someone is not following the rules of language, we just shrug and walk away: Nobody is fined or put in jail. Noncommunication is not a *punishment*. This is because (roughly) language is more like chess than it is like driving: One may opt out of chess or language, but one may not opt out of the driving laws. The only "punishment" for moving a chess piece in violation of the chess rules is losing the game, but this does not matter to someone who is not interested in playing by the rules anyway. To most people it is more important and useful to "play" the "language game" than it is to play chess. Although real sanctions are perhaps typical of paradigmatic rule systems, such as driving laws, they are not necessary to all rule systems; thus the lack of real sanctions in language does not, contrary to Ziff, show that language is not a rule-related activity.

But there is even a further complicating factor. According to Searle, it need not even be the case that all rules direct behavior, that is, make it the case that people must, may, or may not act in certain ways. *Regulative rules*, in Searle's terminology, direct behavior but *constitutive rules* need not. Not all the rules of chess, for example, tell players what may, must, or cannot be done; some set up definitions of special terms used in other rules (for example, "A square is 'under attack by an enemy piece' when that piece can move to the square on its next move" (Knight 1973, p. 25)). Searle thinks that certain rules of English are constitutive rules, for example, the rule to the effect that saying (under certain conditions) "I promise to ———" constitutes a promise to do the action named.

Even though one finds items such as the "rule" of chess mentioned in what are called lists of rules or rule books, it does not seem to me that these are really genuine rules; rather, they are definitions of terms used elsewhere in genuine rules. Perhaps the question of whether or not these are, properly, rules is the familiar and uninteresting question of stipulating a meaning (in this case, for 'rule') when ordinary usage is unclear. More important, however, if these are merely definitions of terms used in other inscriptions or reports of rules, then they will not form any part of systems of tacit rules.

Cultural Regularities

It is easy to think of examples of merely regular action. Everyone breathes more than twice a minute, although there is no rule in existence to this effect. But why should we think that no such breathing rule exists? We can write

Everyone must breathe more than twice a minute.

Why not say that this sentence reports a rule and that the great regularity we find in human breathing behavior is rule related? In a similar way, *every* regularity of action could be counted as rule related, because we can state a similar "rule" for any regularity. But this would be an absurd consequence; surely it is not the case that there is a rule corresponding to *every* regularity of action. What we need is some way to decide when rules really exist and when they do not. Otherwise, the notion of rule-related behavior would be trivial, because it would simply be equivalent to regular behavior.

One feature of the breathing regularity that inclines us to think that no rule corresponding to it exists is that there is a perfectly sufficient biological explanation for why people act this way. Similarly, the fact that people tossed out of windows accelerate toward the earth at a certain regular rate is surely not rule related, because it has a physical explanation. If a regularity has a purely biological or physical explanation, we are disinclined to speak of rules—at least, in literal, non-metaphorical ways. We can say, of course, that there is a "rule" that robins fly south in the winter or that the sun rises a little later each day in August, but this is speaking only loosely. We might think that only cultural or individual regularities in the behavior of conscious beings, where there is no biological or physical explanation, can be rule related. If the regularities exhibited by English speakers have no biological or physical explanation, then that is some grounds for thinking that they are rule related.

But this way of thinking is full of difficulties. First, is this restriction to conscious beings justified? One might think that the reason that robins and heavenly bodies cannot behave in rule-related ways is that they can hardly be *motivated* by the existence of rules. But conscious motivation, as we will shortly see, is perhaps not necessary for rule-related behavior; we can speak perfectly well of rule-related behavior when the behaver is not motivated by a rule.

Another difficulty here is that the cultural explanation of a regularity (as opposed to a biological or physical explanation) is not always a good reason to think that the behavior is rule related. Imagine that American truck drivers usually wear baseball-style hats, whereas English truck drivers usually wear flat cloth caps. This would clearly be a cultural regularity; we hardly would think that there is a genetic difference between the truck drivers that explains their wearing different hats. We would guess that this difference is just a matter of custom and that members of a group wear the kinds of hats they do only because they unconsciously imitate each other. But this would not appear to be a matter of rule-related behavior.

Nevertheless, it is not perfectly clear that this sort of cultural learned regularity is not rule related. Social scientists seem to be in the habit of speaking of such regularities as the result of tacit social rules. An additional problem is that some behaviors of subhuman, probably unconscious organisms are now thought to be matters of cultural regularity, not the result of innate biological preprogramming. Suppose that robins of a particular group migrate to a particular place because they learn to do so from other robins in that group; should we then speak of unconscious rule-related behavior in robins?

More problems: It is questionable whether or not a regularity that has a biological explanation should therefore be judged as a mere regularity, not a rule-related one. Recall from our discussion of the innateness controversy that there are some philosophers who think that certain regularities of language behavior are innate, not learned; but they often say that what is genetically given is (in some sense) knowledge of rules.

Motivation

Suppose that, when asked why they stop at red lights, most truck drivers report that they do so because there is a driving law that requires it and that they are able to state the law approximately. When asked, on the other hand, why they rest their arms on the window ledge, they say that they do not know or that it is comfortable to do so; in any case, none ever says that there is a rule to this effect.

Now suppose that a particular truck driver always stops at red lights but cannot state and does not know of any rule to this effect. Perhaps his motivation is to avoid collision with traffic going the other way, or perhaps he is consciously or unconsciously imitating other drivers. A rule surely exists requiring his action, but because he is unaware of it, he is not *guided by* the rule; he is merely acting in a way that *fits* it. Quine distinguishes the two cases this way:

> Imagine two systems of English grammar: one an old-fashioned system that draws heavily on the Latin grammarians, and the other a streamlined formulation due to Jespersen. Imagine that the two systems are . . . equivalent, in this sense: they determine, recursively, the same infinite set of well-formed English sentences. In Denmark the boys in one school learn English by the one system, and those in another school learn it by the other. In the end the boys all sound alike. Both systems of rules fit the behavior of all the boys, but each system guides the behavior of only half the boys. . . . Fitting is a matter of true description; guiding is a matter of cause and effect. Behavior fits a rule whenever it conforms to it; whenever the rule truly describes it. But the behavior is not guided by the rule unless the behaver knows and can state it. (1972, p. 442)

But can a rule exist, which people's behavior fits, if *nobody* is ever guided by it? I think that we can imagine a certain sort of case in which this might be so. Imagine that there is an obscure traffic law on the books, long forgotten, forbidding the driving of cars longer than 100 feet. It is hard to imagine how such a law would come to be part of the driving code, because nobody would do what this law forbids even if it did not exist. It is clear that this rule would exist, however, so we could properly say that drivers regularly act in ways fitting this rule, though nobody would be guided by it.

But the status of an informal tacit rule, one without inscription, that nobody is guided by is more troublesome. How could we find out that it exists? There would be no place where it is written down, and it would have no status establishing it as an "official" rule. Nobody would claim its existence as a reason for her regular action. The mere existence of regular behavior should not count as reason to think that an informal tacit rule exists.

The problem with seeing language as rule related can now be faced squarely. Those philosophers who believe that there are language rules must admit that the rules are (with the exception of those noted above by Ziff) tacit and informal. When linguists are able to figure out what the rules are and write them down, these writings would be reports, not inscriptions, and would be quotable and consciously used for guidance in linguistic behavior only by the few who learn a second (or third, etc.) language from them. Almost nobody who is a native speaker of the language, then, would be *guided* by these rules, in the sense that Quine understands this term. Everyone would be acting merely in accord with these rules. But then there would be no reason at all to think that such rules exist. This sort of behavior seems to be a clear case of merely regular action.

Going on in the Same Way

But perhaps Quine is seeing rule guidance too narrowly. In order for it to be proper to think of the existence of tacit rules at all, one must have reason to think that at least some behavior is rule guided; but must people who are rule guided be able to state or even know about the existence of a rule that guides them? Searle argues that one can "follow a rule," that is, act guided by it, not merely fitting it, even if one does not know the rule. He offers as argument the following example, which involves the pronunciation of words ending with 'ger'. In some common dialects of English, pronunciation of those words not formed from a verb include the phoneme /g/, but pronunciation of those formed from a verb do not include that phoneme. (A *phoneme* is one of the set of basic units of sound necessary in a language to distinguish one word from another.) The phoneme /g/ is the hard "g" sound, such as is heard in the pronunciation of 'going' at the beginning of the word but not at the end. You can probably hear this difference if you say aloud the words 'singer' (formed from the verb 'sing', no /g/) and 'finger' (not formed from a verb, pronounced with a /g/). Searle argues:

I want to claim that this is a rule and not just a regularity, as can be seen both from the fact that we recognize departures as 'mispronunciations' and from the fact that the rule covers new cases. . . . Thus, suppose we invent a noun "longer" from the verb "to long". "Longer" = df. *one who longs*. ['= df.' means *is by definition*.] Then in the sentence, "This longer longs longer than that longer," the initial and terminal "longer" have no /g/ phoneme in their pronunciation, the interior "longer" ho ·ever has the hard /g/. Not all English dialects have this rule, and I do not claim there are no exceptions—nonetheless, it is a good rule. It seems obvious to me that it is a rule, and that it is one which we follow without necessarily knowing (in the sense of being able to formulate) that we do. . . . Two of the marks of rule-governed as opposed to merely regular behaviour are that we generally recognize deviations from the pattern as somehow wrong or defective and that the rule unlike the past regularity automatically covers new cases. Confronted with a case he has never seen before, the agent knows what to do. (1970, p. 42)

Searle's reasoning here is that behavior that has these two "marks" can be adequately explained only by the postulation of internalized learned but unconscious and unformulated rules. The same sort of reasoning is behind the supposition by those who believe that some of language has an innate basis, that what is genetically programmed is best seen as a set of unconscious and unformulated rules. If these rules can be said to "motivate" behavior at all, then they should be said to provide unconscious motivation only.

As we have already seen, however, our recognition of right and wrong ways of doing things, of "correct" and "deviant" cases, does not necessarily show that we are operating under rules; it may just be our conformist reaction to unusual behavior.

The second "mark" of rule-related regular behavior that Searle mentions is that the behavior is carried on to new cases in the same way. Unfortunately, however, the fact that a regularity is continued in a new sort of case is not a sure sign of rules as opposed to mere regularities. We can imagine that the truck driver who regularly rests his arm out the window would do the same when he, for the first time, drove a farm tractor with an enclosed cab or was a passenger in a bus. Regularities that are habits carry on to new cases, and there is no need to think of rules in those cases. And if, as some philosophers argue, without rules nothing *counts* as going on in the same way, then this "mark" would be useless, for we would first have to know the rule that governs some sort of action *before* deciding whether a particular action goes on in the same way.

After our long and tortuous search through various proposals for sure tests for when a regularity is rule related as opposed to merely regular, we have come to an impasse. Although we have seen that various characteristics are often associated with paradigm cases of rule-related or merely regular behavior, none of them seems decisive. Perhaps the concept is just a mess, without clear criteria of application; but more likely, this is an unanswered question that needs further philosophical work. In any case I leave the question undecided and pass on to a related and more powerful way to understand the basis of the regularities of language: the notion of *convention*. This gives us a useful and illuminating way to explain what kind of regularity the regularities of linguistic behavior are and what they are for.

Suggested Readings

Knight, Brian M. 1973. *Fascinating History of Chess Pieces and Internationally Recognized Laws of Chess*. Montreal: Chess Nut Books.

Quine, W. V. O. 1972. "Methodological reflections on current linguistic theory," in *Semantics of Natural Language*, Donald Davidson and Gilbert Harmon, eds. Boston: Reidel, 442–454.

Russell, Bertrand. 1921. *The Analysis of Mind*. London: Macmillan.

Searle, John. 1970. *Speech Acts*. Cambridge: Cambridge University Press.
   Searle's arguments for the centrality of rules in language. See especially chapter 2, part 5. A discussion of constitutive versus regulative rules is also found here.

Winch, Peter. 1958. *The Idea of a Social Science and Its Relation to Philosophy*. Boston: Routledge & Kegan Paul.
   A classic extended argument for the rule-relatedness of language and for the necessity of taking rules into account in order to understand any rule-related activity.

Ziff, Paul. 1960. *Semantic Analysis*. Ithaca: Cornell University Press.
   Ziff's arguments against the centrality of rules in language are in the appendix to chapter 1.

8

Conventions

We now look at a powerful and provocative theory that tries to explain in greater detail and specificity exactly what sort of social arrangement the existence of natural languages actually represents. This theory was developed in detail in a recent influential book by David Lewis; its outline is sketched here.

The first notion to understand is that of a *coordination problem*. Suppose that you and I want to meet at a bar every Tuesday night and that there are two bars in town that are possible, equally good choices. It does not matter which bar we go to, so long as we go to the same one, so that we meet. This is a coordination problem, defined by Lewis as

> a situation of interdependent decision by two or more agents in which coincidence of interest predominates and in which there are two or more proper coordination equilibria. (1969, p. 24)

A *coordination equilibrium* is a combination of actions by all agents such that no agent would be better off had any one agent acted differently. Thus, in the current example, if we both go to El Grubbo Cafe, that is a coordination equilibrium, because nobody would be better off if I alone had acted differently and had gone to Sleezy's Bar instead or if you alone had gone to Sleezy's. A second coordination equilibrium is achieved if we both go to Sleezy's.

We can imagine different kinds of ways in which this problem can be solved, how we can manage to arrive both at a coordination equilibrium and at the same bar. We might happen each week, just by blind luck, both to go to the same bar. Or I could telephone you and suggest Sleezy's (or the other bar), and you could agree. This is a solution to our coordination problem by agreement (and something similar to the establishment of a rule by inscription). Or suppose (implausibly) that Parliament, appreciating our difficulty, passes a law requiring us both to go to El Grubbo. This solves our coordination problem by the creation of a rule by an empowered authority. Or we can eventually wind up doing the same thing if one of us merely imitates the other. (Other kinds of ways, which I will not go into, are discussed by Lewis.)

Conventions

But there is a different way, the most interesting one, in which a solution may come about. Suppose that we try to meet despite the absence either of prior agreement or rule and that just by luck we succeed when we both just happen to show up at Sleezy's. Now, by next Tuesday there is still no rule, and we stupidly have again neglected to form an agreement; but I reason that because we succeeded in getting together at Sleezy's last week, you are most likely to try that again, and you think the same; so we both go to Sleezy's. We have solved our coordination problem again, but this time not by mere luck. We have both reasoned matters out. We each expect the other to go to Sleezy's, and so we each go there. Note that it is also reasonable for me to think that you will go to Sleezy's because you expect me to go there and for me to think that you will think I will go there because you expect me to think that you will go there, and so on ad infinitum. Of course, I do not go through this infinite chain of reasoning (it would take me an infinite amount of time) but each link is justified, if I were to reason that way. This sort of infinite chain of justified expectations is called *mutual knowledge*.

Once we have this mutual knowledge, we have solved our coordination problem. We can now manage to meet every Tuesday. This kind of solution to the coordination problem is called by Lewis a solution by *convention*.

Solutions by convention are widespread and important in our everyday lives. For example, suppose that you are driving down a virtually deserted road and you see a car approaching you from a distance. Were it not for convention, you might have a fatal coordination problem: If you try to go by the other car on your left and the other driver tries to pass you on her right, you would be in trouble. The law about keeping to the right is, of course, designed to solve this coordination problem; but given the existence of a convention, the law is hardly necessary. Each of you has good reason to want to avoid collision, and each of you has good reason to think the other wants the same. Both of you know the convention for doing this: Keep right. Each of you has reason to think the other knows this. Both of you reasonably believe the other knows this (and so on). So (most of the time) you pass each other safely, each on your own right, not necessarily because each of you obeys the traffic rules (on this straight deserted road both of you are probably exceeding the speed limit) but because of the existence of a convention. There are countless ways our lives are facilitated (or even made possible) by conventions. (It has even been suggested that morality has its source in convention.)

One complication needs to be noted here. Suppose that we get into the habit of meeting at Sleezy's, but for the following reason: I *falsely* think that you live near Sleezy's and that you have no car and thus that you cannot go to El Grubbo; and you falsely think the same thing about me. We both go to Sleezy's because we expect the other to go there and want to meet. But it seems that this is not exactly meeting by convention, because we do not *think* that this arrangement is a convention; we think that it is a necessity. I do not expect you to be there because you expect me to be there. I do not expect you to expect me to be there because you expect me to expect you to be there (and so on). Lewis thought that this sort of behavior is in fact not conventional behavior; he specified that the participants in a convention must know that what they are doing is conventional; their motivation must include the realization that their behavior is conventional (and the realization that the other participant's behavior is similarly motivated, and so on). Thus our meeting at Sleezy's because of our mistaken beliefs is not conventional behavior.

This restriction makes conventional behavior analogous to rule-following behavior, and Lewis's amendment is analogous to Quine's strong position on behavior *guided by rules:* The participants must know the convention (or rule) as a convention (or rule) and must be motivated to act because they know it (and are able to state it) and recognize it as a convention (or rule).

Just as this strong position on rules makes it doubtful that language behavior is guided by rules, similarly it makes it seem that language, at least large parts of it, cannot be conventional. As we have seen, some philosophers think that significant parts of natural language are not *arbitrary* solutions to coordination problems, because they think that those parts of language are innately, genetically determined. Similarly, they hold that the innate structures (rules?) that regulate all languages are not *consciously* recognized as motivations for our usual language behavior. They do not *believe* that some significant parts of their own language behavior are the result of conscious application of arbitrary, socially developed solutions to coordination problems. Thus, whether or not they are correct, given the last restriction Lewis added, it would follow that *their* language behavior, at least, is not entirely conventional. If they are right in the innateness hypothesis, then significant parts of everybody's language behavior are not conventional.

But, the innateness hypothesis aside, most people certainly do not give a thought to the underpinnings of language we have discussed; thus we can hardly say that they recognize it as a convention or are motivated to act in the linguistically regular way they do because of the way conventions solve coordination problems. Given Lewis's restriction, then, almost no ordinary language behavior is conventional.

It is possible that language had its historical origins in conscious attempts to solve coordination problems. We can imagine our primitive ancestors wanting, for example, to have ways to signal each other about something and developing arbitrary verbalizations that each would expect the other to understand in certain ways. But suppose that by now we give little or no thought to the coordination problems that language actually solves but use language instead out of mere imitation of each other and habit (compare why you now drive to the right). It would follow again, by Lewis's amended definition, that language is not now conventional, because we are now anyway, unmotivated by coordination.

But one might wonder whether Lewis's last restriction is correct. Can some behavior be conventional even though the participants do not think that it is? Perhaps this is still another empty question about how to define a technical term. 'Convention' is a philosopher's technical term that we can define any way we like; thus there is no use arguing about the "proper" definition.

I think that it is best merely to distinguish *overt* from *covert* conventional behavior. The participants in overt conventional behavior meet Lewis's strong restriction: They realize that they act as they do because each realizes (or would realize, if asked) that it is the arbitrary coordination equilibrium the other will also choose (and so on). Covert conventional action may be of several sorts:

1. It is conceivable that people are really *motivated* to act as they do because their action is an arbitrary socially invented solution to a coordination problem, although they do not realize this and would not think so if asked. (This assumes what is perhaps implausible: that we can have unconscious motivation.)

2. It might be that the historical origins of regular behavior patterns were conscious arbitrary social solutions to coordination problems— overt conventions—although by now everyone acts as they do merely on the basis of habit and imitation.

3. There exist arbitrary solutions to coordination problems that were *never* conscious motivations. Good examples come from unconscious nonhuman organisms. Certain bees get their food from the

nectar of certain flowers and provide those flowering plants with pollination. At some point in their evolution, the flowers managed to evolve certain color patterns to attract the bees, and the bees managed to evolve attraction to those color patterns. The color patterns "chosen" by the bees and by the flowers are arbitrary—so long as the pattern the flowers "choose" is the same one the bees "choose." There are strong analogies between this case and the coordination problem of choosing the same bar. An important difference, however, is that nothing here is conscious and everything here is innate. We can, if we like, call this a case of covert convention. There are also cases among nonhuman organisms of culturally transmitted, learned covert convention, for example, the learned arbitrary song that local groups of birds develop to recognize each other.

Conventional Signaling

Now let's turn to the special form of interaction between persons that Lewis calls *signaling*. Roughly, we can think of signaling as communication. One can, by actions of various sorts, convey something to another in all sorts of ways. You hear me sniffle; the information is conveyed to you that I have a cold. As I walk down the hall, you might be signaled by my noisy tread to walk quickly and silently the other way (if you do not want to see me). Signals can be signals *that* something or other is the case or signals *to* do something or other or both. My noisy walking is a signal *that* I am coming and a signal *to* head the other way.

Much of our signaling to one another rests merely on regularities. The natural fact of the matter is that people generally sniffle when they have a cold, and so this mere regularity underlies the signal you get from my sniffle. Much of this kind of signaling is unintentional, although I could, of course, sniffle on purpose just in order to communicate to you that I have a cold.

Consider, however, the kinds of things that we want to signal intentionally. I can intentionally signal you to take your umbrella by showing up in front of you soaking wet, relying on various obvious regularities and on your knowing these. But how do I signal you to take your umbrella tomorrow? that the forecast is for rain tomorrow? Again there are possibilities (based on mere regularity) with various degrees of plausibility, but clearly the most reliable and easiest ways are those that use language: I *tell you* that the forecast is for rain or *urge you* to take your umbrella tomorrow. Telling you stands a good chance of signaling you that the forecast is for rain, and urging you signals you to take your umbrella tomorrow. These reliable and convenient ways are cases of *conventional signaling*. Here is why.

First, in conventional signaling there is a widespread congruence of interest on the parts of the signaler (call her the *speaker*, although this can be done in writing) and of the one signaled (call him the *audience*, although this can be done by reading). People often want to signal others and want to be signaled.

Second, it does not really matter what method we use for signaling. Only a limited amount of signaling can be done by relying on natural regularities, but any one of a huge number of arbitrary actions could count as a signal, so long as both the speaker and the audience understand and subscribe to the same method. Intentional signaling is thus a coordination problem with an infinite number of coordination equilibria.

Conventions produce a solution to the coordination problem. The speaker wants to signal the audience, and the audience wants to be signaled. One of the many coordination equilibria has somehow been established as the conventional one, and when the speaker produces these actions, the audience, understanding the existing conventions for signaling, takes these actions to be a sign that the speaker wants to signal the audience in a certain way, and therefore the audience receives the signal. The speaker is motivated to use just those conventional actions to signal because she reasonably believes that the audience will take them in this way.

Speech and writing are good modes for conventional signaling (although they are not the only modes). Their particular form is highly arbitrary, so that instances of them are unlikely to be confused with other sorts of behavior. Speech is handy; writing sends signals even in the absence of the signaler. They are immensely—infinitely—variable. Thus we have language.

Suggested Reading

Lewis, David K. 1969. *Convention: A Philosophical Study*. Cambridge: Harvard University Press.

9

Speech Acts

Meaning as Use

The philosophical sources for the sort of analysis of meaning I hinted at at the end of chapter 8 are influential works by J. L. Austin, H. P. Grice, and John Searle. These works have spawned an entire tradition in the philosophy of language, called the *speech act theory* of meaning. The central strategy here is to see language as a *tool* for *doing things* and to explain what bits of language mean in terms of what they are used to do.

Suppose that Sally says, "It is raining outside"; what is she doing by making this noise? We can imagine all sorts of things. Under various circumstances she might thereby:

report to the hearer that it is raining outside
get the hearer to believe correctly that it is raining outside
get the hearer to believe falsely that it is raining outside [she is lying or mistaken]
get the hearer to believe that it is Tuesday [because his competence in English is slim and he takes her to be saying that it is Tuesday]
get the hearer to believe that it is Tuesday [because he believes that it rains only on Tuesday]
get the hearer to take his umbrella
get the hearer to stay around awhile
get the hearer to leave
get the hearer to think that she is stupid
insult the hearer
please the hearer
surprise the hearer
wake the hearer up
cause war to break out in Guatemala [How? I leave it to your imagination]
practice her English

practice her lines in a play
see if the microphone she is speaking into is turned on
do nothing at all except make that noise [if nobody is listening]

In fact, anyone might just do anything at all by uttering any sounds in any language, or not in any language, given the appropriate circumstances. The problem is that some of these things Sally might do have nothing at all to do with the meaning of what she says. In other cases the meaning of what Sally says has some connection with what she does by saying it, but it seems altogether implausible that we could explain what the meaning of her utterance is by examining the list of things she might do by uttering it, because the list is limited only by our imagination and because the list for one utterance would not distinguish it from any other one (we could imagine the same list for any other utterance). This makes the prospects for explaining what each utterance type or token means in terms of what one might do by saying it look dim indeed, and similarly for the prospects for explaining in these terms in general what language meaning is.

Grice attempts to deal with this sort of problem by specifying that only certain sorts of things that one does with utterances are the ones that explain its meaning.

First, it is clear that if we are interested in what Sally means when she said "It is raining outside," we should ignore all the things she might thereby have done *unintentionally*. If her utterance was not intended to insult the hearer or to start a war in Guatemala, then these effects are not relevant to what she meant by uttering the sentence token. So we restrict the list to those things she intended to do.

Second, we can restrict the list to cases in which the action is the result of an effect on a hearer. Grice wants this restriction because he thinks that someone's meaning something by a bit of language essentially involves the speaker's having the intention to affect a hearer in some way. Any sentence at all could be used to test a microphone, and whatever (if anything) it means is not relevant; but the meaning of the sentence is crucially involved when the effect of uttering the sentence on a hearer is considered. (But it is not *always* relevant. Try to think of a case when an effect *on a hearer* is intended but the meaning of the uttered sentence is irrelevant. The list of intentions contains some cases of this sort.)

Third, Grice wants to restrict the list to the kinds of things that are intentionally done to hearers in a certain kind of way: by means of revealing to the hearer the speaker's intentions to do these things. When I say to you, for example, "Please pass the salt," I intend to get you to pass the salt, and the way I try to accomplish this is by revealing to you that I have this intention. I think that my saying "Please pass the salt" will get you to pass the salt because I think that my saying "Please pass the salt" will get you to see that I want you to pass the salt and because I think that your seeing this will result in your passing the salt. A speaker can achieve certain kinds of effects on a cooperative hearer by means of getting the hearer to realize that the effects are desired by the speaker. This, according to Grice, is the primary way language is used, and it is the capacity for use in this way that makes a bit of language mean what it does.

These restrictions go some way toward fixing up the initial implausibility we noticed in the attempt to explain meaning by giving an account of what one does with language. The problem was that one might do just anything with just any bit of language, so this approach did not seem to lead us any closer to an understanding of what bits of language mean. Given these restrictions, however, only some of the vast number of things that can be done with language are relevant to what the speaker means by a particular token.

To summarize Grice's position, then, we can say that the meaning of a language token consists in its intentional use by the speaker to accomplish her desire to get the hearer to do something by revealing to the hearer that the speaker has this intention. What a speaker S means by a particular token utterance on a particular occasion, then, is explained in terms of S's intentions: to reveal to the hearer H that S wants H to respond in a certain way and thus to get H to respond in this way.

Some more examples may clarify this. Suppose that I say to you, "It is raining outside," intending thereby to (1) get you to realize that I want you to believe that it is raining outside, and thus (2) get you to believe (if you trust me) that it is raining outside. These intentions constitute what I mean by that sentence. Similarly, if I say to you, "It is time you were off," what I mean by that is constituted by my intentions to (1) get you to realize that I want you to leave and thus (2) get you to leave (if you are cooperative).

These examples seem to show that Grice's theory is plausible, for giving these intentions does seem to be relevant to what the speaker means by what she says.

Illocutionary and Perlocutionary Acts

There are, however, several objections that show that Grice's theory needs fixing, despite its initial plausibility. The objections all have the form of producing imaginary examples in which someone says something with the proper Gricean sorts of intention, but these intentions apparently do not have anything to do with the meaning of the sentence.

Here is one such example. Suppose that Sally says to Fred, "It is raining outside," with the following intentions: (1) She wants to get Fred to realize that she wants him to take his umbrella, and (2) she wants thereby to get Fred to take his umbrella. These intentions fit Grice's pattern for indicating the meaning of her utterance, but is this *what she meant* by that utterance? It seems not. Of course, we can say that, by Sally saying "It's raining outside," she meant to get Fred to take his umbrella (by getting him to realize that she wanted to get him to take his umbrella), but 'meant' here seems to mean only *intended*, as when we say, "By connecting those wires, he meant to fix his TV." These intentions tell us Sally's motivations in saying what she did, but they do not tell us what she took the words she uttered to mean. They give the speaker's intentions, but they do not give the speaker's meaning of the token utterance.

To see how to fix up Grice's theory, let's begin by spelling out in greater detail exactly what we suppose Sally's intentions were: (1) She wanted to get Fred to realize that she is trying to *inform* him that it is raining outside, and thereby (2) she wanted to get Fred to realize that she is trying to get him to take his umbrella, and thereby (3) she wanted to get Fred to take his umbrella. It appears in this case that intention 1 is relevant to what Sally meant by those very words—to what she took them to mean in English—whereas intentions 2 and 3 are not.

Here is another objection that is somewhat similar:

> A man suddenly cried out 'Gleeg gleeg gleeg!' intending thereby to produce a certain effect in an audience by means of the recognition of his intention. He wished to make his audience believe that it was snowing in Tibet. . . . According to Grice . . . the madman meant . . . something by 'Gleeg gleeg gleeg!', and so . . . the madman's cry must have meant . . . something, presumably that it was snowing in Tibet. But the madman's cry did not mean anything at all; it certainly did not mean it was snowing in Tibet. (Ziff 1967, p. 51)

We have already limited the relevant actions to those that intentionally get a hearer to do something, but we should make a further limitation to narrow down the field to exactly those actions that reveal what the speaker meant by the words uttered. Here is how this can be done.

When Sally says, "It is raining outside" to Fred, one of the things she intends to do is to *inform* him that it is raining outside. This is different from getting him to *believe* that it is raining outside—she may successfully *inform* him of that even though he does not believe what she informs him of. The act of informing him is successful as soon as Fred understands her words and takes them to be a sign that she is attempting to inform him that it is raining outside. Her success at this intention consists *entirely* of his recognition of her intention to do this act. This act, then, is of a peculiar sort: Its success is nothing but the hearer's recognition of the speaker's intention to do it.

Here is another example of this peculiar kind of act. Suppose that Fred says, "Please pass the salt," intending to get Sally to pass the salt. One of Fred's intentions in uttering what he does is to *request* that the salt be passed. Just as soon as Sally recognizes that Fred has this intention, this intention has been successfully accomplished: Fred has successfully requested that the salt be passed. Now, Fred does not just want to make this request; he also wants (thereby) to get the salt passed. But success at *this* intention—getting Sally to pass the salt—does not consist *entirely* of her recognition of it. Sally might realize that Fred wants her to pass the salt, but, not feeling cooperative, she might not pass the salt. Only *one* of Fred's intentions here is of the peculiar sort we have noted: Its success consists entirely of the hearer's recognition of that intention. That intention is to request that the salt be passed.

This peculiar sort of verbal intentional act regarding a hearer is called, in the literature of the speech act theory, an *illocutionary act*, and the intention to do this sort of act is called an *illocutionary intention*. Fred in this example has the illocutionary intention to perform the illocutionary act of *requesting* of Sally that she pass the salt. (The original source of the terms 'illocutionary' and 'perlocutionary' is Austin (1962).)

Fred also has the intention to get Sally to pass the salt, and if this intention succeeds, he gets Sally to pass the salt. But this intention and this act are not illocutionary: The success of this intention does not consist entirely of her recognition of the intention. Sally might recognize that Fred has this intention in saying what he does and yet not pass the salt. This sort of act that one does intentionally to hearers by means of language is called a *perlocutionary act*, and the intention to do it is called a *perlocutionary intention*. Perlocutionary acts are performed by means of illocutionary acts.

Here are some other examples of illocutionary acts.

Sally *orders* Fred to stand at attention. She can do this only if she is in the appropriate relation to Fred, say, a superior officer. Sally succeeds in her intention to order Fred to stand at attention as soon as he hears and understands the utterance as an order that he stand at attention.

Sally *predicts* to Fred that the Blue Jays will win the game. When Sally gets Fred to understand that she is trying to predict this, then she is successful. Whether or not he believes what she predicts and whether or not her prediction is true are other matters.

Let's consider each of the things on the list of what Sally might do so saying "It is raining outside":

> report to the hearer that is raining outside

This, as we have seen, if done intentionally, is an illocutionary act.

> get the hearer to believe correctly that it is raining outside
> get the hearer to believe falsely that it is raining outside
> get the hearer to believe that it is Tuesday
> get the hearer to take his umbrella
> get the hearer to stay around awhile
> get the hearer to leave
> get the hearer to think that she is stupid
> insult the hearer
> please the hearer
> surprise the hearer

Each of these might be done intentionally or unintentionally. If done intentionally by means of the illocutionary act of informing the hearer that it is raining outside, they are all perlocutionary acts.

Suppose that Sally intentionally surprises the hearer or wakes the hearer up by (suddenly and loudly) making the noise "It is raining outside." These are all intended effects on the hearer, but they are not illocutionary acts: Their success does not consist in the hearer's recognition of her intention. Nor are they perlocutionary acts: They are not accomplished by means of the performance of an illocutionary act. They are accomplished merely by making noise.

The rest of the list is:

> practice her English
> practice her lines in a play
> see if the microphone she is speaking into is turned on
> do nothing at all except make that noise

Because these are not intended effects *on a hearer*, they are neither perlocutionary nor illocutionary acts.

Not every sort of intention, as we have seen, is an illocutionary intention and, in fact, there are certain sorts of act that cannot be illocutionary acts. (Can you figure out why this is so?) There is a wide variety of illocutionary acts one *can* accomplish, however, and a much wider variety of possible perlocutionary acts. Here are samples of each kind (Alston 1964, p. 35):

Illocutionary	Perlocutionary
report	bring x to learn that . . .
announce	persuade
predict	deceive
admit	encourage
opine	irritate
ask	frighten
reprimand	amuse
request	get x to do . . .
suggest	inspire
order	impress
propose	distract
express	get x to think about . . .
congratulate	relieve tension
promise	embarrass
thank	attract attention
exhort	bore

The right-hand list names actions that surely can be perlocutionary acts, but one can do each of these acts in other ways also. One can, for example, embarrass (perlocutionary) somebody by reporting to him (illocutionary) that his breakfast is on his tie, but there are also nonillocutionary means of embarrassing someone, for example, by getting him to do something foolish in public.

A good test to distinguish illocutionary acts from perlocutionary acts is that illocutionary acts can be named in sentences of the form 'I hereby _____' (for example, 'I hereby report that _____', 'I hereby request _____'). This sort of construction is called a *performative*. The reason this works as a test is that all the hearer has to do in order for an illocutionary act to be accomplished is to hear and understand the utterance; thus the speaker accomplishes the acts merely by speaking them. You cannot say 'I hereby get you to think that _____' because more hearer compliance is necessary for accomplishment of this perlocutionary act.

Speaker's Meaning and Sentence Meaning

Now, at last, we are in position to understand what all this has to do with speaker's meaning: The speech act theory says that speaker's meaning is specified by the illocutionary intention behind the speech act (but not by the perlocutionary intentions). (The restriction of relevant intentions to illocutionary ones was not made explicitly by Grice. It was invented earlier by Austin, and added to Grice's theory later, for example, by Searle, to fix it up.)

The reason why the speech act theory looks like a promising way to explain meaning is that it seems that we do get some understanding of the meaning of what Sally says when we consider her illocutionary intentions in saying it. Note that perlocutionary intentions seem in general to have little or nothing to do with this sort of meaning. The objection we encountered is solved. Recall the objection: Sally says, "It is raining outside," attempting to get Fred to see that she wants him to take his umbrella and, as a result, to take it. But this intention does not specify the meaning of her utterance. Now we can see that the nonspecificity is a consequence of the fact that the intention is perlocutionary: Only illocutionary intentions are supposed to specify meaning. Sally's illocutionary intention, presumably to report that it is raining, does specify the meaning of her utterance.

Look at Ziff's objection. Note that the madman's intention is a perlocutionary one (getting his audience to believe something). Again, it is no wonder that this intention does not specify the meaning of his utterance. However, we can alter Ziff's objection somewhat so that the madman *does* have illocutionary intentions:

> A man suddenly cried out "Gleeg gleeg gleeg!" intending thereby to *report* to his audience that it is snowing in Tibet. So the madman's cry must have meant something, presumably that it is snowing in Tibet. But the madman's cry did not mean anything at all; it certainly did not mean it is snowing in Tibet.

We can still argue that, even though this sort of intention might specify what the madman meant by saying, "Gleeg gleeg gleeg!" it nevertheless has nothing to do with what 'Gleeg gleeg gleeg!' means. That sentence might be uttered with any sort of illocutionary intention whatever, but this does not succeed in making it mean anything.

The point here is that, even if the speech act theory gives an account of *speaker's meaning*, it fails to tell us anything about *sentence meaning*.

Grice does recognize the difference between speaker's meaning and sentence meaning and tries to give an account of the latter. He thinks that what the sentence meaning of x is "might as a first shot be equated with . . . what 'people' (vague) intend . . . to effect by x" (Grice 1957, p. 385). This is not a specific account of what sentence meaning might have to do with speaker's meaning, but we can see what Grice has in mind. His idea is that the sentence meaning of a particular utterance token can be explained not by the illocutionary intentions of the speaker of that token but rather by the illocutionary intentions people in general have when uttering tokens of that type.

Thus, were another madman to utter "Please pass the salt," intending thereby to report that one of Wyoming's chief agricultural products is dry edible beans, his intention tells what he means by it, but what his utterance really means is given by the illocutionary intentions people in general have when uttering it, namely, to make a polite request that they be handed the salt. Similarly, because people in general do not say "Gleeg gleeg gleeg!" to carry out any sort of illocutionary intentions at all, that utterance does not have any sentence meaning, whatever the madman happens to mean when he utters it.

But Grice's attempt to explain sentence meaning will not work. On Grice's view the sentence meaning of an utterance is a statistical matter; what a sentence means is given by the illocutionary intentions of most of its speakers. But a simple statistical theory will not do because (as we saw in chapter 1) there are myriad sentence types and it is easy to construct a sentence that we are confident has *never* been uttered, for example, 'My third cousin enjoys carving symbolist poetry stanzas on watermelon rind'. We have no trouble telling what that sentence means, despite the fact that there is nothing that people in general intend when they utter it, because nobody ever utters it.

But the speech act theory can handle this, although it must modify Grice's vague suggestion somewhat in order to do so.

First, we should note that the association of illocutionary intentions with sentences is not, as Grice seems to hold, a matter of mere statistical regularity. As we saw earlier, language can be seen as a matter of convention; one can learn conventions without observing regularities, for example, by being told the "rules." Recall, however, Ziff's point that language is almost never learned this way. Usually, we learn by listening and doing; thus there does seem to be an element of abstraction from statistical regularity. More important, however, to know language is to know a *structure* that allows us to construct brand new meaningful utterances and to understand them by combining a large but limited number of words in a large but limited number of kinds of grammatical combination. We can say, then, that to know a language is to know the conventions that make any meaningful combination of these elements in these forms usable to reveal illocutionary intentions. This is why we can figure out what illocutionary intentions *would be* associated by these conventions with any grammatically constructed sentence, despite the fact that nobody ever says it.

We can say, then, that the sentence meaning of any English sentence is its *conventional illocutionary act potential,* that is, that the conventions of English provide, for each of the possible English sentences, an illocutionary act that (depending on the circumstances) that sentence would perform. "Please pass the salt," then, is the conventional way of making the request that the salt be passed, and "It's snowing in Tibet" is the conventional way of informing someone (in certain circumstances) or warning him or her (in other circumstances) that it is snowing in Tibet. "Sit down" is in some circumstances a polite request and in others an order.

Conventional Illocutionary Act Potential

But now let us consider one additional objection to Grice's theory. This example was proposed by John Searle.

Suppose that an American soldier is captured by the Italians during World War II and that the soldier wants the Italians to believe that he is a German officer so that they will release him. He wants to tell them that he is a German officer, but he knows no Italian, and the only sentence in German he remembers is a line of poetry, "Kennst du das Land, wo die Zitronen blühen?" In German this means, *Do you know the land where the lemon trees bloom?* but the soldier knows that the Italians know no German. He utters this line of poetry, intending to get them to think that he is saying that he is a German officer, that is to report (falsely) that he is a German officer.

According to the Grice account this German sentence type does not have this sentence meaning; but it follows from Grice's theory that the soldier means that he is German officer by the token he utters, that is, that this gives the speaker's meaning. But because the soldier knows perfectly well that his sentence does not mean that he is a German officer, it is plainly false that he means *I am a German officer* by what he says. So this is a counterexample to Grice's theory of speaker's meaning.

This example differs from the "Gleeg gleeg gleeg!" example. The speaker of "Gleeg gleeg gleeg!" thought, we can assume, that the conventions of the language he was speaking did associate this utterance type with the intention to inform that it is snowing in Tibet; we were willing to admit in that case that the madman really meant *It is snowing in Tibet* by "Gleeg gleeg gleeg!" But because the soldier knows that the conventional sentence meaning of his utterance is not *I am a German officer,* he does not mean this by what he says.

This gives us the key to amending Grice's view about speaker's meaning to fit these two cases. We should say, then, that what is relevant to the speaker's meaning of what he utters is not only his illocutionary intentions but also what he believes the conventional sentence meaning of his utterance in the language he is speaking to be. Thus, when the speaker has illocutionary intentions but does not think that the sentence he utters is one of those which the conventions of the language he is speaking designate as a way of achieving those intentions, then those intentions do not tell us what the speaker means by what he says. In Searle's amended version of Grice's theory, both of these elements are built into his account of an illocutionary act:

> In the performance of an illocutionary act the speaker intends to produce a certain effect by means of getting the hearer to recognize his intention to produce that effect, and furthermore, if he is using words literally, he intends this recognition to be achieved in virtue of the fact that the rules for using the expressions he utters associate the expressions with the production of that effect. (Searle 1965, pp. 230–231)

Now, the madman is wrong about the conventions of English, and the meaning of his sentence is not what he means by it. The soldier knows what the conventions of German say about his sentence; nevertheless he does not mean what that sentence conventionally means in German.

We now are in position to explain sentence meaning more specifically. The (tacit) conventions of a language provide for each of its sentence types an associated illocutionary act (or several sorts depending on context). Thus these conventions give each sentence type an illocutionary act potential. The conventions of a language, then, permit utterance of a sentence only when the speaker has the intention to perform the appropriate illocutionary act; thus tokens uttered by a speaker conventionally signal the speaker's illocutionary intentions. If the speaker has illocutionary intentions other than those associated with his sentence, then he is violating those conventions— not "playing the game" correctly. He may do this because he is mistaken about the conventions (for example, the madman) or because he wants to mislead the hearer about his real intentions (a liar) or even because he wants to make use of his hearer's mistakes about or ignorance of those conventions (the soldier). Here we have, then, at least the outlines of an answer to the question raised earlier—an account of what the social "game" of language is *for* and what sorts of actions its "rules" permit and forbid.

Speaker's Meaning and Privacy

Before we leave this topic, it is appropriate to consider how the notion of speaker's meaning we have evolved fares as an account of language when confronted with the considerations raised earlier about the possibility of a private language.

The original speech act theory developed by Grice ran into problems. Grice wanted the speaker's meaning of an utterance to be a consequence merely of the intentions the speaker had to affect the hearer. Because (given exotic enough circumstances) we can imagine any sort of intention associated with any sort of noise (or writing) a speaker may produce, this does not seem like a language at all; and explaining what intentions just happen to be associated with a particular noise seems far removed from the notion of linguistic meaning. But the version of the speech act theory we have now come to, while still making speaker's intentions central to speaker's meaning, is a different story. Intentions, we assume, are private items; thus any attempt to explain speaker's meaning by association with these private items must run into the problems discussed earlier about privacy. But note that public conventions play a crucial role in the evolved version of the theory. Sentence meanings are, after all, a public matter, involving public conventions. But what about speaker's meanings?

Recall that the problem with privacy is, in a nutshell, that meanings in a language are not just individual associations of events but are systematic, perhaps regular or rule-governed or conventional associations. I cannot mean this sort of sensation by 'S' unless it makes sense to say that I can correctly (or incorrectly) continue to associate 'S' with sensations of the same type. Without the possibility of a public test, there is no right or wrong of the matter.

In the current version of the speech act theory, the speaker's meaning of an utterance is given by the speaker's intentions to produce (certain kinds of) effects on the hearer by virtue of what the speaker believes to be the fact that the noises she makes have certain conventional associations with these intentions. In the "Gleeg gleeg gleeg!" case, the speaker is mistaken in believing that there is a conventional association between informing that it is snowing in Tibet and his words. That this is a mistake is a publicly verifiable matter, because the real conventions of language are public property. We still want to say that the madman's intentions give his *speaker's* (not *sentence*) meaning because at least *he believes* that his sentence has this conventional use. The publicity of the conventions provide an objective test whereby the speaker's belief that his sentence has this conventional use can be shown to be wrong; but it is exactly his being wrong that constitutes the fact that the speaker's meaning of his words is different from their sentence meaning.

Beliefs and intentions, we might assume, are private matters; thus the whole enterprise of using these to explain speaker's meaning might get us into private-language problems. In the madman's case perhaps there was just an accidental, one-shot association of beliefs and intentions with his utterance, but might someone have an idiolectic *system* of regular utterance-intention associations? There seems to be no reason why not. I can, if I like, utter "Gleeg gleeg gleeg!" regularly whenever I wish to inform hearers that it is snowing in Tibet; I might, were I mad enough, believe that this conforms to a public convention of English. I might even create a private rule for myself (by inscribing it on my wall) to utter this whenever I fall prey to that intention and act according to that rule. In a sense this would then be a private language, with regular speaker's meanings. But can there be private *conventions* for language? This appears not just impossible but nonsensical. A convention is, as we have seen, essentially an interpersonal mechanism. Speaker's meanings depend on speaker's beliefs about conventions, but they cannot themselves be conventional. Insofar as we see conventions regarding illocutionary act potential as the essential core of meaning, we must deny that speaker's meaning is full-fledged language meaning.

Suggested Readings

Alston, William P. 1964. *Philosophy of Language*. Englewood Cliffs: Prentice-Hall.
    A later expression of the speech act theory. See especially chapter 2.
Austin, J. L. 1962. *How to Do Things with Words*. Cambridge: Harvard University Press.
    Austin is one of the grandfathers of the speech act theory. Despite the later date of publication, his views were expressed in lectures before Grice's article. Parts of this book are reprinted in [9].
Grice, H. P. 1957. "Meaning." *Philosophical Review* 66(3):377–388.
    Reprinted in [7, 9].
Searle, John. 1965. "What is a speech act?" in *Philosophy in America*, Max Black, ed. Ithaca: Cornell University Press, 221–239.
    A readable source for a later expression of the speech act theory. Reprinted in [5, 9].
Searle, John. 1970. *Speech Acts*. Cambridge: Cambridge University Press.
Wittgenstein, L. 1963. *Philosophical Investigations*. Oxford: Basil Blackwell.
Ziff, Paul. 1967. "On H. P. Grice's account of meaning." *Analysis* 28(1):1–8.

10

Animal and Machine Language

Animals and Language

Recently, among philosophers and the general public there has been a good deal of interest in animal languages. The questions here are whether animals already have what should be called a language and whether they can be taught language. Information and speculation have been emerging at a great rate from studies by naturalists of animal behavior and from the experiments of those who are trying to teach language to animals. Aside from their intrinsic fascination, the studies are of interest to us especially because of what they say or presuppose about what language is.

The claims regarding animal language are quite controversial. One of the areas of controversy concerns exactly what the animal in question is doing or can be taught to do. This is more a scientific question than a philosophical one, although, as we shall see, it has its philosophical aspects.

The widespread desire to attribute language to animals can promote wishful thinking—jumping to unjustified conclusions. Some people want to stress our continuity with some parts of the animal world or are attracted by the notion that animals are like us, can do what we can. They may be motivated by ecological concerns or by the attractiveness of the feeling that humans are not alone in the universe (think of the popularity of the movie *E.T.*), or maybe they are simply animal lovers. Pet owners almost invariably think that their animals can do more than they really can; many otherwise sensible people converse freely with their pets and are convinced that the pets have absurdly high levels of comprehension.

A famous case of misinterpretation of evidence and exaggeration of animal abilities illustrates (some critics claim) faults in some recent research. A horse called Clever Hans was put on show for his apparent ability to do arithmetic. After his trainer presented an arithmetic problem to Hans, the horse would stamp his foot the number of times equal to the answer to the problem. What was really happening was finally discovered: When the trainer had counted the right number of stampings, he unconsciously gave Hans an almost imperceptible sign, which caused the horse to stop stamping. Apparently the trainer was not a conscious fraud; he actually believed that Hans could do arithmetic. But Clever Hans was not that clever.

But even when there is agreement about what an animal can do, there is another source of disagreement. Everything found in animals falls short, of course, of full human language in various ways. But the motivations mentioned lead people to emphasize our closeness with animals by awarding animals the prize of calling their limited behavior language; but those who share the older view that humans are substantially and importantly above—different in kind, not just in degree, from—the rest of the animal kingdom prefer not to call what animals do language.

This disagreement may be (again!) only about the proper application of the word 'language' and related terms. As it should be clear by now, there are many different complex features of language and language use, and we normally call something language when it has all these complexities, as all human languages apparently do. Animal behavior showing only some of the features of human language might be called language, but this term is somewhat extended when so applied. The question of whether this and related words are correctly applied cannot be answered, because these words do not have defining characteristics that rule these more limited phenomena in or out; sharpening the definition to include *or* exclude more limited animal behavior is redefinition. The more fruitful question to consider is, How close can animals get to full human language?

Suppose that you have managed to train your dog, Arnold, to woof in a certain characteristic way when he wants to go outside. We can say, then (using scare quotes liberally in order to indicate that words are being used in an extended sense), that this kind of woof "means" that Arnold wants to go out; and that Arnold "means" *I want to go out* or *Please let me out* when he utters this woof and that Arnold thus has at least a one-"word" "language."

It is not altogether absurd to use words such as 'language', 'means', and 'word' when we describe Arnold's behavior. One reason this seems plausible is that Arnold's noises give us information about Arnold. But this is not a good reason. Arnold pants when he is hot, but we are not tempted at all to say that his panting is another word in his language and that by panting he means that he is hot. A kettle rumbles before it starts to boil, and we might want to say that this rumbling means that the kettle is about to boil. But *this* sense of "means" has little to do with linguistic meaning; there is no temptation to say that this rumbling is a word in the kettle's language. The fact that some state of an object transmits information about that object is perhaps necessary, but it is surely far from sufficient for imputing language to that object.

Teaching Chimps to Talk

A more plausible case for animal language has been presented by experimenters who have claimed to have taught language to higher primates. These animals lack the vocal apparatus to make the rich variety of noises humans use in spoken language; thus attempts to teach them language have concentrated on other techniques, for example, getting them to produce the signs with their hands that deaf people use to communicate (American Sign Language) or picking up and displaying various differently colored and shaped plastic pieces to correspond to different words and phrases in English.

One research project taught a chimpanzee a large vocabulary of such signs, including "words" for water and for bird. A chimp that has been trained to give the correct signs in response to various objects does not have much of a language—this is merely Arnold's woof again. The significant claim was that the chimp, when first exposed to a duck, signed 'water' *plus* 'bird' in response and responded to ducks with that combination ever afterward.

This *appears* to show that what the chimp had is much closer to language than Arnold's woof. Arnold's behavior, even if it included many regular "signings," does not exhibit the structure that we have already examined in human languages, which makes it possible for us to use and understand combinations of words we have not previously encountered. This (and other) reports claim to have found such combinatory abilities in animals.

Critics of this example claim that the experimenters did not tell the full story, which, given their usual interactions with the animals, was probably something similar to the following. The chimp in question had been subjected to a huge amount of training and was reinforced (by a bit of food or by the affectionate or enthusiastic response of the trainer) whenever a bit of signing was taken by the trainer to be correct. This reinforcement produced a chimp who responded often with correct signs, just as your training of Arnold has. But another effect of this reinforcement was that the chimp constantly produced a great deal of random signing behavior. Now, when the chimp was taken out in a rowboat with ducks nearby, it, as usual, must have been signing appropriately and randomly at a great rate. It is plausible to think that among the chimp's great variety of signs on this occasion, it produced the sign for water (possibly responding to the water in the lake) and just happened to produce immediately afterward the sign for bird (perhaps in response to the ducks or maybe just at random.) The trainer, judging that 'water' plus 'bird' was a correct sign for the ducks—indeed, a creative and important one—no doubt responded enthusiastically, reinforcing this behavior and causing the 'water' plus 'bird' response to ducks afterward.

If this is what happened, then the experiment showed less than what was claimed. A more significant result would have been the production of regular, spontaneous, nonrandom but not reinforced appropriate new combinations of words. This would be evidence of language structure. If the critics are right, this is a case of poor experimental design, perhaps of the unintentional Clever Hans variety. We cannot decide whether the critics are correct about this case or about many other claims of structured language in primates without careful investigation into experimental details. My point is to show how important structure is in demonstrating language competence and to indicate how evidence might (or might not) demonstrate this.

Naturalists have reported that there are naturally occurring animal "languages" that exhibit exactly this sort of structure. Consider, for example, the well-known case of the "language" of honeybees. When a scout bee has found a patch of nectar-laden flowers, it returns to the hive and performs a figure-eight "dance" that the other bees sense: They feel the movements of the dancing bee with their legs or sense the movements and buzzing made by the dancing bee's wings with tactile hairs and antennae. The angle of the dance corresponds to the angle between the sun and the direction of the food; the size of the figure danced and the vigor of the wiggles and buzzing of the dancer correspond to the distance and concentration of sugar in the food. Having sensed the scout's dance, other bees fly directly to the newly found food source.

The scout is transmitting information to the other bees by a "language" with structure. It communicates the distance, direction, and concentration of the food within a wide range of each variable with a large variety of different possible "sentences." Here we have at least an analogy with the structure of human language.

Human language is (at least to some extent) a learned social artifact. If the bee dance is entirely instinctive, this represents a significant difference between their "language" and ours. But complex *learned* communicative behavior has also been observed in animals. All white-throated sparrows in a certain area, for example, sing a few similar songs that are different from the songs of the same species living in other areas. The local dialects are learned by young birds from the older ones in that area; birds raised in isolation from others do not develop this dialect. Different dialects of birdsong probably have a territorial function: Cardinals who sing one dialect react aggressively when they hear songs of a different dialect; the strength of this reaction is proportional to the distance of the population that sings the other dialect.

This example shows that some animal communication shares some features of conventional language behavior: The birds "solve" a coordination problem. They are better off when they can tell members of their own tribe from outsiders, and they accomplish this by means of an arbitrary (learned, not instinctually given) signal.

Is Arnold's behavior conventional? For it to be *overtly* conventional, we have to credit Arnold with various sorts of belief and desire, for example, the belief that you will let him out once you know that he wants to be let out and the even more complex beliefs that his behavior is an arbitrary solution to a coordination problem and that you also know this. Care must be taken here not to commit what can be called the *Walt Disney fallacy*; probably some of these things are a bit too much to attribute to Arnold's doggy brain. It is even more implausible to attribute complex beliefs and intentions to puny bird brains. Is it plausible to attribute intentions to animals at all?

It might be the case that this question is not relevant to the issue of whether or not animals have language. One moral that philosophers have drawn from the private language argument and from the considerations of radical translation is that whatever (if anything) is going on in the minds of noise makers is irrelevant to the question of what those noises mean or to the question of whether or not those noises constitute a language at all. On the other hand, it seems that noise makers must at least have a mind containing some sorts of intention and belief in order to credit them with a language. Parrots and tape recorders make noises that mean things in English, but they clearly are not therefore linguistically capable. Their noises have sentence meaning because they are the same noises that are made by people (who do have minds thus stocked).

Perhaps the most we would feel confident in saying is that Arnold and the birds are acting in a *covertly* conventional manner. As we have seen, this might not make them different from humans if human language conventions are also covert.

The Mental Lives of Other People

The question of intentions and mental states in general in animals is one that animal lovers might be interested in in its own right, but the question is of philosophical interest primarily because consideration of it can give us insight into what is involved in attributing mental states to other *people* or, indeed, to oneself. It is philosophically useful as a tool to help us understand what is involved in the concept of mentality in general.

A traditional way to think about mental states is to take them to be features of internal, private mental life. It seems that in your own case, after all, you know that *you* have intentions associated with your utterances because you notice them through the internal sense called *introspection*. Other philosophers have argued, however, that this interior noticing is not the way you discover the presence of your own mental states. (Does it feel some particular way inside whenever you have a particular intention?) In any event this sort of direct awareness (if it exists at all) is surely no help at all in finding out that other people (or other animals) have mental states, because we cannot see directly into other people's consciousnesses the way we are supposed to be able to see into our own. So what justifies our attribution of mentality to other people? In the literature this is called the *problem of other minds*.

Those philosophers who think that we discover the presence of mental states in our own case by private introspection see this as a problem and produce all sorts of ingenious arguments to try to solve it; but others react differently to this "problem": They argue that, because we clearly *do* know that other people have mental states, there must be a way other than private introspection to discover the existence of mental states. If mental states are some private inner item of consciousness, then we have no reason whatever to attribute them to other people. But clearly we do; therefore they are not some private inner item of consciousness.

These philosophers argue that saying something about another person's mental state, and even about our own mental states, is justified by the way the person behaves. This is denied by philosophers who think that we discover our own consciousness and the existence of our own mental states only by introspection.

This sort of approach to mentalistic attributions would seem to open the door to attributing mental characteristics to higher animals and even to complicated machines. If Arnold's behavior justifies the attribution to Arnold of a mental life, then if we can build a machine that exhibits all the complexities of Arnold's behavior, we should attribute a mental life to that machine as well.

Historically, the view of many philosophers and perhaps of most thoughtful nonphilosophers is that, even if some of the higher animals can be counted as having a mental life, it is inconceivable that a machine could be built to have consciousness. Perhaps this view has something to do with the fact that the brains of higher animals are fairly similar to ours but that machines must be made of entirely different stuff; it used to be inconceivable that something made out of machinery could be conscious. It was understandable that philosophers in the sixteenth century should think this way, because machines then were (so to speak) simpleminded: Nothing made of crude gears, levers, and pulleys could possibly behave in the ways that would justify attributing it consciousness. Nowadays, however, when computers can begin to approach the kinds of things we can do, it might be time to change our minds about this.

What is it, then, about our behavior that accounts for our attributing (unobservable) mental lives to each other? Here is one suggestion, by the contemporary philosopher Paul Churchland:

> Theorists postulate unobservable entities, and specific laws governing them, because occasionally this produces a theory that allows us to construct predictions and explanations of observable phenomena hitherto unexplained. . . . Consider now the network of general principles—connecting mental states with one another, with bodily circumstances, and with behavior—that constitutes folk psychology. ["Folk" psychology here is contrasted with scientific psychology. It means the sort of "theory" of mind that everyday folks, not just scientists, believe.] This 'theory' allows us to explain and to predict the behavior of human beings better than any other hypothesis currently available, and what better reason can there be for believing a set of general laws about unobservable states and properties? . . . [T]he hypothesis that a specific individual has conscious intelligence is . . . plausible to the degree that the individual's continuing behavior is best explained and predicted in terms of desires, beliefs, perceptions, emotions, and so on. Since that is, in fact, the best way to understand the behavior of most humans, one is therefore justified in believing that they are 'other minds'. And one will be similarly justified in ascribing psychological states to any other creatures or machines, so long as such ascriptions sustain the most successful explanations and predictions of their continuing behavior. (1984, pp. 71–72)

Churchland does not believe, however, that folk psychology is the best theory for humans; he thinks it will be replaced by a neurophysiology that will be better at explaining and predicting human behavior.

Propositional Attitudes

Suppose that a thermostat is set for a temperature higher than that in the room, and thus it turns on the furnace. We know exactly how the thermostat works: It contains a sensing element connected to a switch; when the sensing element registers a temperature lower than the one we have set, it causes a switch to be thrown that turns on the furnace. We do not say that the thermostat *believes* that the temperature in the room is lower than the temperature we have set or *desires* to turn on the furnace to remedy this situation. Why not?

One suggestion is that thermostats behave so simply. They are describable perfectly adequately without any need to invoke psychological states in their insides. All we need to describe the workings of a thermostat is an account of how inputs (room temperatures and thermostat settings) are related to outputs (switching the furnace on and off). It may, however, be fruitful, indeed necessary, to describe the activity of much more complex machines and of the higher animals in psychological terms.

But complexity alone is not sufficient for attribution of psychological states. A nuclear reactor is surely much more complex than a thermostat, but we do not think of it as having psychological states. Churchland argues that a certain *kind* of complex behavior justifies the attribution of mentality. In humans some internal states do not merely relate input to output; they are also related *to each other* in systematic ways, depending on their *propositional content*—on what they are about. (Sometimes philosophers call this sort of state "intentional." I avoid this word because it encourages confusion with two other uses: first, with the ordinary word "intentional," meaning *on purpose*, and, second, with the philosophers' word "intensional," meaning *nonextensional* (explained in chapter 14).)

Some of our psychological states might be said to have propositional content. These are called *propositional attitudes*. They are distinguished from nonpropositional psychological states by being describable with 'that' plus a sentence (the expression of a proposition), for example, a belief *that* Bolivia is in South America, the fear *that* nobody loves you. Hunger, pain, "floating anxiety," etc. are not "that" anything, not propositional attitudes. They are not *about* things or states of affairs in the world. Certain philosophers argue that the necessity of attributing propositional attitudes to us (and perhaps to other things) is the central factor in attributing to it a mental life. Because these propositional attitudes have "content" that can be expressed in a sentence that has logical relations to other sentences, these propositional attitudes can have special systematic relations to each other.

For example, we drink something not merely because we think it is water but also because we want to drink some water. We can believe that something is water yet behave toward it in different ways, depending on whether we want to water the plants or drink it. These internal states are related because they are all *about* water. Our complex behavior, it is argued, necessitates the postulation of internal states with *logical relations* to each other, when, for example, the propositional content of one *entails* that of another or is *inconsistent with* it. (One proposition *entails* another when it is impossible, because of the logic of the propositions, for the first to be true and the second false. For example, the proposition that there is a dog behind the door entails the proposition that something is behind the door. Two propositions are *inconsistent* if it is impossible, as a matter of logic, for the two to be true at once. For example, the propositions that there is a dog behind the door is inconsistent with the proposition that nothing is behind the door.) These features, which essentially involve the notions of *truth* and *falsity*, properties of propositions, show that what we are dealing with are propositional attitudes. 'Proposition' and 'propositional attitude' are defined and discussed later. For the moment we can think of propositional attitudes as certain sorts of psychological states, the ones we describe when we say that someone thinks that _____ or knows that _____ or fears that _____ or hopes that _____, where the blank is filled by a whole sentence (which expresses a proposition). Other psychological states are not propositional attitudes: Someone is afraid of cats (not afraid *that*); someone is sad or hungry.

Can Animals or Machines Have Propositional Attitudes?

One never needs to postulate psychological states in thermostats or in nuclear reactors, but people who work with computers routinely say things such as "It doesn't like the fact that this disk is formatted wrong" and "It thinks that the data is in that file but it is mistaken." Is this just a picturesque metaphor? Is this the Walt Disney fallacy transposed from cute animals to machines?

A typewriter cannot be mistaken; why not? Of course, it can print a sentence such as "The capital of Brazil is Cleveland," but because it cannot have any internal states about Cleveland or Brazil or anything else, it cannot believe anything about them. Because its behavior never necessitates the postulation of internal states related to propositions, we do not see it as having internal states that are true or false.

Nor can it lie, because it cannot intend to deceive, for to have this intention is to have an internal state that is a relation to a proposition—it is to believe a proposition false and to desire that someone else believe it true.

The question of whether or not it is necessary to impute internal psychological states to anything nonhuman is a hotly debated one. Many people think that some higher animals show just the sorts of complexity of behavior that require internal states. Here is an example, from chimp research:

> Several of the psychologists who have taught sign language to apes have reported actual lying. When confronted with a pile of feces on the carpet, or a cast-iron sink ripped from the wall, the delinquent apes claim "So-and-so did it," blaming a human companion. . . . Matata . . . a female pygmy chimp . . . returned to the social group for breeding and found herself subordinate to Lorel, a female she had easily dominated in earlier years. The situation lasted for some days, until Matata happened to be alone in the outer cage with Lorel and the child of a still more dominant female. Matata reached up and yanked on the child's leg, where it dangled on the net above her. The little chimp squealed, of course. All the other animals came pounding out of the inside cage, including the adult male and the child's bristling mother. As they emerged Matata glared at Lorel and barked. The dominant mother swung round and attacked innocent Lorel. From that day on, Matata again lorded it over Lorel. (Jolly 1985, p. 74)

Computers are approaching the state in which it might be similarly plausible to impute mental states to them. The movie *2001: A Space Odyssey* portrayed a computer whose behavior seemed to justify fully that imputation: The computer felt fear, lied, etc. Of course, the movie is still science fiction, but we are probably not terribly far from being able to build a computer that could act much like that one.

The question here is not centrally what it is technically possible to build but rather whether such a machine, if built, would properly be said to have propositional attitudes and thus to *mean* something by the sentences it puts out. A general and highly controversial argument against the possibility of any computer with a mental life is the following: Any computer, no matter how complex, would be made out of smaller pieces; we could understand the workings of any huge and complex future computer, then, by analyzing its workings into a large number of little operations of these tiny subsystems. Nobody thinks that any of these tiny subsystems needs to be explained by invoking propositional attitudes: A microchip that adds numbers in your pocket calculator does not *think about* the numbers; it merely inputs, stores, and outputs electrical states. Therefore anything made out of these little pieces, no matter how complex or humanlike its behavior, could also be understood without invoking propositional attitudes.

But critics of this argument agree that it is unnecessary to impute propositional attitudes to little bits of electronic machinery but deny that it follows that it is unnecessary to think this way about complex information-processing systems made entirely out of these little bits. *We*, after all, might turn out to be a highly complex system of tiny subsystems (not silicon microchips, of course, but neurons, etc.; not "hardware" but "wetware") whose functions are nonpsychologically describable; but this would not imply that a human is not appropriately described as having a mental life and, by consequence, as nonlinguistic.

Suggested Readings

Bennett, Jonathon. 1967. *Rationality*. Boston: Routledge & Kegan Paul.
    A discussion of bee language and its philosophical implications.
Churchland, Paul. 1984. *Matter and Consciousness*. Cambridge: MIT Press.
Dennett, Daniel. 1978. "Intentional systems," in his *Brainstorms*. Cambridge: MIT Press, A Bradford Book, 3–22.
    A sophisticated discussion of the question of the philosophical possibility of thinking and talking computers.
Jolly, Alison. 1985. "A new science that sees animals as conscious beings." *Smithsonian* 15(12):66–75.
    A summary of some research on bee communication and a general discussion of attribution of language and consciousness to animals.
Rising, Trudy, and Jim Rising. 1982. *Canadian Songbirds and Their Ways*. Montreal: Tundra Books.
    A discussion of bird language behavior in a fairly superficial popular-science work.
Searle, John. 1981. "Minds, brains, and programs." *The Behavioral and Brain Sciences* 3:417–424. Reprinted in *The Mind's I*, Daniel Dennett and John Hofstadter, eds. New York: Basic Books, 353–373.
    A sophisticated discussion of the philosophical possibilities of thinking and talking computers.
Sebeok, Thomas A. 1980. "Looking in the destination for what should have been sought in the source," in *Speaking of Apes*, Thomas A. Sebeok and Jean Umiker-Sebeok, eds. New York: Plenum, 407–427.
    A discussion of the claim that the Clever Hans fallacy is committed by advocates of chimp language. This anthology also contains wide-ranging critical discussions of claims about interspecies language.

II
Language and Things

11

Function and Object

Names of Things

The speech act theory explained in chapter 9 was the beginning of a full theory of meaning, but only the beginning. To see why this theory does not go far enough, consider its analysis of any declarative sentence, for example, 'Fred is bald.' What the speech act theory tells us, in essence, is that tokens of this sentence are conventionally usable for reporting to someone that Fred is bald. But we have left untouched some clearly central questions. The sentence is *about* a particular person—it *refers* (using 'Fred') to him, and it says something about him. What is it for parts of a sentence to be about things? What is it for a sentence as a whole to say something about them? What is it for the sentence to say something *true* about them?

We have already seen the beginnings of one attempt to answer these questions: the idea theory of meaning. This theory relies on the view that, when I say "Fred is bald," my words are connected to ideas I have; and the idea corresponding to 'Fred' is (somehow) connected to Fred. Similarly, other words in the sentence are connected to other ideas (for example, to *baldness*), which in turn are presumably connected to things (bald things). The whole sentence expresses a connection in my mind among these ideas; and if what I say is true, the things in the world related to these ideas are similarly connected.

Several of the earlier chapters have, however, discussed problems with this sort of account of the way language is connected to the world. Let's make a fresh start on these questions by trying, at least for the time being, a shortcut that might make things simpler. Let's investigate the connection between words (and sentences) and things, leaving out the detour through ideas. It seems now that this more direct approach may get us closer to an understanding of language because, even though the consideration of psychological states seems a plausible way to explain speaker's meanings, it appears that sentence meaning is more basic to language.

The direct approach has the additional attraction of great intuitive plausibility. To be sure, language is connected with speakers' and hearers' mental states, but it is perhaps even more obvious and basic that it is connected with the world, with the things and states of affairs that our mental states are about. When Sally expresses her belief that Fred is bald, intending to get the hearer to believe this too, by saying "Fred is bald," it seems that what is *basic* here—what we should begin any theory of language by explaining—is the connection between what Sally says and the way the world is, the connection between that sentence and Fred and between the sentence and the fact that Fred is bald.

Most of the rest of this book is concerned with an attempt to begin to explain this word-world connection. Much of what is said draws on the work of Gottlob Frege (1848–1925), a German mathematician and philosopher who is regarded as the father of contemporary philosophical logic.

What is the connection between 'Fred' and Fred? The answer is simple: 'Fred' is the name of Fred. The word 'Fred' functions in the sentence 'Fred is bald' by making the sentence be about Fred. It points to—refers to—him.

There are various ways of pointing at or referring to things. For the time being, let's call any piece of language that refers to something a *name*. 'Stinky' is Fred's nickname, and so 'Stinky' is also a name of Fred. Because Arnold is Fred's son, another name of Fred is 'the father of Arnold'.

Functions for Names

We can immediately note that names work in a variety of ways. 'Fred' names Fred in a simple way, but 'the father of Arnold' names the same person in a more complex way, combining a simple name, 'Arnold', with 'the father of'. Taken alone, 'the father of' is an *incomplete symbol:* It does not name anything until we add a name to its end. When a name is supplied to fill in the blank in 'the father of _____', it becomes a name itself. (This is not quite right, as I point out in chapter 13, but it will do for now.)

It is useful to think of 'the father of _____' as a *function*. The analogy here is with the notion of function in arithmetic: '9' is the name of a number, but x^2 is a function. What that means is simply that, when the function is supplied with a number (in the place marked by the x) the function turns into the name of a number. Thus, when x^2 is supplied with the number 3 to fill the place marked by the x, it becomes 3^2, one name for the number 9. The result when a function is thus *completed* is called its *value;* what completes it by filling the hole is called its *argument.*

Of course, the function x^2 does not relate arguments to values haphazardly. The fact that it has a uniform "meaning" no matter what argument is given to it is a consequence of the *systematic* way it pairs values with arguments. A sample of these ways is given in the following table:

Table for x^2

Argument	Value
−1	1
0	0
1	1
2	4
9	81
⋮	⋮

x^2 might be called a *number → number function;* given a number as argument, the number function yields a number as value. Similarly, we can call 'the father of' an *object → object function,* abbreviated $o → o$. That means that 'the father of' takes an object as argument and yields an object as value. (An object is abbreviated by o.) Thus, when the name of an object is placed into a blank in an expression, the result is the name of (another) object. 'Arnold' is the name of the argument object; 'the father of Arnold' names the value object.

The notation I use in this chapter, the following notation for functions, and the trees analyzing sentences (introduced in what follows) are not standard logical notation. I use them because I think they are easily learned and clearly represent the structural features they analyze and are in these ways superior to standard notation. For readers already familiar with standard logical notation, however, I sometimes, when things get a bit more complicated, give the equivalent standard logical notation. If you are not familiar with modern symbolic logic, you can safely ignore these.

Just as the meaning of a numerical function consists in the systematic way it relates argument numbers to value numbers, the meaning of 'the father of _____', an object → object function, is given by the systematic way it relates objects given to it as arguments to objects yielded as values. A sample of these pairings:

Table for 'the father of _____'

Argument	Value
Arnold	Fred
Prince Charles	Prince Philip
Johann Christian Bach	Johann Sebastian Bach

We can illustrate the simple structure in which this function takes an argument object and yields a value object by means of a tree, analogous in some ways to the syntactic trees introduced in chapter 1; here, however, we have a *semantic tree:*

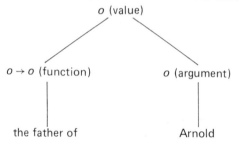

Predicates

We have made some progress, using the notions of a simple name and of an $o \to o$ function, in understanding part of the sentences 'Fred is bald' and 'The father of Arnold is bald'. But what about the rest of each? The word 'bald' is not a name; it does not refer to anything, at least not in the clear way that 'Fred' and 'the father of Arnold' do. In a sense, though, 'bald' does "point to" something, not any particular individual thing but a group of things—the group of bald things—although it does not exactly refer to them in the way the name 'the group of bald things' clearly does. The phrase 'is bald' is not a name either.

Frege's suggestion for understanding predicates, such as 'is bald', is to see them as functions also. (If you have forgotten what a predicate is, refer back to chapter 3.) Like 'the father of', 'is bald' takes an object as argument. Unlike 'the father of', 'is bald' does not yield an (ordinary) object as value: 'Fred is bald' is not straightforwardly the name of an object. Frege argued (in a number of ways that I cannot go into here) that this function yields as value one of the two *truth values* (True and False). Thus, given that Fred in fact is bald, the function 'is bald' yields True as value given Fred as argument. This sort of function thus is an object → truth value function, abbreviated $o \to v$. It yields the truth value True when the object *satisfies* the predicate, and False when it does not. In a sense, then, this complicated function "names" the truth value True.

Thus we can draw a tree for 'Fred is bald', using v as the abbreviation for the truth value:

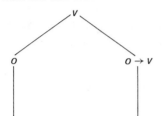

And another one for 'The father of Arnold is bald':

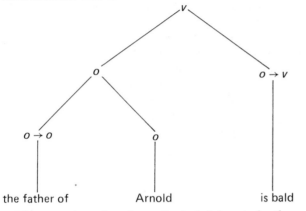

The meaning of each predicate is taken to be the systematic way the predicate relates argument objects to truth values. You can get some idea of why this and the general strategy of seeing predicates as $o \to v$ functions are plausible when you compare predicates to the other functions we have examined. Suppose that Fred is bald but Arnold is not. Thus the function 'is bald' yields True as value given Fred as argument, and False as value given Arnold as argument. Given any bald person as argument, the value of this function is True; and given any nonbald person, False. Thus this predicate gives the relation between objects (persons in this case) and truth values in a systematic way, depending exactly on whether or not that person is bald, is among the bald things. Predicates with different meanings yield different object → truth value pairings. For example, the predicate 'is stupid' might give True as value given either Arnold or Fred as argument. The particular way each $o \rightarrow v$ function relates objects to truth values thus plausibly constitutes the meaning of that predicate, just as the particular object $\rightarrow$ object pairings yielded by 'the father of' gave its meaning.

We have looked at predicates taking one name as argument, but there are also predicates that take two or more names. In 'Brutus killed Caesar', 'killed' is a *two-place predicate*. We can see this as a more complex sort of function. 'Killed' first takes one object (named by the grammatical object of the verb, Caesar, the object killed), yielding a one-place predicate, 'killed Caesar'; then this second predicate takes an object (named by the grammatical subject of the verb, Brutus, the killer), yielding a truth value as value. Thus 'killed' is a function with the following structure: Given an object, it yields a (one-place) predicate. We can abbreviate this as $o \rightarrow (o \rightarrow v)$. Look carefully at this function: The left-hand side tells us that a name is needed to refer to the argument; the right-hand side tells us that the value is referred to by a predicate. Loosely, a two-place predicate takes a name as argument and yields a predicate as value. (Strictly, we have been taking objects, not names, as arguments or values for functions with an 'o' in them; thus we should speak not of predicates but of what they name—perhaps *properties*—as arguments or values of functions with an '$o \rightarrow v$' in them. A predicate is a bit of language; a property is not.)

Here, then, is the tree of 'Brutus killed Caesar':

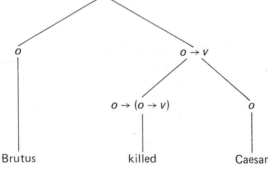

And of 'Brutus killed himself':

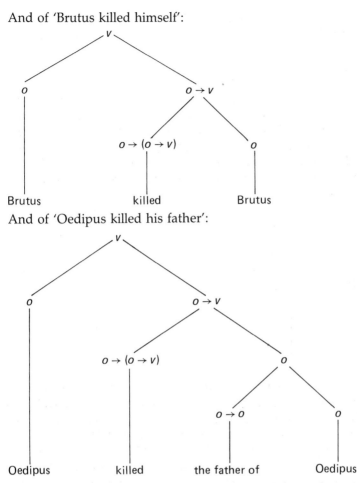

And of 'Oedipus killed his father':

Before you continue, you should look carefully at these trees and make sure you understand how they work. Try constructing the tree for 'Fred's father killed himself'.

I have been speaking of *satisfaction of a predicate* so far; but what does this amount to? So far, the only relation of bits of language and the world that we have been relying on is *naming*, the relation between a name and a particular thing. It is useful for our purposes to conceive of the world as containing not only particular things but also *sets*, that is, collections, of things. Tom, Dick, and Shirley are particular objects, and we can conceive of them as collectively constituting a set: {Tom, Dick, Shirley}. The braces are standard notation for a set consisting of the objects named inside. There is also a set of bald things: {Fred, Dick, Yul Brynner, . . . }. To say that Dick is bald, then, is to say that Dick is one of the *members* of the set of bald things.

Adverbs

Now consider adverbs in English: How can they be given a functional construal? What adverbs do is to take predicates as arguments and yield other predicates as values. For example, 'slowly' takes the predicate 'runs' as an argument and yields the predicate 'runs slowly' as a value. Adverbs are thus functions from one predicate to another, of the form $(o \rightarrow v) \rightarrow (o \rightarrow v)$. The tree for 'Fred walks slowly' is:

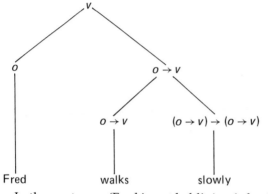

In the sentence, 'Fred is not bald', 'not' also functions as an adverb. What 'not' does in this sentence is to turn the predicate 'is bald' into the predicate 'is nonbald'. ('Not' also has a different important use, as a $v \rightarrow v$ function. This is discussed in chapter 12.) This predicate is satisfied by anything that is outside the set of bald things, which is in other words in the set of nonbald things, that is, the set of things including everything in the universe except the bald things. Thus:

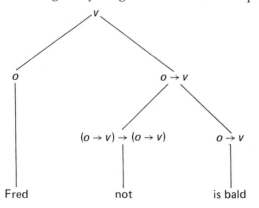

Now consider the sentence 'Fred is a fat professor'. We could construct this tree for it, using the predicate 'is a fat professor':

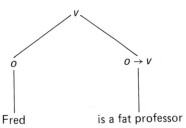

Fred   is a fat professor

But to say that Fred is a fat professor is to say that he is fat *and* a
professor. But note that this sort of decomposition is not always correct. To say that Dumbo is a small elephant is not to say that Dumbo
is small and an elephant. Small elephants are large. A more detailed
analysis of semantic form than the one in this chapter would need to
take account of this difference.

What is 'and'? It is a curious sort of function. Combining the predicate 'is fat' with 'and' yields 'is fat and'; combining 'is fat and' with
another predicate ('is a professor') yields a predicate, 'is fat and is a
professor' (or, for short, 'is fat and a professor', or, even shorter, 'is a
fat professor'. Because 'is fat and' combined with another predicate
('is a professor',) yields a predicate ('is a fat professor'), 'is fat and' is
an adverb, symbolized by $(o \rightarrow v) \rightarrow (o \rightarrow v)$. Because 'is fat' combined
with 'and' yields this adverb, the structure of this 'and' as a function
must be that it takes a predicate and yields an adverb. Thus 'and' is a
function of the form $(o \rightarrow v) \rightarrow [(o \rightarrow v) \rightarrow (o \rightarrow v)]$. (Basic symbolic
logic has no equivalent way of decomposing predicates in this sort of
way. In standard form this sentence would be analyzed as a conjunction of two sentences: Fred is fat *and* Fred is a professor: *Ff* & *Pf*.) Look
at this function carefully, and you will see that it takes a predicate and
yields an adverb. Thus the tree for 'Fred is a fat professor' is:

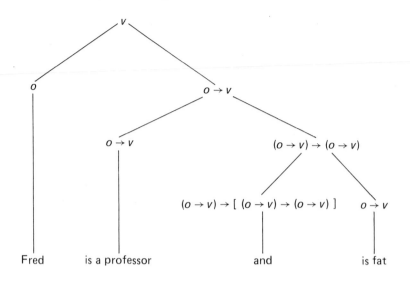

The Function and Object Theory of Meaning

The philosophical attractiveness of the system we have started to develop for understanding the meanings of sentences is that it has—so far, at least—managed to explain things without any recourse to mental entities. There are only three things whose existence we have needed to assume so far: (1) *individuals,* particular items in the objective, external world; (2) *sets,* collections of individuals; and (3) *linguistic entities.* The first two things are real objective parts of the external world (although there has been some philosophical debate about the reality of sets); the third thing consists of conventional connections between linguistic items and (a) sets or individuals, (b) truth values, or (c) other linguistic items.

The aim of this theory is to explain what each sentence type in English means, and so far we have been able to manage this without relying on mental objects as explanatory entities. The advantage this gives us is that it avoids those problems we saw raised by any idea theory of meaning: Meanings, according to the present theory, are not "in the head," so we do not need to worry about the private language argument difficulties or about the apparently unscientific enterprise of what understanding others' meanings would be if meanings were "in the head" (remember our consideration of radical translation.)

It is clear, however, that the "function and object" account of meaning we have so far is incomplete in a couple of ways. First, it aims at explaining meaning by using the notions of reference and truth; this will not explain all the ways language works, for it will not deal with the use of language for informing, asking questions, making requests, etc. These are the features of language that the speech act theory was designed to deal with, and the speech act theory does require explanatory entities such as people's intentions. Perhaps intentions and other mental entities are unavoidable, then, in a *complete* account of what language is about. But we saw that the speech act theory had nothing to say about why it is that what a speaker informs a hearer of is true or false or about the connections between any question, request, act of informing, etc. and the external world. Filling this gap is the job of the current theory.

The second sort of incompleteness of the function and object theory so far developed is that it does not even do the job it was designed for. It is clear that the list of functions so far accumulated is incomplete for anything similar to a fine-textured analysis of language in detail. This introductory book can provide only a rough sketch of a few other main items necessary for semantic analysis. Most of the rest of this book discusses how—and whether—a functional analysis such as the one we have begun might deal with problems and puzzles that arise from the theory we have begun to develop.

12

Quantifiers

Why Quantifiers Are Not Names

Bertrand Russell gave this good advice:

> A logical theory may be tested by its capacity for dealing with puzzles, and it is a wholesome plan, in thinking about logic, to stock the mind with as many puzzles as possible, since these serve much the same purpose as is served by experiments in physical science. (1905, pp. 484–485)

Here are some examples of the first sort of puzzle with which we confront our theory:

1. 'Something is tall' is certainly true, and so is 'Something is not tall'. But how can these sentences both be true? For 'Fred is tall' and 'Fred is not tall' cannot both be true.
2. Consider the following dialogue:
   Hal: What did you see in the drawer?
   Sal: I saw nothing in the drawer.
   Hal: You saw *that* in the drawer? Funny, when I looked it was empty.
3. Nothing is better than steak; but hamburger is better than nothing; therefore, hamburger is better than steak.
4. No cat has two tails. Every cat has one more tail than no cat. Therefore every cat has three tails.

Of course, these puzzles throw nobody into deep confusion: It is clear that they all result from a mistaken way of thinking about the words 'something', 'nothing', 'every', and 'no'. Everyone knows that a mistake is being made in each case, but it is not obvious what sort of mistake this is and how a theory of meaning might explain it.

In all four cases there is the same sort of mistake, namely, that we take a bit of the sentence ('something', 'nothing, or 'no cat') as a *name*, as a word that refers to a particular individual entity, but these words do not work like that.

Suppose that Fido is in the doghouse and that I say, "Something is in the doghouse." Is 'something' one way of naming Fido? Suppose that Fido has left the doghouse and that Rover has gone in there instead; then the sentence 'Something is in the doghouse' is still true. Maybe we should say that 'something' is a peculiar sort of name in that it is the name of *everything*, not the name of the set of all things but the name of each thing. To understand 'something' in this way is to think of it like the name 'Fred', which is, in a certain sense, ambiguous: There are many individuals named Fred, and different tokens of that word type can refer to one or another of them, although each token refers only to one, not to that spatially and temporally spread-out and discontinuous thing that is the set of all things to which that name can refer. But this way of thinking of 'something' leads to just the sort of mistakes that occurred in the four puzzles.

The mistake of trying to treat 'nothing' as a name would lead to the following tree for 'Nothing is in the drawer':

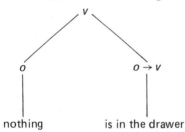

This tree indicates that the sentence is true if there is an object (note the *o* in the tree) that is in the set of things-in-the-drawer. Therefore it would follow from the truth of this sentence, thus analyzed, that the set of things-in-the-drawer is not empty, that is, that the drawer is not empty. But clearly this does not follow, and this is the incorrect analysis of the sentence. But this is the only model for analysis the theory has provided so far.

A similar problem is raised by 'everything'. 'Everything' is not the name of the class of all things, for the sentence 'Everything is purple' is false, not because the set of all things is not purple (do sets have color?) but because there are some items in the set of all things that are not purple. To deal with sentences such as these, the simple function and object theory is insufficient. One way to deal with the meanings of such words as 'something', 'nothing', and 'everything' (called *quantifiers* in logical theory) is to expand the simple function and object theory.

How Quantifiers Work

What the word 'something' does in the sentence 'Something is purple' is not to point to a particular thing but rather to tell you that at least one thing, never mind which, is an argument of the function 'x is purple' that yields the value True. The sentence 'Something is purple' is true because this glass of grape Kool-Aid is purple; but 'something' is not the name of this glass of grape Kool-Aid, for that sentence would be true even if this glass of grape Kool-Aid were not purple, provided that something else, *anything* else, were purple. What this sentence says, then, is not that some particular thing is a member of the set of purple things but rather that there is at least one thing, never mind which one, that is a member of that group.

There are many sentences that mean more or less the same thing as 'Something is purple': 'At least one thing is purple', 'There exists a purple thing', 'One or more things is purple', and so on. We can ignore the small differences in meaning among these sentences and emphasize their basic similarity. All of them are true, provided (roughly) that there exist one or more things to which the predicate 'is purple' applies, that is, that there is something in the set of things that satisfies the predicate. Another way of putting this is to say that the set of things that satisfy this predicate is *not empty.*

Sentences that make assertions such as these are called *existential sentences.* The word 'existential' here is the adjective that comes from the word 'existence'; the sentences are called existential because they assert the existence of one or more things of a certain sort.

Sentences that make assertions about *everything* are called *universal sentences.* Examples of universal sentences are 'Everything is purple' and 'All ducks waddle'.

These quantifiers, then, are a different sort of function: one that takes a predicate—an $o \rightarrow v$—as argument and yields a truth value as value; abbreviate this function as $(o \rightarrow v) \rightarrow v$. Thus, for example, in 'Something is purple' the word 'something' is a function that yields True if and only if its argument function ('is purple') is satisfied by one or more things in the universe:

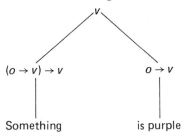

In standard form this is expressed by $(\exists x)(Px)$. The $\exists$ is called the *existential quantifier*; x is an *individual variable* or *placeholder*, analogous to the x in x^2.

Similarly, in 'Everything is purple' 'everything' is a function from predicates to truth values. It yields the value True when each thing in the universe satisfies that predicate:

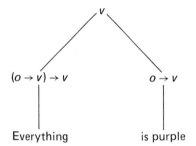

In standard form this is written $(\forall x)(Px)$. The $\forall$ is one way of notating the *universal quantifier*.

How do we analyze the sentence 'Some grape is purple'? This is equivalent to the sentence, 'Something is a grape and is purple'. Thus we can employ the analysis for combining predicates using 'and' with the analysis for the quantifier 'something' (to test your mastery of the system, you might try to produce this tree on your own before looking at it):

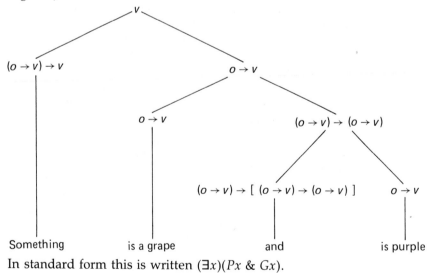

In standard form this is written $(\exists x)(Px \ \& \ Gx)$.

Now consider the sentence, 'All ducks waddle'. It appears that this is a universal sentence, asserting something about each thing in the universe, but what is it asserting about each thing? Not that each thing is a duck or that it waddles; rather, that *either* each thing waddles *or* it is *not* a duck. In other words, everything either waddles or else it is a *non-duck*. Thus "All ducks waddle' is equivalent in logical form to the semi-English sentence 'Everything waddles or is a non-duck'. Here, 'or' is a function of the same sort as 'and', namely, $(o \rightarrow v) \rightarrow [(o \rightarrow v) \rightarrow (o \rightarrow v)]$. Its tree is:

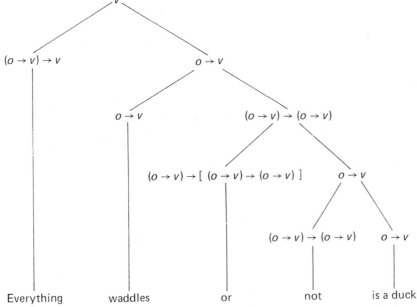

In standard notation this sentence is expressed $(\forall x)(Wx \lor {\sim}Dx)$. The $\lor$ means *or*, and the $\sim$ means *not*. This is logically equivalent to $(\forall x)$ $(Dx \supset Wx)$. The $\supset$ means "if . . . then." Thus this second formulation may be translated most directly into semi-English as 'Everything is such that, if it is a duck, then it waddles'.

'Nothing is purple' can be analyzed in terms of the mechanisms already available, for it is equivalent to 'Everything is non-purple', and so the following tree represents its logical form:

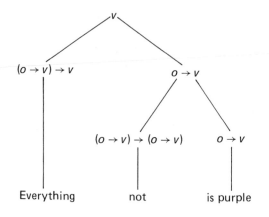

Everything   not   is purple

Negating a Sentence

Note that 'Nothing is purple' is the *negation* of 'Something is purple'. To say that one sentence is the negation of another is to mean that, if the first is true, then the second is false, and if the first is false, then the second is true. That is, the two sentences must have opposite truth values. An easy way of creating the negation of any sentence is to attach 'It is not the case that' to the front of it. Thus all three items in the following list are negations of 'Something is purple':

> It is not the case that something is purple.
> Nothing is purple.
> Everything is non-purple.

The negation of 'Fred is fat' can be expressed, as we did in the last chapter, as 'Fred is not fat'; here the 'not' is a function taking the predicate 'is fat' and yielding the predicate 'is non-fat'. But one can equivalently express the negation of 'Fred is fat' as 'It is not the case that Fred is fat'. This means the same as 'Fred is not fat'. But this sort of equivalence marks one of the significant differences between quantified sentences and nonquantified sentences, for 'It is not the case that something is fat' is *not* equivalent to 'Something is not fat'. To see this, note that

(12.1)   Something is not on my desk.

is true, because my wastebasket, for example, is not on my desk. But

(12.2)   It is not the case that something is on my desk.

is false, because my coffee cup is on my desk. Thus sentences (12.1) and (12.2) do not mean the same thing—they are not equivalent. Sentence (12.2) but not sentence (12.1) is the negation of

(12.3)   Something is on my desk.

Compare the nonquantified sentences

(12.4)   My wastebasket is not on my desk.
(12.5)   It is not the case that my wastebasket is on my desk.

Here, if sentence (12.4) is true, then sentence (12.5) must be true also. If sentence (12.4) is false, then sentence (12.5) must be false also. They must have the same truth value—they mean the same thing and are equivalent. *Both* sentences (12.4) and (12.5) are negations of

(12.6)   My wastebasket is on my desk.

Sentences (12.1) and (12.4) incorporate the negation 'not' in a way we are already familiar with: 'Not' is an adverb, turning one predicate into another. But sentences (12.2) and (12.5) use the negating part of the sentence in a different way. In general, this way, which always yields the negation of the sentence it is prefixed to, is a sort of function we have not seen so far: It takes a *whole sentence* as argument and changes its truth value to the opposite. We can thus see it as a function of the form $v \rightarrow v$ and represent sentences (12.4) and (12.5) differently:

Sentence (12.4)

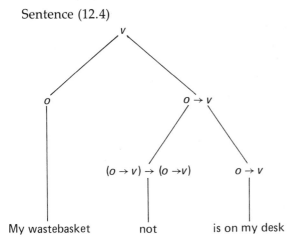

Sentence (12.5)

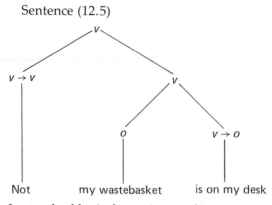

In standard logical notation no distinction is made between wide and narrow scope of negation in nonquantified sentences. This is not a problem, however, because the two are logically equivalent anyway. Both sentences (12.5) and (12.6) could be symbolized $\sim Db$, where b is an individual constant—the symbol for a name—standing for my wastebasket.

The Scope of a Negation

Logicians say that the 'not' in the logical form of sentence (12.4) has *narrow scope* in that it is a function taking as argument only a small part of the sentence; in sentence (12.5) the 'not' has *wide scope* because it takes a wider portion of the sentence—in fact, all the rest of it—as argument. You can see this by comparing how the 'not's interact in the trees of the two sentences.

It turns out that wide or narrow scope makes no difference in this nonquantified sentence: Sentences (12.4) and (12.5) mean the same thing. But wide or narrow scope does make a difference in quantified sentences:

Sentence (12.6)

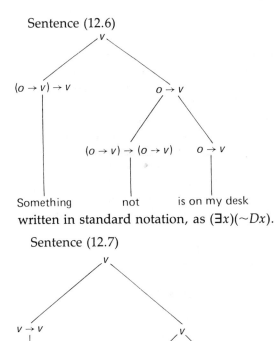

written in standard notation, as $(\exists x)(\sim Dx)$.

Sentence (12.7)

in standard notation, $\sim(\exists x)(Dx)$.

In sentence (12.6), the 'not' has narrow scope, and in sentence (12.7) the 'not' has wide scope. This *does* make a difference here: Sentences (12.6) and (12.7) can have different truth values because they are not logically equivalent.

Now, at last, we can see exactly how to solve one of the puzzles at the beginning of this chapter:

1. 'Something is tall' is certainly true, and so is 'Something is not tall'. But how can these sentences both be true? For 'Fred is tall' and 'Fred is not tall' cannot both be true.

The reason why 'Fred is tall' and 'Fred is not tall' cannot both be true is because one is the negation of the other. 'Fred is not tall' means the same thing as 'It is not the case that Fred is tall'. It makes no difference whether the 'not' has narrow or wide scope in a nonquantified sentence. But the scope of 'not' makes a difference in quantified sentences. The negation of 'Something is tall' is 'It is not the case that something is tall' ('not' has wide scope). But 'not' in 'Something is not tall' has narrow scope, and because this is a quantified sentence, 'Something is not tall' is not the negation of 'Something is tall', and both sentences can be true. (In fact, they both *are* true.)

The fact that the negation of a quantified sentence has 'not' in wide scope but not in narrow scope and that this distinguishes them from nonquantified sentences comes up in the next chapter in connection with a different sort of puzzle.

Suggested Reading

Russell, Bertrand. 1905. "On denoting." *Mind* 14:479–493.
    This article is more germane to the content of chapter 13 than to the content of this chapter. The article can also be found in [2, 6, 7].

13

Definite Descriptions

The Problem of Nonreferring Definite Descriptions

Another family of puzzles facing the theory of meaning so far developed involves nonexistence, expressions that do not refer to anything.

I consider first the problem with nonreferring *definite descriptions*. (I discuss nonreferring proper names in chapters 17 and 18.) A definite description is, roughly, a noun phrase beginning with 'the', for example, 'the daughter of Fred'. Definite descriptions and proper names are both *singular terms*, that is, they refer (if at all) to exactly one thing.

We began by thinking of definite descriptions, such as 'the daughter of Fred', as composed of a name ('Fred') that is the argument of an object → object function ('the daughter of'). This explains how 'the daughter of Fred' has meaning. The function 'the daughter of' yields as value (refers to) Fred's daughter when supplied with Fred as argument. Fred exists and has exactly one daughter, and so the meanings of both 'Fred' and 'the daughter of Fred' give our theory no trouble.

But consider the sentence, 'The daughter of Igor is attending college'. If Igor has no daughter, never has and never will, 'the daughter of x' yields no value given Igor as argument; 'the daughter of Igor' is a nonreferring singular term:

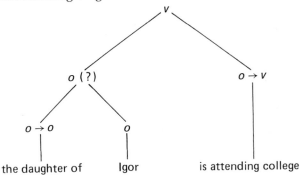

The same sort of problem would arise if Igor has two or more daughters; then there would equally be nothing referred to by 'the daughter of Igor'.

Why is this a problem? I have been attempting to explain the meaning of linguistic items, such as 'the daughter of Igor', by seeing them as object → object functions. In this case, however, the function 'the daughter of' yields no object as value given Igor as argument. Remember that a function is nothing but a systematic relationship between arguments and values; if a particular argument yields no value in a function, then that function is defective. The number → number function x^2 is well defined because it yields a value for *every possible* argument; but 'the daughter of x' is not.

Frege's Answer

Frege saw this problem and suggested the following solution: Suppose that we see this sort of function in this case as yielding the *null set* as value, that is, the set with nothing in it, the *empty set*. This expands the notion of what sort of function 'the daughter of x' is: Sometimes it yields exactly one object, a *unit set*, as value and sometimes the null set. In either case we can say, at least, that it is well defined: It yields some set or other as value with Fred or with Igor as argument:

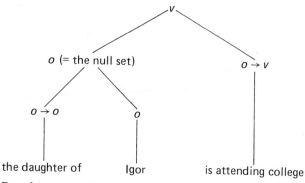

But this suggestion encounters grave difficulties. Suppose that Fred and Sally are married and that they have exactly one daughter, Mildred. In that case 'the daughter of' yields the same value (Mildred) with Fred or with Sally as argument. (This is no problem: Note that x^2 yields the value 36 with 6 or with -6 as argument.) Thus 'the daughter of Fred' and 'the daughter of Sally' refer to the same thing. The daughter of Fred *is* the daughter of Sally; Fred and Sally have the same daughter.

But suppose that Lulu, like Igor, has no daughter. On Frege's suggestion 'the daughter of Lulu' refers to the null set, and so does 'the daughter of Igor'. Because these two expressions yield the same object—the null set—as value, we must say that they refer to the same thing and that the daughter of Lulu *is* the daughter of Igor; Lulu and Igor have the same daughter. (Given that they have never met, Lulu and Igor would be surprised to hear this.) By the same line of reasoning, what these two expressions refer to is also the referent of 'the present King of France' and of 'the mountain made out of pure gold', given that these expressions similarly yield the null set as value. Thus it follows that the joint daughter of Lulu and Igor is the present King of France and is also the world's only golden mountain. This would surprise Igor and Lulu even more.

If this is not a sufficiently intolerable consequence, consider the following. Is 'the daughter of Igor is attending college' true or false? Given that Igor has no daughter, that sentence seems false. But on Frege's suggestion 'the daughter of Igor' refers to the null set; is the null set attending college? Well, perhaps. Let's try to make Frege's suggestion work.

Suppose that the entire attendance list at Very Small University is the following: Alice, Bertha, and Calvin. The set of objects that satisfies the predicate 'attends VSU' is thus {Alice, Bertha, Calvin}. So it seems that subsets of that three-member set satisfy that predicate: the unit sets {Alice}, {Bertha}, and {Calvin} and the sets of two members, {Alice, Bertha}, {Alice, Calvin}, {Bertha, Calvin}. But the null set is (by virtue of a stipulation by set theorists) a subset of *every* set; so it is also a subset of that set of three members. Thus it follows that the null set satisfies the predicate 'attends VSU' and thus is also to be counted among the attenders of VSU (and, of course, of every other university as well.) It appears, then, that Frege's suggestion would make it *true* that the daughter of Igor (= the null set) is attending college—in fact, *every* college. Another surprise for Igor, who by now is thoroughly nonplussed.

The quote from Russell at the beginning of chapter 12 likened logical puzzles to experiments in physical science. The job of our theory is to explain the semantics of language, and puzzles such as sentences containing nonreferring definite descriptions provide experiments to test proposals. A theory will fail if it turns out not to be true to the facts; the facts in this case include the truth or falsity of sentences in real English. It appears that Frege's suggestion has failed, because it has consequences that are too far from these facts. (As we will see later, what I have been calling Frege's suggestion was not his last word on the matter.)

Russell's Analysis

In a classic work in modern philosophy of language, Russell attempted to show how we can understand definite descriptions in such a way that the theory we have so far is consistent with the facts. Russell proposed that all definite descriptions, referring or not, be dealt with not as $o \rightarrow o$ functions but rather in a more complex way. According to Russell's theory the sentence 'The daughter of Igor is attending college', is to be understood as equivalent to the following paraphrase: Something and no more than one thing is a daughter of Igor and is attending college. Alternatively: There exists *exactly* one thing that is a daughter of Igor, and it is attending college. Thus, if Igor has no daughters or more than one daughter, the sentence is false; or if Igor has exactly one daughter but she is not attending college, the sentence is false.

The word 'something' in the first paraphrase indicates that a quantificational analysis of that sentence is in order. Let's try:

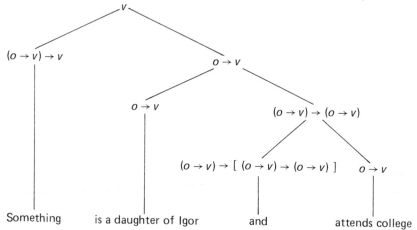

which in standard notation is written $(\exists x)(Dx \ \& \ Cx)$. You might have noticed that there is a further functional decomposition possible here: The predicate 'is a daughter of Igor' might further be analyzed into a function that takes an object, Igor, as argument to yield this predicate. A function of this sort would be of the form $o \rightarrow (o \rightarrow v)$. This sort of function has not previously been encountered, but it and others I have not described would be necessary in a system of functions that would produce a thorough analysis of English logical form. I omit it here and simply take 'is a daughter of Igor' as an unanalyzed predicate, for the sake of keeping the trees relatively simple and comprehensible.

The problem here is that what the diagram says is that the set of things that are both Igor-daughters and college-attenders is not empty—that there exists *at least* one such thing. Recall that the standard reading of the quantifier 'something' yields True if the predicate is satisfied by one or more objects. The sentence understood this way, then, is true if there is one such thing, but it is also true if there are two or more such things. So this does not get 'The daughter of Igor attends college' straight, because that sentence is not true if there are two or more such things; there has to be *exactly* one thing and no more for that sentence to be true.

What we need instead is a way of saying that there is *exactly* one thing that is a daughter of Igor—that there is *uniquely* one thing. 'Uniquely' is an adverb, transforming the predicate, 'is a daughter of Igor' into 'uniquely is a daughter of Igor'; thus:

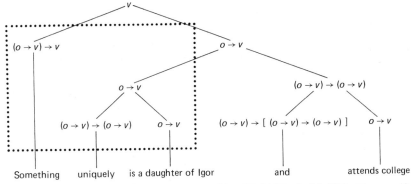

In standard notation this is expressed by $(\exists x)((Dx \ \& \ (\forall y)(Dy \supset x = y))$ $\& \ Cx)$. The part of the sentence $(\forall y)(Dy \supset x = y)$ can be rendered into semi-English as, 'For anything, if it is a daughter of Igor, then it is quantitatively identical with x'. This means that there is at most one daughter of Igor.

The dotted-line box encloses the contribution of 'the daughter of Igor'. You can see why Russell called the definite description an "incomplete symbol." We might call a name (or a function-plus-argument) a "complete symbol," but a definite description amounts to a complex function that needs an argument (a predicate) to complete it.

One of the puzzles Russell noted about definite-description-containing sentences, which his theory is designed to solve, is the following:

By the law of excluded middle, either 'A is B' or 'A is not B' must be true. Hence either 'the present King of France is bald' or 'the

> present King of France is not bald' must be true. Yet if we enumerated the things that are bald, and then the things that are not bald, we should not find the present King of France in either list. (1905, p. 485)

It is clearly a consequence of Russell's account of definite descriptions that 'The present King of France is bald' is false: There does not exist exactly one thing that is the present King of France and that is bald. If we take it, as Russell advocates, that 'The present King of France is bald' is false, then we must surely take it that the negation of that sentence is true. The puzzle arises because we take the negation of 'The present King of France is bald' to be 'The present King of France is not bald'. But the second sentence on Russell's analysis is also false, because it is equivalent to the assertion that there exists uniquely one thing that is the present King of France and it is *not* bald.

Russell's answer to this puzzle is that we are mistaken if we take 'The present King of France is not bald' to be the genuine negation of 'The present King of France is bald'. Because 'The present king of France is bald' is equivalent on his view to 'Something is uniquely the present King of France and bald', its genuine negation is, rather, 'It is not the case that something is uniquely the present King of France and bald' or, in other words, '*Nothing* is uniquely the present King of France and bald'. (Recall the discussion of the negation of quantified sentences in chapter 12.)

Of course, there is a certain ambiguity in English in denying that

(13.1)   The present King of France is bald.

is true. We may mean either

(13.2)   There is a unique present King of France, but he is not bald.

or

(13.3)   Nothing is a bald unique present King of France.

But sentence (13.3), not sentence (13.2), is the genuine negation of sentence (13.1). Sentences (13.1) and (13.2) could not both be true, but they are not negations of each other; sentences of these forms might both be false. Genuine negations must have opposite truth values. Sentences of a form such that it is logically impossible that both be true (although both may be false) are called *contraries*. Our discussion in the last chapter shows why sentence (13.2) is not the negation of sentence (13.1): 'Not' in it has narrow scope, and this does not yield a genuine negation of a quantified sentence. Thus it is possible (in fact, actual) that both sentences (13.1) and (13.2) are false. This does not violate the logical law that the negation of a false sentence is true.

The scope difference between sentences (13.2) and (13.3) may be seen in the difference between the trees showing their logical form. For sentence (13.2) we have

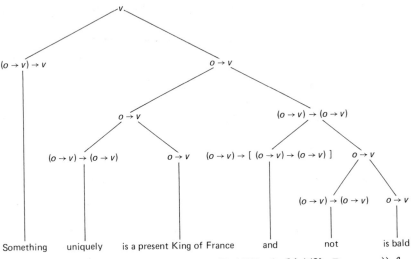

In standard notation this is written $(\exists x)((Kx\ \&\ (\forall y)(Ky \supset x = y))\ \&\ \sim\!Bx)$. And for sentence (13.3) we have

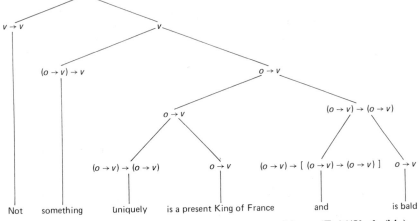

In standard notation, this sentence is expressed by $\sim\!(\exists x)((Ks\ \&\ (\forall y)(Ky \supset x = y))\ \&\ Bx)$.

The sort of theory we are aiming at is tested for adequacy by seeing whether it produces the correct *truth conditions* for sentences in English. We look at two well-known criticisms of Russell's theory in this light.

Referential and Attributive Uses

A set of what are sometimes taken to be counterexamples to Russell's analysis are presented by Keith Donnellan. Here is an example of the Donnellan sort. I spent a frustrating few minutes with a color-blind friend of mine, who kept insisting, "The big red book on the top shelf has the article you are looking for." In response to my continuing insistence that there was no big red book on the top shelf, he finally got up and brought me the big *green* book from the top shelf. "This is the one I meant, you idiot!" he exclaimed triumphantly.

On Russell's theory, 'the big red book on the top shelf' does not refer, and my friend's sentence 'The big red book . . .' is false. But Donnellan's article (included, in fact, in that big green book [9]) argues that, despite the fact that nothing fits such a definitive description, nevertheless the speaker has a particular thing in mind, and the thing he has in mind, despite his mistake in describing it, is what 'the big red book on the top shelf' means.

Now compare this to a use of a definite description when the speaker has nothing particular in mind. I can say with perfect confidence, "The fastest runner in Brazil can beat me in any race," not having any idea who the fastest runner in Brazil is. When I say this, I do not need to have any particular person in mind; I mean just *whoever* happens to be the fastest runner in Brazil, and my definite description refers to whomever that happens to be.

Donnellan argues that cases of these sorts illustrate two different ways definite descriptions may work. The second example fits Russell's analysis: I imply that there is exactly one object that fits a certain description and intend to refer to whatever (whomever) that is. Donnellan calls this the *attributive use* of the definite description.

But in the first example my friend's use of the definite description is intended to apply to the particular thing he has in mind, not to just whatever satisfies the description he utters. Had it turned out that some other book was in fact the only big red book on the shelf, he would not have agreed that he was talking about that one. He did not succeed in communicating to me which book he had in mind, but nevertheless, on that occasion the book he had in mind was the one he meant, the book that his use of that definite description referred to. Donnellan calls this the *referential use* of the definite description. Russell's analysis does not fit this sort of use, for my friend's words were not intended to pick out just whatever fit a certain description but were aimed at a particular thing.

In a sense Russell encouraged this distinction, speaking of the difference between knowing things "by immediate acquaintance" and knowing things only "as what has such and such properties" (Russell 1905). Russell thought that definite descriptions are appropriate only for things known in the second way; Donnellan's argument is that sometimes they are used also for things known in the first way.

Nevertheless, it seems that this is not exactly the point. What we are interested in here is the truth conditions for a sentence containing a definite description, not in the psychology of the speaker on particular occasions of its use. Perhaps the psychology of the speaker is relevant to the *speaker's meaning* of the utterance, but the task here is to provide an account of *sentence meaning* and the hope is that a truth-conditional semantics can give this. However, my friend was acquainted with the book, and the very words he uttered in fact failed to refer; and thus we can say that, despite his intentions, what he said was false. Perhaps there are two sorts of ways we can know about things, but it seems clear nevertheless that this is not relevant to the sentence meaning of what we say.

Strawson's Objection

Another well-known objection is due to P. F. Strawson:

> Now suppose some one were in fact to say to you with a perfectly serious air: "The king of France is wise". Would you say, "That's untrue"? I think it's quite certain that you wouldn't. But suppose he went on to *ask* you whether you thought that what he had just said was true, or was false; whether you agreed or disagreed with what he had just said. I think you would be inclined, with some hesitation, to say that you didn't do either; that the question of whether his statement was true or false simply *didn't arise*, because there was no such person as the king of France. . . . So when we utter the sentence . . . we simply *fail* to say anything true or false because we simply fail to mention anybody by this particular use of that perfectly significant phrase. (1950, pp. 330–331)

Russell replies:

> Mr. Strawson . . . admits that the sentence is significant and not true, but not that it is false. This is a mere question of verbal convenience . . . I find it more convenient to define the word

"false" so that every significant sentence is either true or false. This is a purely verbal question; and although I have no wish to claim the support of common usage, I do not think that he can claim it either. Suppose, for example, that in some country there was a law that no person could hold public office if he considered it false that the Ruler of the Universe is wise. I think an avowed atheist who took advantage of Mr. Strawson's doctrine to say that he did not hold this proposition false, would be regarded as a somewhat shifty character. (1957, pp. 338–339)

It seems to me that Russell's way of dealing with definite descriptions matches the facts of English usage a bit better than Strawson's does; you can make up your own mind about this. A theory must be tested against the facts of usage, as I have been insisting; but the problem here is really that there seem to be no hard facts of usage in English about the truth or falsity of sentences containing nonreferring definite descriptions, no "rules, habits, conventions governing its correct use, on all occasions, to refer or to assert" (Strawson 1950, p. 327). (By contrast, Frege's suggestion did contradict some hard facts. Recall how surprised Lulu and Igor were.)

When some facts are ambiguous, this does not mean that there is no reason to prefer one theory over another, however. So far, the truth-conditional semantics we have been pursuing, which treats sentences (at least assertions, as opposed to questions, orders, etc.) as true or false and explains their meaning on this basis, has achieved remarkable success. Perhaps, then, the best way to settle this question is to continue to see just what theoretical power a truth-conditional semantics has. If it can cope with puzzles and successfully explain the semantics of language, then it is the theory we want.

Suggested Readings

Donnellan, Keith. 1966. "Reference and definite descriptions." *Philosophical Review* 75(3):281–304.
   Also found in [5, 10].
Russell, Bertrand. 1919. *Introduction to Mathematical Philosophy*. London: Allen & Unwin, ch. 16.
   A readable presentation of Russell's ideas on definite descriptions. Chapter 16 is also available in [2, 4, 5, 9].
Russell, Bertrand. 1905. "On denoting." *Mind* 14:479–483.
   Russell's classical work on definite descriptions. Reprinted in [2, 6, 7].
Russell, Bertrand, 1957. "Mr. Strawson on referring." *Mind* 66:385–389.
   Russell's reply to Strawson's "On referring" (1950). Reprinted in [7].
Strawson, P. F. 1950. "On referring." *Mind* 59:320–344.
   Objections to Russell's views. Also found in [7].

14

Extensionality

Extensional Contexts

In the last three chapters I have been attempting to build a theory of meaning based on the idea that referring expressions mean what they do merely by virtue of what they refer to, that is, that their contribution to the meaning of sentences they occur in is entirely to "tie" these sentences to the things (or sets of things) they name. Proper names are simply names of individual things; predicates name sets of things and are propositional functions that give the value True when the argument names an individual in that set, and False otherwise. Functions, such as adverbs, and quantified sentences and definite descriptions make things more complicated but do not require more basic apparatus than our theory provides.

The theory as developed so far is thoroughly *extensional*; that is, it attempts to explain the meanings of bits of language entirely on the basis of their *extensions* (their referents). The extension of a proper name is the thing it refers to; the extension of a general term and of a predicate is a set of things. The extension of a sentence is its truth value.

We have begun to consider the ways this extensional theory can be saved from problems of nonexistence. Russell's analysis of definite descriptions helps do this (although as we will see shortly, other problems about nonexistence arise). Let us turn now to the second major sort of problem for an extensional theory: the (apparent) existence of *nonextensional contexts*.

A *context* is merely a bit of language with a hole in it. 'The son of _____' is a context; filling its hole with a singular term makes the expression itself a singular term. Certain contexts become *sentences* when their holes are filled with predicates or with singular or general terms or with whole sentences. For example, '_____ is bald' (a predicate) becomes a sentence when its hole is filled by a singular term; 'Fred _____' becomes a sentence when its hole is filled by a predicate; 'The sky is blue and _____' becomes a sentence when its hole is filled by a sentence (among other ways). You can think of a context as equivalent to a *function*; I speak of the *argument* (what goes into the hole) and the *value* (the referent given the insertion of an argument) here as well.

I call two bits of language *coextensive* when they have the same referent. If 'Fred' and 'Stinky' are two names of Fred, then 'Fred' and 'Stinky' are *coreferential singular terms* and are coextensive; similarly, if Fred is the stupidest civil servant in Ottawa, then 'the stupidest civil servant in Ottawa' is coextensive with 'Fred' and with 'Stinky'. Every animal that has kidneys has a heart, and every animal with a heart has kidneys; because the set of renates (animals with kidneys) is identical with (contains exactly the same things as) the set of cordates (animals with hearts), the two general terms 'renates' and 'cordates' are coextensive, and so are the two predicates 'is a renate' and 'is a cordate'.

(You should be warned that some of the literature does not use 'extension' in exactly this way. Sometimes philosophers use 'extension' to mean the set of things that satisfy a predicate but not the reference of terms or the truth values of sentences; thus only predicates can be said to be coextensive. These other philosophers would speak instead of coreferring terms and of sentences with the same truth values.)

The theory (so far) claims that the referent of a sentence is its truth value. Thus two sentences with the same truth value have the same referent—are coextensive. Any true sentence is coextensive with any other true sentence; and any false sentence with any other false sentence.

A context is *extensional* when the referent of its value depends entirely on the referent of its arguments. Thus 'the son of _____' is an extensional context; it is a context that takes singular terms as arguments and yields singular terms as values. The referent of a value of this context depends entirely on the referent of the singular term inserted. If 'the son of Fred' refers to anyone at all, then what it refers to is the same thing (person) referred to by any singular term obtained when any singular term coextensive with 'Fred' is taken as value. Thus, because 'Fred' is coextensive with 'Stinky' and with 'the stupidest civil servant in Ottawa', 'the son of Fred' is coextensive with 'the son of Stinky' and with 'the son of the stupidest civil servant in Ottawa'.

Consider the context '_____ is bald'. This context takes singular terms as arguments and yields sentences as values. The referent of a sentence is its truth value; thus this context would be extensional if its truth value depended entirely on the referent of its argument. We can test for the extensionality of this context by trying various arguments. If two coreferential singular terms taken as arguments can ever yield different truth values for the sentence, then the context is nonextensional.

(Another common term for 'nonextensional' is 'intensional'. As I mentioned in chapter 10, this is a confusing term because of its similarity with 'intentional'—note the difference in spelling. Because of this confusion, I do not use the term 'intensional', always using 'nonextensional' instead.)

But if coextensive arguments always produce sentences with the same truth value, then this context is extensional. In the philosophical literature this test for the extensionality of a context whose value is a sentence is described this way: The context is extensional if and only if coreferring terms are substitutable *salva veritate* (a Latin term that means, here, *keeping the same truth value*).

It is easy to see that this context is extensional. Given that 'Fred', 'Stinky', and 'the stupidest civil servant in Ottawa' are coextensive, then 'Fred is bald', 'Stinky is bald', and 'The stupidest civil servant in Ottawa is bald' all have the same truth value, whatever that truth value is. If that person is bald, then all three sentences are true; if he is nonbald, then they are all false. One can always substitute coreferring terms in this context salva veritate.

Similarly, '_____ inhabit the reptile house at the Bronx Zoo' is an extensional context. It makes a sentence when a general term is taken as argument, and its truth value is determined wholly by the referents of (the set of objects referred to by) that general term. Replacement of any general term in that context by a coextensive general term leaves the truth value unchanged. If 'Renates inhabit the reptile house at the Bronx Zoo' is true, then so is 'Cordates inhabit the reptile house at the Bronx Zoo'.

An extensional context that takes a term (singular or general) as argument is called a *referentially transparent context*. So far, we have not encountered any contexts that take terms as arguments that are not extensional; but we will encounter some later. Contexts taking terms as arguments that are *not* extensional are called *referentially opaque contexts*.

Other contexts take predicates as arguments. The two predicates 'is a renate' and 'is a cordate' are coextensive. Thus replacement of one predicate by the other in the extensional context 'Fido _____' leaves that sentence true (given that Fido is a dog; if Fido is an amoeba, then 'Fido is a renate' and 'Fido is a cordate' are both false.)

Some contexts can take whole sentences as arguments, for example, '_____ and ducks waddle'; thus taking the sentence 'Snow is white' as argument yields the value 'Snow is white and ducks waddle'. Because 'Snow is white' and 'Grass is green' are both true, they are coextensive. Use of either sentence as argument yields a value with the same referent: 'Snow is white and ducks waddle' is true, and so is 'Grass is green and ducks waddle'. '_____ and ducks waddle' is an extensional context: Given *any* true sentence as argument, it would be True, and given any false sentence as argument, its value would be False.

An extensional context that takes whole sentences as arguments is called a *truth-functional context*. We have not yet encountered contexts that take sentences as values that are nonextensional; these will be examined shortly. Such a context is called *non–truth functional*.

Nonextensional Contexts

Extensional contexts are exactly what we would expect if the extensional theory is correct. An extensional theory sees sentences as built out of referring components; their truth value is determined wholly by the referents of the component expressions. But the existence of nonextensional contexts in a natural language would mean trouble for the extensional theory. It would show that a theory of meaning cannot rely on reference alone. English is apparently not an extensional language; it contains a variety of nonextensional contexts. If this is the case, then an extensional theory is not adequate. I examine several sorts of apparently nonextensional contexts.

In the purely extensional theory so far developed, the referent of sentences has been taken to be their truth value; this makes all true sentences have the same referent (True), and all false sentences have the same referent (False). But this view will not do, for there are contexts that take whole sentences as arguments, yielding (larger) whole sentences as values, but that are not extensional. Here is one example: the context 'Fred went to the store and then _____'. Suppose that

(14.1)   He went home.

and

(14.2)   He woke up that morning.

are both true. Now, inserting sentence (14.1) into the context yields

(14.3)   Fred went to the store and then he went home.

which, we suppose, is true. But inserting sentence (14.2) in the context yields a false value:

(14.4) Fred went to the store and then he woke up that morning.

Examples such as this one can be taken to show that the referent of a sentence cannot be merely its truth value, because different true sentences contribute differently to the meaning of sentences in which they are inserted. What we need to do is to define the reference of sentences more finely so that 'He went home' and 'He woke up in the morning' do not have the same referents.

States of Affairs

There is a way to do this. Intuitively, it is clear that sentences (14.1) and (14.2) name different *facts,* different *states of affairs.* It is understandable that insertion of one sentence yields a different truth value from substitution of the other: They name different facts, and the truth values of sentences (14.3) and (14.4) depend not merely on the truth values of sentences (14.1) and (14.2) but also on what states of affairs sentences (14.1) and (14.2) name.

What is a state of affairs? Suppose that we take it to be the satisfaction of the predicate by an object. 'He went home' names the state of affairs that is the satisfaction by him (Fred) of the predicate 'went home', that is, that Fred belonged (at a particular time) to the set of things that went to Fred's home. Similarly, 'He woke up in the morning' names the state of affairs that consists of Fred's belonging to the set of things that woke up that morning. These are different states of affairs, for they involve Fred's membership in two different sets. In this view it is no problem that the substitution that changes sentence (14.3) into sentence (14.4) changes its truth value, for the sentences involved in this substitution ((14.1) and (14.2)) are no longer seen as having the same referents: They have different referents to two different states of affairs.

(You might have noticed that the switch from truth values to states of affairs as the referents of sentences might result in a change in the salva veritate test for extensionality. Now we should see not only if a replacement in a context in a sentence leaves the truth value of that sentence intact but also whether it leaves it naming the same state of affairs. This is a stronger test, but we can continue to apply the weaker test (salva veritate), because anything that fails this test will certainly fail the stronger test: Any two sentences with different truth values must certainly name different states of affairs, although it does not follow that two sentences that have the same truth value name the same state of affairs.)

Note that the term 'state of affairs' is somewhat misleading; it seems to imply that it is something that makes up part of the actual world. But false sentences also name states of affairs: The state of affairs named by 'Pigs fly' is the inclusion of all pigs in the class of flying things. This is not true of the real world, and so we have to speak here of states of affairs that *obtain* and those that do not in the real world.

Verbally different sentences can name the same state of affairs. Because 'Fred' and 'Stinky' corefer, 'Fred woke up this morning' and 'Stinky woke up this morning' name the same state of affairs. Because the set of cordates is identical with the set of renates, 'Cordates reproduce sexually' names the same state of affairs as 'Renates reproduce sexually'; similarly, the set of things that satisfy the predicate 'is a cordate' is identical with the set of things that satisfy the predicate 'is a renate'; so substitution of one predicate for the other in a sentence should leave it referring to the same state of affairs.

This proposal saves the extensional theory from the counterexample indicated by sentences (14.1) and (14.2) and from others also. Consider the context that takes sentences as arguments: 'That _____ caused the house to burn down' (a *causal context*). With the true sentence 'The house was struck by lightning' as argument, a true sentence results; but with the true sentence 'Snow is white' as argument, a false sentence results. In this context as well it is clear that it is not only the truth value of the argument that contributes to the sentence but also the state of affairs that it names. 'The house was struck by lightning' and 'Snow is white' share the same truth value (True) but name different states of affairs. Once we have decided that the referents of sentences are states of affairs, this problem of nonsubstitutability salva veritate is similarly eliminated, because it seems that any sentence naming the same state of affairs as 'The house was struck by lightning' could be substituted for it, salva veritate, in 'That the house was struck by lightning caused the house to burn down'. For example, 'That the house was struck by electrical discharge caused it to burn down' is true, and so 'That Fred's pride and joy was struck by lightning caused Fred's house to burn down' is equally true (given that 'Fred's house' and 'Fred's pride and joy' corefer).

The move from truth values to states of affairs as the referents of sentences saves the theory from these sorts of counterexamples and at small expense. As I have noted, the theory is attractive partly because of its small ontology (the small number of kinds of existent it postulates), and this change does not add to its ontology. We do need to recognize the existence of states of affairs, but that is no problem because they apparently can be understood merely on the basis of the theory's existing ontology: States of affairs are analyzed as (*reduced to*) individuals, classes, and class membership.

This is the first of several problems an extensional theory of meaning will have to face. Why, you might be wondering, should we try to save the extensional theory at all? What is so good about extensionality in a theory? One of the things that is so good about it is the small ontology of explanatory entities just mentioned. This is always desirable in a theory. But a more important benefit of an extensional theory of meaning is that it sees meaning as a public thing, as the relationship between public words and the public world. Nonextensional theories, on the other hand, postulate intermediaries between word and world, such as the idea theory (chapter 2) did or the internal representations mentioned in chapter 3 and brought up again in chapter 19 did in response to an apparent failure of extensionality. These sorts of things are apparently private and subjective; thus they raise the problems discussed in the chapters on the private language argument and radical translation; they remove language from the public world, making it unfit for scientific study; perhaps they reduce all meaning to speaker's meaning. This is what is at stake in abandoning the word-world extensionality we are pursuing, and this is why we should try to keep it.

The next problem to be faced is an important, different sort of context that appears nonextensional, even when states of affairs are seen as the referents of sentences.

Suggested Reading

Quine, W. V. O. 1960. *Word and Object.* Cambridge: MIT Press, sections 30 and 31.

15

Modal Contexts and Possible Worlds

Possibility and Necessity

The first sort of nonextensional context I examine occurs inside what are called *modal sentences*. Modal sentences are (loosely) those sentences that contain the words 'necessary' and 'possible', for example:

It is possible that snow is blue.
Aristotle is necessarily human.

The terms 'necessary' and 'possible' are used in these sentences in a fairly special sense, which needs explanation.

What we are talking about here are *metaphysical* possibility and necessity. Whatever is necessarily false is not possibly true—is impossible; whatever is necessarily true is not possibly false. These terms are used in a special sense in these phrases, one you may be unfamiliar with. To say that something is metaphysically impossible is not to say that it is merely unbelievable or inconsistent with the way we know the world works or even with the most basic laws of science. It is difficult to define these terms; the best that can be done is to give some examples.

1. The sentence, 'The largest green book on this shelf is not green' expresses something impossible because, for that sentence to be true, there would need exist a book that is green and not green.

2. It is impossible that someone can simultaneously be a bachelor and married, because 'bachelor' means someone who is unmarried (plus male, etc.).

3. It is necessary that $2 + 2 = 4$ and impossible that $2 + 2 = 5$. Of course, if the symbol '5' actually meant 4, then the sentence '$2 + 2 = 5$' would be true, and it is possible (although false) that the symbol '5' means 4. But this means only that it is possible that the expression '$2 + 2 = 5$' expresses something true (if the symbol '5' means something different from what it in fact does). But even under these circumstances, that would not make it true that $2 + 2 = 5$. $2 + 2$ would still equal 4, only we would write that truth differently.

4. It is possible that I can fly around the room by waving my arms, although it contradicts the known laws of physics and physiology.

5. It is possible that Aristotle may not have been a philosopher, even though (let's suppose) his personality and training made his being a philosopher psychologically inevitable and even though it is historically true that he was a philosopher. Perhaps it is necessary that Aristotle was a human.

Why Modal Contexts Are Nonextensional

Let's see, first, why modal statements seem to involve referentially opaque contexts. Consider the following context: 'It is necessary that Aristotle is _____'. Using the referring term 'Aristotle' as argument, we get the following:

(15.1)   It is necessary that Aristotle is Aristotle.

It seems plausible to think that sentence (15.1) is true. It is necessary, after all, that each person be him/herself. Now, suppose that Aristotle was in fact the greatest philosopher; then 'Aristotle' and 'the greatest philosopher' are coreferring singular terms; using 'the greatest philosopher' as argument, we get

(15.2)   It is necessary that Aristotle is the greatest philosopher.

But sentence (15.2) is false. It is not necessary that Aristotle was a philosopher at all; and it is possible that there has existed a philosopher who is greater than Aristotle.

Because sentences (15.1) and (15.2) are values obtained from the context 'It is necessary that Aristotle is _____', with coreferring singular terms as arguments, and because sentence (15.1) is true and sentence (15.2) is false, it follows that that context is not extensional; that is, it is referentially opaque.

Similarly, the context 'It is possible that _____ not have kidneys' is apparently nonextensional. That context takes general terms as arguments; the general terms 'renates' and 'cordates' are coextensive; but

(15.3)   It is possible that cordates not have kidneys.

is true, but

(15.4)   It is possible that renates not have kidneys.

is false. Nothing could possibly at once be a renate and not have kidneys. 'Renates' *means* animals that have kidneys.

Similar examples show that the context 'It is possible that an animal with kidneys not _____' is nonextensional, for the predicates 'has kidneys' and 'has a heart' are coextensive; but substitution of one for the other in this context (with appropriate grammatical adjustments) changes the truth value of the resulting sentence.

It is easy to see that modal contexts that take whole sentences as arguments are nonextensional (when we take the extension of a sentence to be its truth value). The sentences, 'Aristotle is Aristotle' and 'Snow is white' are both true; thus they are coextensive. 'It is necessary that _____' is a modal context taking sentences as arguments. Placing the first sentence in that context yields

(15.5)   It is necessary that Aristotle is Aristotle.

which is true; but placing the second sentence in that context yields

(15.6)   It is necessary that snow is white.

which is false.

Even if we take the extension of a sentence to be a state of affairs, modal contexts still can be nonextensional. To see this, replace 'Aristotle is Aristotle' (true, necessary) with 'Aristotle is the greatest philosopher (true, not necessary; names the same state of affairs) in sentence (15.5).

Quotational Modal Contexts

If modal contexts are really nonextensional, then the extensional theory as developed so far must be rejected or amended. But there is an argument to the effect that modal contexts are really extensional; if this argument is sound, then the theory is saved.

Consider the following context: 'Seymour said, "_____ is stupid" '. Clearly, coreferring singular terms are not substitutable in this context salva veritate: 'Fred' and 'Stinky' are, we assume, different names for the same person and thus corefer; but we can imagine that

(15.7)   Seymour said, "Fred is stupid."

is true but

(15.8)   Seymour said, "Stinky is stupid."

is false. This sort of context is called *quotational*; it reports the very words Seymour uttered by directly quoting them. It is obvious why substitution of coreferring terms in this context changes the truth value: The truth of the sentence depends not on what the argument refers to but on exactly what word is used to refer to it.

It is easy for an extensional theory to take account of quotational contexts, however. In sentences (15.7) and (15.8) the words 'Fred' and 'Stinky' are clearly being *mentioned*, not *used*. The distinction between mention and use of a bit of language is a useful one; in case it is not clear, compare the following examples:

(15.9)   'Fred' starts with an F.

is true and *mentions* the name 'Fred'.

(15.10)   Fred starts with an F.

is false, because people do not start with letters; the sentence *uses* the name 'Fred'.

(15.11)   'Eggplant' makes Arnold laugh.

and

(15.12)   Eggplant makes Arnold laugh.

might both be true if both the name and the food make Arnold laugh. Sentence (15.11) *mentions* the word 'eggplant' and sentence (15.12) *uses* it. (A puzzle: In the sentence 'Beef Wellington is so called after the Duke of Wellington', is 'Beef Wellington' mentioned or used?) Careful writers enclose words mentioned in a sentence in quotes. You may have noticed that this book uses single quotes for this (and double quotes for reporting the very words somebody said). These are widespread conventions of philosophical writing.

In sentence (15.11), what does the linguistic expression including the two single quotes and the word 'eggplant' refer to? It does not refer to eggplants; the sentence does not say that eggplant makes Arnold laugh. Because it says that the *word* 'eggplant' makes Arnold laugh, it is clear that that linguistic expression refers to the word 'eggplant'. We can say, then, that quoted expressions—words mentioned, not used—refer to words, not to (other) things. Thus 'eggplant' refers to eggplants, but ' 'eggplant' ' refers to 'eggplant'. (Look carefully at all those quotes.)

Given this distinction, quotational contexts in English give an extentional theory no problem. In sentence (15.7), because the word 'Fred' is inside quotation marks, it is mentioned, not used; thus it does not refer to Fred, but rather to the word 'Fred'. Sentence (15.8), then, does not substitute a coreferring term for a term in sentence (15.7) because 'Stinky' does not refer to what 'Fred' refers to: 'Stinky' refers to the word 'Stinky', and 'Fred' to the word 'Fred'. Thus quotational contexts do not produce counterexamples for an extensional theory.

The argument to save our extensional theory from the apparent counterexamples provided by modal contexts is that modal contexts should be thought of as essentially quotational. The idea is that, for example,

(15.1) It is necessary that Aristotle is Aristotle.

is really a way of saying

(15.1q) The sentence, 'Aristotle is Aristotle' is necessary.

and, for another example, that

(15.2) It is necessary that Aristotle is the greatest philosopher.

really says

(15.2q) The sentence, 'Aristotle is the greatest philosopher' is necessary.

Sentences (15.1q) and (15.2q) thus more clearly express the real logical form of sentences (15.1) and (15.2), respectively. The fact that sentence (15.1q) is true and sentence (15.2q) is false can be easily admitted and explained: They do not use 'Aristotle' and 'the greatest philosopher'; they mention these words. The sentences refer to the words, not to the person. Thus it is no problem that sentence (15.1) is true and sentence (15.2) is false: Sentence (15.2) is not obtained by substituting a coreferential singular term in sentence (15.1). The context 'It is necessary that Aristotle is _____' turns out to be an extensional context after all, once we realize that the terms in this context are mentioned, not used. Substitution of another name for Aristotle is not substituting a coreferential term, because what the term 'Aristotle' refers to is the word 'Aristotle'; and the term 'the greatest philosopher' does not refer to 'Aristotle'; thus it is not coreferential. (But quotational contexts are not always nonextensional. The context

'_____ is bald' is true.

is extensional. Try substituting coreferring singular terms in the blank to see that the sentence does not change truth value.)

The quotational account of modal sentences gives an interpretation of them such that what is really being said to be necessary, possible, etc. are *sentences*, not (directly) the way things are. Part of the motivation behind this account has been that philosophers of an empiricist bent have thought that there is nothing in our experience of the external world to account for any distinction between what is necessarily true (that is, what could not be false) and what is true but possibly false (that is, what could be false). All that our sense experience tells us about the world is what is true and false, period. Why, then, do we count some sentences as expressing necessary truths and others as expressing merely *contingent truths*, which are possibly but not actually false? Their answer is that those sentences we count as necessarily true are analytic—sentences that are true merely because of the meanings of the terms involved. Some of them are merely true by definition. For example, 'All male siblings are brothers' is true because 'male sibling' means the *same thing* as 'brother'. Others are true merely because of the meanings of the logical terms involved: 'It is raining or it is not raining' is true merely because of what the logical words 'not' and 'or' mean. Similarly, 'Aristotle is Aristotle' is true because of its logical form and the logic of the word 'is'. We do not need to examine the way the world is to find out that these sentences are true: Their truth is guaranteed by the meanings of the words involved. We count these sentences as necessarily true because we know that, however the actual world happens to be or might have been, these sentences will turn out to be true; this sort of nonempirical knowledge is explained by the fact that the meaning of the words in the sentences guarantees that they will be true no matter what.

This account of modal sentences attributes necessity, possibility, etc. to sentences; thus, when we say that something is a necessary or contingent truth, what we are really saying is that some *sentence* is analytically or synthetically true.

There are several problems with this attempt to account for modal sentences. One of them is that many contemporary philosophers have come to doubt the reality of the distinction between analytic and synthetic sentences; some of the reasons for this doubt were discussed in chapter 6. But even philosophers who grant the validity of this distinction do not by and large think that analyticity provides a good account of necessity. Some philosophers have argued that certain sentences are synthetic but nonetheless necessary: The truths of arithmetic, for example, do not seem clearly to be a consequence of the meanings of the words involved and yet seem to be necessary truths. The truth of '2 + 2 = 4' does not seem to be a consequence of the meanings of the "words" in that sentence—if they meant something else, for example, if '4' really meant 5, then that sentence would no longer state a truth—but however we state it, it is still necessarily true that 2 + 2 = 4. We seem to have here a necessary *fact*, not just a sentence whose meanings guarantee its truth no matter what. Again, there are some sentences in higher mathematics whose truth or falsity is entirely unknown, despite the fact that nobody has any difficulty understanding the meanings of the words involved. For example, the conjecture called Fermat's last theorem has not yet been shown to be true or false (and it may not be possible to show its truth or falsity). The theorem says that there are no solutions of $x^n + y^n = z^n$, where x, y, and z are integers and n is an integer greater than 2.

If the argument that modal contexts are really quotational contexts fails, then modal contexts really are nonextensional, and the extensional theory as developed so far fails. I now examine a way of adding to the theory to allow for modal contexts.

Possible Worlds

An influential and powerful way to understand modal statements is called *possible-world semantics*. The term 'possible world' is closely associated with Gottfried Leibniz (1646–1716); the development of the contemporary view, however, is credited largely to the contemporary philosopher Saul Kripke.

We have been thinking of the world to which language refers as a large set of individual objects that fall into groups. 'Fred is bald' is true because 'Fred' refers to one of these objects and because the predicate 'is bald' is satisfied by a set of objects (the bald ones), Fred among them. This is the actual world. Now, when we want to affirm that, despite Fred's baldness it is possible that he not be bald, we can think of a *possible world*—a world containing, like the actual one, Fred and a set of bald things but in which, unlike the actual world, Fred does not belong to the set of bald things.

A possible world is not another planet. It is a way things might have been, a consistent set of states of affairs. Because it is possible that snow not be white, there is a possible world in which it is not white. In one possible world Fred is bald and snow is green; in another possible world Fred is not bald and snow is white, and so on. We are to think, then, of a vast number of different possible worlds in which the individuals in our actual world belong or do not belong to the sets of things they belong to in our actual world.

Each different combination of individuals and their set membership/nonmembership constitutes a different possible world. It is also possible that Fred not exist at all; so there are some possible worlds in which Fred does not exist. There are also some possible worlds that contain things that do not exist in the actual world. The actual world is said to be one of the set of possible worlds, distinguished from the others by the fact that it is actual.

Suppose it is necessary that Fred be human. That means that it is not possible that Fred is nonhuman; that is, there is no possible world containing Fred in which Fred is a member of the set of nonhumans.

Another way of putting this is that Fred is human in all possible worlds, although there are some possible worlds in which Fred does not exist (and in some of these possible worlds no humans exist).

To sum up, a sentence is true when the object referred to by the subject belongs in the set referred to by the predicate in the actual world. A sentence is possibly true when there exists at least one possible world in which it is true. (Because the actual world is counted as one of the set of possible worlds, anything actually true is also possibly true.) A sentence is necessarily true when it is true in all possible worlds. (If it is true in all possible worlds, it is true in the actual world; thus all necessarily true sentences are true.) A sentence that is necessarily false is true in no possible world (and thus also false in the actual world). A sentence is false but possibly true when it is false in the actual world but true in some other possible worlds (for example, 'Snow is green').

This way of speaking appears to expand the ontology (the set of things postulated to exist) in the extensional theory. Now we have not only the objects that actually exist but also other possible objects; and we have not only the set of actually bald things but also other different sets of bald things, the sets of bald things in other possible worlds. In a possible world in which Fred is not bald, the set of bald things is different from the set of bald things in the actual world in that it has different members: Fred is not in that set. (There may, of course, be other differences in membership also.)

Now let's see how this apparatus helps with the problems of modal contexts. First, let's look at the problem of the nonextensionality of modal contexts that take predicates as arguments. Recall that the supposition that predicates refer to sets ran into problems because coextensive predicates are not substitutable into modal contexts salva veritate. For example,

(15.13)   It is necessary that each creature with a heart is a cordate.

is true, but

(15.14)   It is necessary that each creature with a heart is a renate.

is false, despite the coextensionality of the predicates 'is a cordate' and 'is a renate'. We can interpret and explain the truth of sentence (15.13) and the falsity of sentence (15.14) using the possible-world semantics: sentence (15.13) is true because in every possible world each creature (if any) with a heart is a member of the set of things that satisfy the predicate 'is a cordate'; that is, it belongs to the set of cordates. Sentence (15.14) is false because there are some possible worlds in which some creatures with hearts are not members of the set of things that satisfy the predicate 'is a renate', that is, that are not renates.

We can fix our theory in such a way that the nonreplacement salva veritate of coextensive predicates in modal contexts is explained and accommodated; but the theory is no longer extensional.

Rigid Designators

Now let us examine the behavior of singular terms in modal contexts. Let us assume, as before, that Aristotle is, in fact, the greatest philosopher. As we observed, the context 'It is necessary that Aristotle is _____', which takes a singular term as argument, is nonextensional:

(15.1)   It is necessary that Aristotle is Aristotle.

is true, but

(15.2)   It is necessary that Aristotle is the greatest philosopher.

is false. According to the possible-worlds interpretation of these modal sentences, what we do, in effect, when considering these two sentences is to think about all possible worlds. In each of them we locate Aristotle and ask whether in that possible world Aristotle is Aristotle and whether Aristotle is the greatest philosopher. Of course, Aristotle's existence is not necessary—he might not have even been conceived; so in some possible worlds Aristotle cannot be picked out because he does not exist there. But in all those worlds containing Aristotle, he is, of course, Aristotle; but in some of those worlds he is not the greatest philosopher. In some possible worlds Aristotle existed but decided not to become a philosopher; in other worlds there happened to exist a philosopher greater than Aristotle. Thus it is necessary that Aristotle is Aristotle, but it is not necessary that Aristotle is the greatest philosopher.

Note carefully what this line of thought involves. In thinking about the truth or falsity of sentences (15.1) and (15.2), what we do is "locate" Aristotle in each possible world in which he exists; the name 'Aristotle' in the subject of both modal sentences refers to him in each of these possible worlds. In sentence (15.1) 'Aristotle' in the predicate does the same job: We merely refer to the same thing twice. This explains why Aristotle is Aristotle in all possible worlds containing Aristotle. In fact, any true sentence of the form $\ulcorner x$ is $y \urcorner$, where $\ulcorner x \urcorner$ and $\ulcorner y \urcorner$ are rigid designators (defined in the next paragraph) and 'is' means *is identical with*, is a necessary truth. See if you can figure out why. (You can ignore those strange quotation marks for the moment; they will be explained in chapter 22.)

A singular term that refers to the same thing in every possible world in which it refers to anything is called a *rigid designator*. Kripke argued that proper names normally are rigid designators, and this view is widely, although not universally, shared by contemporary philosophers. (I examine Kripke's argument and an alternative view in the next chapter.)

But compare the function of the definite description 'the greatest philosopher'. In the actual world as well as in some other possible worlds, that singular term refers to Aristotle. In some possible worlds that term does not refer to anything—in those worlds in which two or more equally great philosophers are greater than all others and in worlds that (heaven forbid!) do not contain any philosophers at all. But in still other possible worlds, that definite description refers to something different from what it refers to in the actual world, say, to Plato in some worlds and to David Hume in others and to somebody who does not exist in the actual world in others. There is no widely accepted name for terms such as these, which refer to different things in different possible worlds; but we might as well call them *flaccid designators* (because 'flaccid' is the opposite of 'rigid'). The explanation of the falsity of sentence (15.2), then, is that the definite description 'the greatest philosopher' is a flaccid designator.

16

Proper Names

Let us now turn to a direct consideration of the semantics of proper names. *Proper names* are names referring to individual persons, places, things, etc. They are capitalized in English. Some examples are:

Sally	Aristotle
Elvis	God
Bob Martin	Earth
Richard Nixon	Halifax, Nova Scotia
Santa Claus	June 24, 1962
Donald Duck	Eastern Michigan University

Russell believed that proper names have the same semantic structure as definite descriptions and are what we now call flaccid designators, although most philosophers believe nowadays that Russell was mistaken. To begin with, let's look at Russell's theory of proper names.

Most of the terms in the list do not mention any characteristics of the things they name; nevertheless, it seems that we must recognize any particular thing by means of some set of characteristics that we associate with it. How, for example, do you know that it is your friend Jane who has just entered the room? There must be some characteristics you associate with her, by which you recognize her—the way her face looks, for example. It has seemed reasonable to many philosophers that one should think of the criteria of application of any term as somehow connected with that term's meaning: In order for some term to have meaning at all to us, we must be able to apply it to what it belongs to. It is natural to say, then, that to know the meaning of a term is to know some set of characteristics that belong to the thing the term refers to and that enable us to "recognize" that thing. (I put 'recognize' in scare quotes to indicate that it is being used in a rather extended sense.) We understand the meaning of the name 'Aristotle', but few of us, perhaps none of us, would be able to recognize him if he came back from the dead and passed us on the street. Nevertheless, those of us who know the meaning of 'Aristotle' do know some characteristics of Aristotle, for example, that he was an ancient Greek philosopher, that he was the pupil of Plato, that he wrote *The Nicomachean Ethics*; even if we cannot recognize him on sight, we could find out that the name 'Aristotle' referred to someone by finding out that these characteristics applied to him.

Thus it has been tempting to think that proper names get the meaning they have by virtue of their association with some set of characteristics the thing named has. This view is called the *descriptivist analysis* of proper names, for it argues that the meaning of each proper name is given by the identifying descriptions associated with it.

If the descriptivist view of proper names is correct, then the semantics of proper names is a good deal similar to the semantics of definite descriptions. According to the descriptivist view, proper names, like definite descriptions, imply that there is exactly one thing that fits a set of characteristics. Unlike definite descriptions, proper names usually do not mention those characteristics; according to the descriptivist theory, however, each proper name is semantically equivalent to some complicated and variable description, and both the proper name and the definite description are flaccid in that both pick out in other possible worlds whatever (if anything) uniquely satisfies the description, which is not always the same thing that they pick out in this world.

In fact, if the descriptivist view of proper names is correct, there is a definite description that is semantically equivalent to (means the same as) each proper name. Suppose, for instance, that the defining characteristics for 'Aristotle' are being a person plus having A, B, and C (whatever these characteristics are). Then, 'Aristotle' is semantically equivalent to the definite description, 'the person who has A, B, and C'.

Objections to Descriptivism

A problem with the descriptivist view is that, at least in certain cases, we often, or always, recognize some individual as the bearer of a particular proper name by means of certain characteristics that clearly are not among the defining characteristics of that individual's proper name. Large black poodles all look pretty much the same to me, and, besides, their frequent haircuts result in such changes in appearance that I would not try to recognize them by looks; thus I identify a poodle as the bearer of the name 'Max' by noticing the nearby presence of Rich, Max's owner. But surely, if 'Max' is defined by certain characteristics, the nearby presence of Rich is not among them. That dog would be—in fact, *is*—still named 'Max' even when Rich is not in its vicinity. I suppose that this is not a serious objection to the theory, though. The descriptivist might reply that I am simply not using what in fact are the defining characteristics for 'Max' and do not even know what they *all* are. (I know at least one of the defining characteristics: being a poodle.) Thus, even though I have never made any mistakes in applying the name 'Max', I really do not fully know what it means.

There is a similar objection to this theory that should be mentioned, although it also does not have much weight. Suppose that I have a friend named 'Sally'. You ask me, What characteristics do I use to recognize someone as Sally? Suppose that I answer, "She is the person with the dark short hair, eyeglasses, and freckles on her nose." But surely these characteristics do not serve uniquely to identify Sally. I know several other people who fit this set of characteristics, and yet I never have any trouble telling which of them is Sally. But I cannot *state* the set of characteristics that I associate with that name and use to identify its bearer. I can state *some* set of characteristics that individuate only Sally, for example, being the only person with eyeglasses and freckles who lives at 55 rue de la Paix, Moose Jaw, Saskatchewan. But these are not the characteristics I use to identify her as the bearer of that name; I regularly judge that someone I meet is or is not that name's bearer without finding out where that person lives. Nor are addresses the name's defining characteristics. Perhaps the defining characteristics of that name have something to do with the way Sally looks; I generally recognize her this way. But I cannot provide a verbal description of the way she looks that is sufficient to identify her. That does not mean, however, that I do not recognize her by these characteristics or that the characteristics I use are not the ones that define her name. It simply means that I cannot give these characteristics a verbal expression.

How do we pick out some individual as the one to whom a proper name belongs? Clearly we check for certain characteristics, although we sometimes cannot say what those characteristics are. But the real question is, Are proper names equivalent in meaning to definite descriptions naming these identifying characteristics?

A more serious problem with the descriptivist view is the following. Suppose that a descriptivist produces the following list of defining characteristics for the name 'Aristotle':

an ancient Greek philosopher
born in Stageira in Thrace

son of Nicomachus
student of Plato
author of *The Nicomachean Ethics*

If the descriptivist is right, then the name 'Aristotle' refers to the unique individual who has *all* these properties. 'Aristotle' would be semantically equivalent to the definite description, 'the ancient Greek philosopher who was born in Stageira in Thrace *and* who was a son of Nicomachus . . .'. Now suppose that our history is wrong and that, in fact, *nobody* has *all* these characteristics; there was someone who had all these characteristics except for having been born near, not in, Stageira. If we apply the descriptivist theory strictly, this means that 'Aristotle' does not refer (and thus, perhaps, that all sentences containing that word are false). But this is absurd. Surely if we found out that there was someone who fit all these characteristics except for not having been born in Stageira, he would still be the person 'Aristotle' refers to.

The descriptivist might reply that this just shows that, contrary to his supposition, having been born in Stageira in Thrace is not a defining characteristic of 'Aristotle'. But we could raise this same objection about *any* of the items on that list; it seems clear that 'Aristotle' could name someone who did not have any one characteristic while having all the rest.

In response to this objection some descriptivists amend their position to claim that *every* member of the collection of defining characteristics need not be true of a unique individual in order that that individual be the one referred to; instead, they propose that whoever fits those characteristics *best* (even if not perfectly) be the one. Perhaps some of these characteristics weigh more heavily than others: Aristotle's writings seem to be the more important defining characteristics of 'Aristotle' than where he was born. This is sometimes called the *cluster descriptivist theory*; it seems to take care of this objection.

But a collection of arguments that have recently reached print have convinced most philosophers that the descriptivist theory, even patched up by the cluster notion, is mistaken. I examine at length these arguments and the theory proposed to replace the descriptivist view.

Naming and Necessity

The first argument, associated with Saul Kripke, is that proper names are rigid designators; that is, they pick out the same individual in each possible world. Descriptions (at least inside modal scopes) pick out individuals in other possible worlds by the characteristics mentioned in the description. (There is, however, an ambiguity in the logical form of sentences using definite descriptions; under one logical interpretation they are rigid designators. This sort of scope ambiguity is discussed in the next chapter.) The sentence, 'It is possible that Aristotle not have been a philosopher' asserts that there is a possible world in which Aristotle is not a philosopher. That sentence picks out Aristotle rigidly: It refers to the same individual in each possible world he exists in. But it picks out philosophers flaccidly: It points to whatever individuals in each possible world happen to be philosophers, and these differ from world to world. But this means that there is no description that means the same as 'Aristotle', because whatever description or cluster of descriptions we give will always pick out one (or more) individuals (or none at all) in each possible world flaccidly. In other words, a proper name always refers to the *same* individual in each possible world, whereas a set of descriptions does not necessarily refer to the same one: It refers to whomever in that world happens to fit those descriptions.

Thus, if someone proposes a set of descriptions equivalent in meaning to the proper name 'Aristotle' to be the *defining characteristics* of that name, we know that this is incorrect, because that set, whatever it is, will pick out whatever fits the descriptions in each possible world, and this does not have to be Aristotle. This amounts to saying that it is not necessary that Aristotle have those characteristics. The sentence 'Aristotle is a philosopher' is true but not necessary. It is possible that Aristotle had *none* of the characteristics mentioned in the proposed list: We can think of a possible world in which we pick out Aristotle—the same person as Aristotle here—and yet he has none of the characteristics mentioned in any proposed list of defining characteristics. This shows that the proper name is not definable in terms of any set of characteristics or even a "cluster" of characteristics.

Now compare proper names to singular terms that *do* have defining characteristics: definite descriptions. The sentence 'The greatest philosopher is a philosopher' is necessary; the subject term picks out whatever in each possible world happens to be the greatest philosopher, and this differs from world to world. But in each world in which this definite description picks out one individual, that individual, of course, is a philosopher. This has to be true, because the definite description picks out that individual on the basis of his/her having that characteristic (plus being greater than all other philosophers there). Thus definite descriptions do have defining characteristics (they mention them, in fact). In this way proper names differ from definite descriptions, and no proper name is ever equivalent to a complicated definite description.

The Twin Earth Argument

Now I turn to a different but related argument for the same conclusion: that the Russellian analysis of proper names is mistaken.

Imagine that there is another planet somewhere far away in space (I am not speaking of a possible world but of a distant, actual planet). This planet resembles Earth so closely that if you were instantaneously transported there, you would not notice any difference. Every person and thing on Earth has its duplicate on this other planet, which we call *Twin Earth,* and everything on Twin Earth exactly matches, in all characteristics, its duplicate on Earth. On Twin Earth some of the people speak a language resembling English so closely that, were you instantaneously swapped with your duplicate on Twin Earth, you could continue the conversation you were engaged in before the swap with no discernible difference. Call their language *Twinglish.*

It follows from this story that on Twin Earth (at the time I write this) there is a president of a large country they call (in Twinglish) 'The United States' who is a former movie actor, dyes his hair, and longs to invade small underdeveloped nations to the south. He and Ronald Reagan on Earth are, however, clearly two different people: They are *qualitatively identical* but *quantitatively distinct.* There is an ambiguity in English when we say such things as 'This is the same as that': We can mean either that there are two things here that are similar—that have the same characteristics—or that there is actually only one thing pointed to twice. Thus 'My car is the same as his' might mean either that our two cars are the same color, make, etc. or that the two of us jointly own one car. To guard against this ambiguity, philosophers have adopted a clear technical jargon. They say that things are *qualitatively identical* when they resemble each other exactly but *quantitatively identical* when they are one and the same thing. Actually, Reagan and Twin Reagan are not precisely qualitatively identical; I explain why not in what follows. To distinguish the two men, we call the man on Twin Earth "Twin Reagan" (although there, in Twinglish, he is just called "Reagan"). On Earth Sally says

(16.1)   Reagan has done something stupid again.

exactly, of course, when her twin on Twin Earth, Twin Sally, utters the corresponding sentence in Twinglish, which sounds exactly the same as Sally's English sentence. And when Fred on Earth says

(16.2)   The largest reptiles that existed anywhere at any time became extinct long ago.

Twin Fred on Twin Earth says the Twinglish match of this. Let's examine these sentences.

To what is Fred referring in sentence (16.2)? If it turned out that there are currently reptiles on Mars larger than our Earth's dinosaurs, sentence (16.2) would be false. We assume that sentence (16.2) is true because the group consisting of the largest reptiles anywhere and at any time is in fact (although Fred does not know it) the group consisting of dinosaurs on Earth *and* their identically sized twins on Twin Earth; but what Fred says is true because all dinosaurs became extinct long ago. The fact that Fred unknowingly referred not only to Earth dinosaurs but also to Twin Earth dinosaurs is a consequence of the semantics of the definite description he uttered: It picks out *whatever* happens to have the characteristic of being the group of largest reptiles.

But compare the sentences uttered by Sally and Twin Sally. Sally, when she utters sentence (16.1) is referring to Reagan, but when Twin Sally makes the same noises in Twinglish, she is referring to Twin Reagan; Sally is *not* referring to Twin Reagan, and Twin Sally is *not* referring to Reagan. This is parallel to other differences between the residents of Earth and of Twin Earth: The citizens of the richest country in the Western Hemisphere of Earth elected Reagan, not Twin Reagan (and conversely for the citizens of the richest country in the Western Hemisphere of Twin Earth). But if this is true, then the proper name in Sally's sentence has a different function from the definite description in Fred's. The proper name 'Reagan', as used by Earth residents, does not pick out *whatever* is the unique bearer of certain general characteristics, for Reagan and Twin Reagan share *all* their general characteristics. (Why do I say that Reagan and Twin Reagan share their *general* characteristics and not *all* their characteristics? The reason is that there are some characteristics that, as we have seen, they do not share. Reagan was elected by Americans, but Twin Reagan was not; *he* was elected by Twin Americans. Reagan and Twin Reagan differ in their relations to particular objects in their worlds, but they do not differ in general characteristics; for example, both dye their hair and both were movie actors.)

Notice that, even if Twin Earth exists, its existence would not change the status of most of the definite descriptions we actually use. This is so because many definite descriptions do not specify their referent in terms of purely general characteristics but include proper names or *indexicals*. (Indexicals are words such as 'this', 'that', and 'here'. They are discussed in chapter 20.) For example, 'the railway station in Halifax' would still refer to exactly one entity, even if Twin Earth existed, because 'Halifax' (in English) is a proper name referring only to Halifax (and not to Twin Halifax); similarly, 'the man in this room drinking a martini' would still uniquely refer because the characteristics mentioned are not purely general, including the indexical reference to a room on Earth, excluding the matching room (and martini-drinker) on Twin Earth.

Nevertheless, there still is a way that even these definite descriptions, including proper names and indexicals, are different from proper names, for it is always possible that there is more than one individual that satisfies the description (for example, more than one man drinking a martini in this room, more than one railway station in Halifax); but because they do not pick out individuals by their characteristics, proper names can never run into the problem of more than one referent. (But you may have noticed that there is a puzzle concerning proper names that refer to *no* individuals; more on this in the next chapter.)

The conclusion of this argument, then, is that, although definite descriptions pick out whatever happens to fit uniquely the description mentioned, proper names pick out particular individuals, whatever their characteristics happen to be. That is, definite descriptions, in general, are flaccid designators, whereas proper names are rigid designators.

Note that, if the Russellian position on proper names was correct, then, strictly, the sentence uttered by Sally would be false—not because Reagan had not done something stupid again but rather because 'Reagan' would be equivalent to a definite description mentioning some general characteristics and Sally's sentence would imply that these general characteristics were uniquely instantiated. But they (given the existence of Twin Earth) would not be uniquely instantiated: They would be instantiated by two things, namely, Reagan and Twin Reagan. Because we are confident that, even if Twin Earth exists, Sally's statement would still be true (provided, of course, that Reagan had just done something stupid), this shows that the Russellian analysis of proper names is mistaken.

Of course, we can assume that Twin Earth does not exist, but this does not interfere with the point of this argument. Given the nonexistence of Twin Earth, Sally's statement is true just as Fred's is. Nevertheless, there is a semantic difference between the two statements, which is demonstrated by the difference between them that *would* obtain had Twin Earth existed. This is not mere idle science fiction; the argument is intended to show that there is a difference even though Twin Earth does not exist. That difference, in a nutshell, is that definite descriptions refer to *whatever* uniquely satisfies a description; but proper names refer only to a unique individual, regardless of what characteristics it (or anything else in the universe) has.

Suggested Readings

Kripke, Saul. 1980. *Naming and Necessity.* Cambridge: Harvard University Press.
Parts of this book are reprinted in [1, 5].
Putnam, Hilary. 1970. "Is semantics possible?" in *Language, Belief, and Metaphysics,* H. E. Kiefer and M. K. Munitz, eds. Albany: State University of New York Press, 50–63.
The Twin Earth argument. Also reprinted in [5, 10].
Searle, John. 1957. "Proper names." *Mind* 67:166–173.
Searle's cluster descriptivist view. Reprinted in [5, 9].

17

More on Proper Names and Definite Descriptions

Scope and Modality

There is a complication in the comparison of definite descriptions and proper names that I have so far ignored. We have been assuming that

(17.1) It is possible that the greatest philosopher may not have been a philosopher.

is false; 'The greatest philosopher' refers flaccidly in each possible world to whoever (if anyone) satisfies the characteristics named. Thus, because whoever is picked out in any possible world by this description is a philosopher, this sentence is false.

But sentence (17.1) is ambiguous; there is a way of understanding it in which it is true. Consider the person to whom we refer in the real world by the following definite description: There is a possible world in which he was forced to abandon his studies by a tragic accident and never became a philosopher at all. In that possible world he is not a philosopher.

A slightly clearer way of expressing this way of understanding sentence (17.1) is

(17.1n) Of the greatest philosopher it is possible that he may not have been a philosopher.

In sentence (17.1n), as in sentence (17.1) under a certain interpretation, we use the definite description to refer to whoever in the actual world fits these characteristics; but then we consider *that individual* in each other possible world to determine the truth or falsity of the modal assertion. In this second reading sentence (17.1) is true. But in the first reading we use the definite description to refer in each possible world to whoever *there* has the characteristics named. We can more clearly express sentence (17.1) in this first reading as

(17.1w)   It is possible that the greatest philosopher may not have been a philosopher.

The difference between sentence (17.1n) and (17.1w) shows that the ambiguity of sentence (17.1) is another case of *scope ambiguity*. Recall the discussion of the ambiguity of the scope of 'not' in chapter 13; what we have here is an ambiguity about the scope of the *modal operator* (in this case 'it is possible that'). When the definite description is *outside* the scope of the modal operator, as in sentence (17.1n), it functions as a rigid designator: We consider that individual, the same one, in each possible world. In sentence (17.1n) the modal operator has *narrow scope* (thus the "n"); but when the definite description is *inside* the scope of the modal operator, as in sentence (17.1w), it functions as a flaccid designator: We consider in each possible world whichever different individual happens there to satisfy the description uniquely. It contains the modal operator in *wide scope* (thus the "w"). We can say, then, roughly, that definite descriptions are flaccid only when inside the scope of a modal operator; outside it, they are rigid.

We should note another peculiarity of English: Some singular terms of the form 'the such-and-such' are, despite appearances, in fact proper names; that is, they are, inside or outside modal scopes, rigid designators. Examples of these are

The Canadian Philosophical Association
The Duke of Kent
The Holy Roman Empire

You can see that they are rigid designators when you consider some wide-scope modal truths containing these singular terms: (1) It is possible that the Canadian Philosophical Association is not Canadian. Suppose that it moved to the United States but kept its name out of respect for tradition. (2) It is possible that the Duke of Kent is not the Duke of Kent. If the British abolished that title, then he would not be. (3) The Holy Roman Empire, as Voltaire quipped, was neither holy, Roman, nor an empire. That is just its name. It is possible that the Holy Roman Empire was not holy, Roman, or empire.

The Causal Theory of Proper Names

In the extensional theory developed so far, how, after all, does it come about that proper names refer? It should be clear by now that, according to the theory, whatever features the referent of a proper name has, these are not relevant to the fact that the referent is referred to by that name. What is it, then, that makes it be the case that 'Ronald Reagan' refers to him? Well, part of the answer is obvious: There are various sorts of ceremony or other activity that make it the case that a person (or thing) has a proper name, for example, baptism and completion and registration of a birth certificate. These activities need not be official ceremonies: Someone may come to be referred to as 'Bud' even though he was baptized and birth-certified as 'Clarence'. Still, we can imagine that some sort of human activity makes it be the case that 'Bud' refers to him. Human acts of various sorts—formal or informal, brief or gradual and long term—can create the conventions that people and things have the proper names they do. Plato lived before Jesus did and was not baptized at all; and the ancient Greeks, in whatever ceremony they used to give Plato his official name, gave him the name 'Aristocles'; 'Platon' was his nickname derived from his physical characteristics, and this later turned into 'Plato' in English. In French Johann Sebastian Bach is called 'Jean Sebastien Bach', and in Italian, 'Giovanni Sebastiano Bach'.

The important and unobvious fact about such proper-naming procedures is, however, that there has to be an actual connection between the thing named and the circumstances establishing that proper name. It is possible to establish the proper name of some individual while not actually in the presence of that individual; for example, one can name one's child by performing the proper birth certificate procedure in a registry office far away from the recipient of that name, but the procedure somehow has to be *connected* with the recipient. One does not need such a connection in order to establish the reference of a definite description.

Once a proper name is established, one need not use it with any sort of *direct* connection with the individual named; we can use the proper names of people who are far away or even dead; all that is necessary is that there be some history of the use of that name which, traced back far enough, leads back to the individual. Whatever procedure is used to give an individual a name causes later uses of that name, which in turn cause other uses, and so on up to the present use. A *causal chain* thus makes it the case now that uses of the name are connected to the individual named. The name itself may change in the course of this chain, as when 'Platon' changed into 'Plato'. Thus this view is sometimes known as the *causal theory* of proper names.

This is all quite vague, and no causal theorist has bothered to figure out what sort of chain is necessary or sufficient to make a name refer. Suppose that I name my goldfish 'Plato' after the philosopher. Tracing back the causal connections between events in which I use 'Plato' to refer to my goldfish, one would run into that goldfish, but one would also eventually run into the philosopher (because his being named 'Platon' is connected in a long and devious way with my naming my fish 'Plato'); but it is clear that on certain occasions when I use that name, 'Plato' refers to my fish, not to the philosopher. That a name refers to that individual which one runs into in tracing back along the causal chain of uses is not enough, but it is difficult to see what else we should say.

In this causal account of the reference of a proper name, it might be tempting to see a justification for the claim that proper names are, after all, equivalent in meaning to a particular kind of definite description: that 'Bertrand Russell' is thus equivalent in meaning to 'the person baptized with the name "Bertrand Russell"'. But this is mistaken. It is metaphysically possible, for example, that Bertrand Russell may not have been baptized 'Bertrand Russell'. Had Bertrand Russell been baptized 'Fred Russell', then 'Fred Russell' would have been Bertrand Russell's name. Had Jane Russell been the only person baptized 'Bertrand Russell', then that would be her name, but that would not have made her the person whom we in fact now refer to when we speak of the philosopher using what in fact is his name. The sentence

(17.2)   It is possible that Bertrand Russell might have been named 'Fred Russell'.

is true; in some possible, not actual, world, Bertrand was baptized and called 'Fred' by everyone. But notice that in sentence (17.2) we refer to him by using the name he *actually* had—the name he was given in the actual world.

Nonreferring Proper Names

One apparent problem for the account I have been developing is the use of nonreferring proper names.

(17.3)   Santa will bring Fred a pony for Christmas.

is presumably literally false (given the nonexistence of anyone called 'Santa'). We have been arguing, however, that proper names refer directly—get their meaning from their connection with some individual thing. There is a problem with nonreferring proper names not shared by nonreferring definite descriptions. Compare the following with sentence (17.3):

(17.4) The jolly fat man who comes down chimneys at Christmas will bring Fred a pony for Christmas.

The definite description in sentence (17.4), according to Russell's analysis, gets its meaning by means of predicates and a quantifier; sentence (17.4) is equivalent to

(17.5) There exists exactly one x such that x is jolly, fat, comes down chimneys at Christmas, and will bring Fred a pony for Christmas.

which is meaningful and straightforwardly false. But sentence (17.3), according to our account of proper names, would be *meaningless*, not false: The proper name 'Santa' does not refer to anything in the actual world. Were it semantically equivalent to the definite description in sentence (17.4), it would refer in some possible worlds, but we have been arguing that proper names have no "descriptive content."

Many proper names refer in the actual world but not in some possible worlds. Because the existence of Aristotle is not necessary, there are some possible worlds in which Aristotle does not exist; in these worlds 'Aristotle' does not refer to anything. Can we say, then, that 'Santa', like other proper names, refers to the same individual in each world containing that individual, with the difference that the actual world happens to be a world not containing this individual?

There are possible worlds in which some individual is named 'Santa'. (There are even possible worlds in which that person comes down chimneys, etc.) But this does not establish the reference for 'Santa' in sentence (17.3). It *does* establish a reference (in some non-actual worlds) for the sentence

(17.6) The man called 'Santa' will bring Fred a pony for Christmas.

which is meaningful, false, and possibly true. But sentence (17.6) (which includes a quotational context—it *mentions*, not *uses*, the name 'Santa') is not equivalent to sentence (17.3). Remember that proper names we *actually* use (as opposed to those we use in other possible worlds) refer to those individuals in *this* world to whom their use is causally connected. It follows, then, that we *never* can use proper names to refer to any individuals who do not actually exist.

It seems, then, that we are stuck with the unintuitive result that sentence (17.3) is not false but literally *meaningless*, just as any sentence with a proper name not connected to some individual is, for example,

(17.7) Glarfnurd will bring Fred a pony for Christmas.

One difference between sentences (17.3) and (17.7) is that we know what is "being said" when someone utters sentence (17.3) but not (17.7). I say more about this difference later.

A consequence of these considerations that might seem even worse than counting sentence (17.3) as meaningless is that we must also count

(17.8)   Santa does not exist.

as meaningless (although it might seem straightforwardly true). But suppose that we are convinced by these arguments and that we accept the perhaps uncomfortable conclusion that sentences (17.3) and (17.8) are meaningless. Consider, however,

(17.9)   Fred believes that Santa will bring him a pony for Christmas.

This sentence *really* seems meaningful; we want to say that it could be true. The intuitive attachment to the idea that sentence (17.9) is meaningful is stronger than in the cases of sentences (17.3) and (17.8).

Sentence (17.9) attributes to Fred what we have been calling a *propositional attitude*. Other propositional attitudes include doubts, desires, and fears. The apparently meaningful occurrence of nonreferring proper names inside psychological attributions—attributions of propositional attitudes—provides a crucial test for the extensional theory. This is the subject of the next chapter.

18

Psychological Contexts

Extensionality and Propositional Attitude Ascriptions

The problem that arose at the end of the last chapter involved the sentence

> (18.1) Fred believes that Santa will bring him a pony for Christmas.

This sentence surely seems meaningful; we want to say that it could be true. The intuitive attachment to the idea that sentence (18.1) is meaningful is stronger than in the cases of sentences involving non-referring proper names, such as

> (18.2) Santa will bring Fred a pony for Christmas.

We now try to come to grips with the problems posed for an extensional theory by sentences ascribing propositional attitudes.

Note that contexts taking sentences as arguments contained in ascriptions of propositional attitudes share with modal contexts (as well as with causal contexts and others) the characteristic of non–truth functionality; that is, sentences with the same truth value are not always substitutable salva veritate. For example, it might be the case that

> (18.3) Arnold believes that snow is white.

is true, but

> (18.4) Arnold believes that Bolivia is in South America.

is false, despite the fact that 'Snow is white' and 'Bolivia is in South America' are both true. We solved this problem earlier by deciding that the reference of sentences is a state of affairs, not a truth value; this works as well in the present case, because 'Snow is white' and 'Bolivia is in South America' name different states of affairs.

When we came to consider modal contexts, we discovered that this addition did not suffice, because in modal contexts sentences naming the same state of affairs are not always substitutable salva veritate. The same thing is true of contexts in ascriptions of propositional attitudes; for example, even though 'Fred' and 'the stupidest civil servant in Ottawa' corefer and because 'Fred is in the room' and 'The stupidest civil servant is in the room' refer to the same state of affairs, we can suppose that

(18.5)   Arnold believes that Fred is in the room.

is true, but

(18.6)   Arnold believes that the stupidest civil servant in Ottawa is in the room.

is false. (These examples also show how the context taking a singular term as argument, 'Arnold believes that _____ is in the room', is referentially opaque, that is, nonextensional.)

Possible Worlds and Propositional Attitudes

We solved these problems for modal contexts by deciding that terms refer not merely to things in the actual world but also to things in other possible worlds. The term 'Fred' refers to Fred in every possible world containing him, and the term 'the stupidest civil servant in Ottawa' refers to different things—to whatever, if anything, satisfies the predicate 'is the stupidest civil servant in Ottawa' in each possible world. Similarly, pairs of sentences that name the same state of affairs in the real world do not always name the same state of affairs in other worlds. In a (nonactual) possible world in which there is a civil servant in Ottawa who is even stupider than Fred (God help the Canadians there!), 'Fred is in the room' names a different state of affairs from 'The stupidest civil servant in Ottawa is in the room'.

This suggests that we try to solve the problem of nonsubstitutability in intentional contexts by a possible-world ontology and semantics. It is not exactly clear how we could produce such an application here, however. The idea, broadly, would be to think that possible worlds, not merely the actual one, should be relevant to the semantics of ascriptions of propositional attitudes.

The term 'propositional attitude' itself suggests that a possible-worlds semantics might do some work in thinking about ascriptions of propositional attitudes, for a *proposition* is something that has a good possible-worlds interpretation. Consider the sentence 'Fred is the stupidest civil servant in Ottawa'. This, as we have seen, is true in some possible worlds (including the actual one) and false in others.

The distribution of truth values that that sentence has in each possible world defines the proposition it expresses. Note that 'Snow is white' is true in a possible world in which 'Grass is green' is false. (That is, it is possible that snow is white and grass is not green.) Thus these two sentences express a different proposition. Two sentences that share the same truth value in each of the possible worlds express the same proposition; that is, if some sentence S is true in all those possible worlds in which sentence T is true, and false in each possible world in which T is false, then S and T express the same proposition. Note that the proposition expressed by 'Fred is the stupidest civil servant in Ottawa' is not the same as the state of affairs named by that sentence; the state of affairs is merely Fred's being the stupidest civil servant in Ottawa *actually*, that is, in the actual world. You might think of the proposition as the set of possible worlds in which this is true.

In thinking about modal contexts taking sentences as arguments, we see that it is the proposition expressed by a sentence, not the state of affairs it expresses, that is directly relevant. Two sentences sharing the same truth value are not always substitutable salva veritate in modal contexts; nor are two sentences that name the same state of affairs. But two sentences that express the same proposition are.

Can we take the phrase 'propositional attitude' literally and think of propositional attitudes as attitudes to propositions? The suggestion here is that the possible-worlds ontology and semantics that solved the problem for modal contexts might do the same job for psychological contexts.

It is strange to think, however, that propositional attitudes involve relations to propositions. On occasion, we can probably say with confidence that a small infant thinks that it is feeding time; but if propositional attitudes are relations to propositions and thus to nonactual worlds as well as to the actual world, then we would seem to be ascribing to that infant some sort of mental relation to possible nonactual worlds; this is perhaps a bit farfetched, because infants can hardly have ideas about what is merely possible.

In any case, it seems that there are good reasons to think that a possible-world semantics cannot do the job with attributions of propositional attitudes that it did with modal sentences. Here is one example to show this. Consider any two sentences in arithmetic that are both true, for example, '7 + 5 = 12' and 'The square root of 36 is 6'. Arithmetic is generally considered to be a domain of necessary truths; all the truths of arithmetic are true in all possible worlds. It follows, then, that all truths of arithmetic express the same proposition. (If you do not immediately see why this is the case, refer again to the account of when two sentences S and T express the same proposition, and figure it out.) All the truths of arithmetic seem intersubstitutable in modal contexts salva veritate. But surely we can imagine a circumstance in which

(18.7)   Arnold believes that $7 + 5 = 12$.

is true, but

(18.8)   Arnold believes that the square root of 36 is 6.

is false. (A peculiarity about this example is that '$7 + 5 = 12$' might be thought to name a different state of affairs from 'The square root of 36 is 6', even though the two express the same proposition. It is not clear, however, that they name different states of affairs; to make it clear, we would have to make some difficult decisions concerning the objects and sets the sentences are about. But, in any case, it does not seem that this line of reasoning will help with the current problem; the next example is one in which two sentences express the same proposition and clearly name the same state of affairs but appear not to be substitutable in a propositional-attitude context salva veritate.)

A different type of example, originally provided by Frege, seems to show the same thing. Consider that

(18.9)   Fred is the stupidest civil servant in Ottawa.

is true in this world and in some other possible worlds.

(18.10)   Stinky is the stupidest civil servant in Ottawa.

is also true in this and in some other possible worlds. 'Fred' and 'Stinky' are names of the same person. Sentences (18.9) and (18.10) thus attribute membership in the same set to the same individual, and thus they name the same state of affairs. Because 'Fred' and 'Stinky' are rigid designators, they each name the same individual here as they do in other possible worlds; so in every possible world containing that person, he is the individual referred to by both 'Fred' and 'Stinky'. It follows that in each possible world, sentences (18.9) and (18.10) have the same truth value. In the worlds in which sentence (18.9) is true, sentence (18.10) is also true; in the worlds in which sentence (18.9) is false, so is sentence (18.10). Thus they express the same proposition.

If propositional attitudes can be explained by a possible-world semantics in the way that modal contexts are, sentences (18.9) and (18.10) should be intersubstitutable salva veritate inside ascriptions of propositional attitudes. But they apparently are not: We can imagine cases in which

(18.11)   Arnold believes that Fred is the stupidest civil servant in Ottawa.

is true but

(18.12)   Arnold believes that Stinky is the stupidest civil servant in Ottawa.

is false.

Perhaps surrounding sentences (18.11) and (18.12) with a little story will make the truth of sentence (18.11) and the falsity of sentence (18.12) clearer. Suppose that Arnold has frequent dealings by telephone with a civil servant whom he learns to call 'Fred'—Fred himself and Fred's secretary call him this over the phone. The abundant stupidity Fred manifests during these conversations leads Arnold to believe that Fred is the stupidest civil servant in Ottawa; thus sentence (18.11) is true. But suppose that Arnold meets Fred at a cocktail party one evening but does not recognize him as the person he knows from the phone conversations. Fred is introduced to Arnold as 'Stinky', and everyone calls him by this nickname at the party. Fred acts just as stupidly there, but Arnold comes to believe mistakenly that *this* person is not a civil servant; his manner, dress, and conversation lead Arnold to believe that he is an interior designer. Thus Arnold does not believe the man called 'Stinky' is a civil servant at all; so it is false that Arnold believes that *Stinky* is the stupidest civil servant in Ottawa. Thus sentence (18.12) is false.

We might also attribute other propositional attitudes to Arnold that demonstrate similar nonsubstitutability, for example:

(18.13)   Arnold hopes that Stinky will design his office.   (true)

(18.14)   Arnold hopes that Fred will design his office.   (false)

(18.15)   Arnold fears he will talk to Fred when he calls Ottawa.   (true)

(18.16)   Arnold fears he will talk to Stinky when he calls Ottawa.   (false)

(The Arnold/Stinky examples are not Frege's. One of his famous examples involved the names 'Morning Star' and 'Evening Star,' names given by the ancients to Venus as it appeared in the morning or in the evening sky, respectively. They did not believe that these were names for the same thing; thus we can say that 'They believed at time t that the Morning Star was in the sky' is true but 'They believed at time t that the Evening Star was in the sky' is false.)

Insofar as the possible-world semantics goes beyond reference to actual things and sets, it has been called nonextensional. But it appears that attributions of propositional attitudes contain contexts that even this addition of nonextensionality cannot take care of.

Another sort of context that appears to demonstrate this sort of nonextensionality is *indirect discourse,* when a sentence says what somebody says. (This is distinguished from *direct quotation,* in which the very words someone said are quoted.) An example of indirect discourse is:

(18.17)   Arnold said that Stinky was charming at the party.

The nonextensionality of sentence (18.17) is illustrated by the change of truth value when a coreferring proper name is substituted, giving

(18.18)   Arnold said that Fred was charming at the party.

'Stinky was charming at the party' expresses the same proposition (and names the same state of affairs) as 'Fred was charming at the party.' Sentence (18.18) is just the substitution of one expression for the other in the indirect discourse context, 'Arnold said that _____'.

In the next chapter, we examine Frege's answer to these problems and other ways of dealing with them.

Suggested Reading

Frege, Gottlob. 1980. "On sense and meaning," in *Translations from the Philosophical Writings of Gottlob Frege,* Peter Geach and Max Black, eds. Oxford: Basil Blackwell, 56–78.
   Sometimes translated as "On sense and nominatum." Reprinted in [2, 5, 6].

19

Sense and Reference

Frege's answer to the problems of nonextensionality raised in the last chapter was to claim that, in addition to their ordinary reference, referring terms have *sense* (in Frege's German, *Sinn*). Roughly, we can think of the sense associated with any term as its *mode of presentation*—the *way* it refers to the objects it does. The sense of an expression is supposed to explain why it is that it refers to what it does. Nonreferring expressions have a sense but no reference. Coreferring proper names have different senses and the same reference. In sentences involving nonreferring proper names, in indirect discourse, and in attributions of propositional attitudes, Frege claimed that such expressions referred to their sense, not to their ordinary reference. The inclusion of senses gives an alternative to "Frege's suggestion" that nonreferring definite descriptions refer to the null set, discussed in chapter 13.

Perhaps the sense associated with an expression can be thought of as a sort of psychological entity—an association in a speaker's mind between that expression and certain circumstances of its use. When telling the story in the last chapter about why Arnold thought that Fred, not Stinky, was the stupidest civil servant in Ottawa, I told about the circumstances in which Arnold learned and continued to use the names 'Fred' and 'Stinky'; we can understand from this story the different modes of presentation of those two words to Arnold— the different psychological associations they had for him. We can see how Arnold *represents* Fred to himself when he calls him 'Fred' and how this differs from his internal representation of Fred when he calls him 'Stinky'.

Some contemporary philosophers hold views somewhat related to this. Recall that earlier in this book I briefly discussed Mentalese, the supposedly innate language of thought in which we represent externals and which we learn to translate into our public spoken language.

Presumably Arnold has different Mentalese "words" that translate into 'Fred' and 'Stinky'.

There are all sorts of difficulties with the view that postulates senses. I take a brief look at just a few.

First, note that the ontological economy of the original extensional theory has been severely compromised. New entities, senses, have to be recognized. This makes a theory including senses less desirable in itself; but, of course, if senses are really needed, we have to accept this consequence.

A second problem, a more serious one, is that a theory recognizing senses apparently loses a clear advantage of a theory without them, namely, the *objectivity* of meaning. The connection between terms and what they refer to is in a way a fact of the external world, subject to scientific determination. The reference of an expression is an external objective thing (although the addition of possible worlds might be thought to compromise this somewhat); and objective conventions connect expressions with the references. But senses are subjective, nonconventional, internal, and perhaps private and vary from individual to individual. This, of course, raises the issues we looked at in the chapter on private language; if senses are private and if they are an unavoidable part of the semantics of natural languages, then natural languages have an important private component. If senses are subjective and private, how could we learn them? (Could anything count as learning them?)

To see why senses seem subjective, note that the difference of sense is supposed to explain nonsubstitutability salva veritate in psychological attributions. Thus the fact that

(19.1)   Arnold believes that Stinky is at the party.

is true and that

(19.2)   Arnold believes that Fred is at the party.

is false is explained by the fact that Arnold gives different senses to 'Fred' and to 'Stinky'; the two names have a different mode of presentation *to him*. But Marvin may know that 'Fred' and 'Stinky' name the same person; he may have the same mode of presentation associated with those words. Then if

(19.3)   Marvin believes that Stinky is at the party.

is true, then so is

(19.4)   Marvin believes that Fred is at the party.

And a third person, Sally, like Arnold, may not know that Fred is Stinky—may have different modes of presentation associated with 'Fred' and 'Stinky'—but may have an entirely different mode of presentation of 'Fred' from the one Arnold has. If modes of presentation have something to do with the special circumstances in which we learn and later use a word, then it is not unreasonable to think that *everyone's* mode of presentation of an expression differs somewhat from everyone else's. Frege wanted senses to be objective, but it is hard to see, given the work they are supposed to do, how this could be the case.

The postulation of senses seems, in fact, to be fairly *ad hoc*, which means *for this particular purpose only*. Theories should not contain ad hoc additions to solve their problems, because they thereby lose explanatory power. How can we tell what sense someone gives some expression, other than by seeing what she is willing to say and to deny? But if this is the only source for telling what sense someone gives to an expression and if two different expressions can have the same or different senses, then senses do not *explain* anything.

Compare the following phony explanation. Suppose that a scientist wants to explain why opium puts people to sleep and postulates a dormative virtue in opium. Valium also puts people to sleep; so the scientist concludes that valium also contains the dormative virtue. Coffee does not put people to sleep, but an "explanation" is easy for this: no dormative virtue. Without any independent characterization of this dormative virtue, without any way of finding out whether it is there or not except by seeing whether it puts people to sleep, and without any *other* things for this concept to do, clearly nothing is being *explained* here at all. This appears to be the case, at least so far as we have characterized the concept for senses. Perhaps, however, the connection of senses to the explanations involved in Fodor's arguments about the "language of thought" gives it more content and explanatory power.

Extensionality Again

In recognition of these difficulties, then, let's try to defend the previous theory, without senses, internal representations, or modes of presentation. One way of putting the problem that led to the postulation of senses was that we wanted to say that

(19.1)   Arnold believes that Stinky is at the party.

is true and so is

(19.5)   Arnold believes that Fred is not at the party.

Now suppose that we take 'Fred' to be in a referentially transparent context in both sentences (19.1) and (19.5). This is exactly the move that the sense theory argues against. But what exactly is wrong with it? On this supposition, given that Fred is Stinky, we can substitute 'Fred' for 'Stinky' in sentence (19.1) to give

(19.2)   Arnold believes that Fred is at the party.

But, the sense theorist will argue, sentences (19.5) and (19.2) cannot both be true at the same time. How can it be true that both sentences (19.5) and (19.2) correctly describe Arnold's beliefs? If these were both true, then Arnold would at the same time believe that Fred is at the party *and* that Fred is not at the party. But Arnold cannot believe both of these things.

Well, why not? Why can't someone have these two beliefs? We can express the *content* of these two beliefs, that is, what Arnold believes, by the sentences

(19.5c)   Fred is at the party.

(19.2c)   Fred is not at the party.

It is logically impossible that these two sentences be true at once, and it is metaphysically impossible that the states of affairs named by these sentences both obtain at once. Why, however, is it impossible that Arnold have two beliefs of which sentences (19.5c) and (19.2c), respectively, give the content?

One reason to think that Arnold cannot have both beliefs at once is that Arnold surely would not *say* both sentences (19.5c) and (19.2c) to express what he believes. If asked, he would surely claim that sentence (19.5c) is false. He might say (or agree to) sentence (19.2c) and to

(19.1c)   Stinky is at the party.

If he *did* say (or agree to) both sentences (19.5c) and (19.2c), then we would not think that he was correctly expressing his beliefs; we would suspect him of misusing the language to tell us what he believed.

But the assumption here is that, if a sentence gives the content of Arnold's belief, then Arnold would say it or assent to it if asked. This assumption is questionable. Why couldn't it be true that people sometimes believe things they do not say and would not say? Surely you believe many things right now that you are not actually saying. Surely, in addition, if you do not understand a sentence, you might deny that it is true, even though it expresses the content of what you believe. But we are to suppose in addition that you might sincerely deny the truth of certain sentences that you understand and nonetheless actually believe.

Recall the discussion of propositional attitudes in chapter 10, on animal and machine language. We assumed that propositional attitudes had contents whose logical relations paralleled the psychological relations among the attitudes. (This, in fact, was a chief reason to think that thought involves an internal, innate language.) One reason why it might be thought implausible that Arnold believes both that Fred is at the party and that Fred is not at the party is that the sentences that express the content of these beliefs, 'Fred is at the party' and 'Fred is not at the party', are logically incompatible; they cannot both be true. On the assumption that the connections between beliefs parallel the connections between the sentences that express their contents, we would think that these two beliefs are *psychologically* incompatible: We just cannot believe both of them at once. But what I am urging now is the thought that psychological laws do not necessarily parallel logical laws. Someone *can* have two beliefs even though the sentences that express their contents are logically incompatible.

We might also expect Arnold to say sincerely

(19.6)   Fred is not Stinky.

And we can take it that this is a sincere expression of his belief. He believes that Fred is not Fred. He does not say and would not agree to the sentence 'Fred is not Fred', but he believes, nonetheless, that Fred is not Fred. This might seem somewhat less implausible to you if you reflect on the fact that on occasion you might have seen Fred on two different occasions and believed that the first person was not the same as (quantitatively identical with) the second. What you mistakenly believed was that someone was not identical with himself. The content of your belief is expressed by a sentence that is not merely false—it is *impossible*. There is no possible world in which anyone is not himself. But nevertheless you believed that Fred was not Fred.

This view advocates that we associate the content of psychological states not with any particular sentences but with their references. This restores a kind of extensionality to attributions of psychological states. If Arnold believes that Stinky is in the room, this means that he is in a particular sort of psychological relation to Stinky (= Fred). Thus Arnold believes that Fred is in the room. We can take it that he also believes that Fred is not in the room; this means that he is in another sort of psychological relation to Stinky (= Fred). Thus he has two beliefs about Fred: That he is and that he is not in the room. One of them is mistaken, of course; but people make mistakes.

Nonreferring Proper Names

Let us now turn to the question of nonreferring proper names in attributions of propositional attitudes. The problem was that

(19.7)   Santa will arrive at Christmas.

is meaningless, not false, if proper names have a merely referential semantics. But what seemed most implausible was that

(19.8)   Arnold thinks that Santa will arrive at Christmas.

would similarly be meaningless; it seems clear that sentence (19.8) might be true. Why might we think that sentence (19.8) is true, even though we know that 'Santa' names nothing? One reason might be that Arnold sincerely utters sentence (19.7).

One must, as I insisted at various earlier points in this book, distinguish what an utterer believes and intends from what the utterance literally means. The fact that a madman utters "Gleeg gleeg gleeg," believing that it is snowing in Tibet and intending to communicate that fact, does not make the sentence he uttered mean what 'It is snowing in Tibet' really means. This madman is suffering from a rare ailment, and we might have no idea from what beliefs and intentions his utterance springs. But when Arnold utters sentence (19.7), what he says is good evidence that he has a common enough set of beliefs and intentions. As we have seen, however, the fact that a particular utterance is merely a reliable sign that the speaker has certain beliefs and illocutionary intentions does not give the utterance sentence meaning; nor does it make the sentence mean what the speaker means by it.

We can grant this much to a sense theorist: Arnold has a *concept* associated with the name 'Santa'; that is, in his mind Arnold associates uses of that name with certain sorts of characteristics. This is nothing new; we saw in chapter 17 that proper names might regularly be related to such concepts. We can even say that the association of 'Santa Claus' with the appropriate concept is a conventional one, not an idiosyncratic quirk of Arnold's. (The madman, on the other hand, has idiosyncratic conceptual associations with his words.) Because we are justified in thinking that Arnold has this concept, we can tell something about Arnold's beliefs on the basis of what he says: It is entirely plausible to think that Arnold thinks that there is a unique jolly fat man who climbs down chimneys at Christmas and who brings presents to good little girls and boys, etc. But Arnold does not believe that *Santa* will arrive at Christmas. He does not believe this because there is no such belief—there is nobody named 'Santa' for such a belief to be about, and beliefs are understood as relations to existing things.

The important point, however, is that the concept associated with a proper name—even if this association is a conventional one—is not relevant to its meaning. What *is* relevant is the conventional *causal connection* between uses of that name and an existing object. Lacking that, 'Santa' has no literal meaning.

We noted in the last chapter that sentence (19.7), when Arnold utters it, is surely different from

(19.9)   Glarfnurd comes down chimneys at Christmas.

even though both are judged to be meaningless. Now the difference is clear. Because of the conventional concept associated with 'Santa', Arnold's utterance of sentence (19.7) tells us something about Arnold's beliefs; but 'Glarfnurd' has no conventional conceptual associations; thus we would not know what to think about Arnold's beliefs if he uttered sentence (19.9). But it does not follow from this that sentence (19.7) is true or that it follows from Arnold's utterance of it that

(19.10)   Arnold believes that Santa comes down chimneys at Christmas.

is true.

Suggested Readings

Frege, Gottlob. 1980. "On sense and meaning," in *Translations from the Philosophical Writings of Gottlob Frege,* Peter Geach and Max Black, eds. Oxford: Basil Blackwell, 56–78.
Sometimes translated as "On sense and nominatum." Reprinted in [2, 5, 6].
Tomkow, Terrance. *Against Representation.* Cambridge: Cambridge University Press (forthcoming).
Arguments for extensionality.

20

Indexicals

Indexicals and Proper Names

An indexical is a "pointing" term; obvious examples are

this	here
that	there
it	then
that one	now

Less obvious examples, but terms that function nevertheless in the same way, are

I	this year
he	that elephant
she	the future
you	yesterday

Indexicals work somewhat similarly to proper names. Sentences in which an indexical does not refer to anything fail to express anything significant. If someone says, "That is a nice big one" but there is nothing being referred to, then the sentence is meaningless. Suppose that the speaker is hallucinating a nice big pink elephant; she is not referring to a hallucinated elephant, for this is not a *thing*. (A hallucinated elephant is not a kind of elephant. To say that someone is hallucinating an elephant is not to claim the existence of an elephant or of anything else. It is just to say that she is visually experiencing in a way that might lead her to false beliefs about what exists.)

Again, the argument about possibility is applicable. Whatever properties the thing referred to by 'that' has, it is possible that this thing has different ones.

Some of the indexicals listed do include some descriptive content. If we are standing by a cage at the zoo, and you say, "That baboon reminds me of Arnold," it is clear that your utterance refers to the baboon at which your eyes are directed, even if your eyes are also directed at the baboon's swing, the bars in front of the cage, etc., because 'that baboon', if it refers at all, must at least refer to a baboon. Thus indexicals can present mixed cases; they are in some ways similar to proper names and in other ways similar to definite descriptions. Suppose, on the other hand, that we are standing in front of a cage full of orangutans; even if I can tell that you mean to refer to the orangutan your eyes are directed toward, your sentence itself fails to refer to anything; thus your sentence itself is, strictly, meaningless. This is the direct analogy between proper names and even these "mixed" (partially descriptive) indexicals and the disanalogy with definite descriptions: According to the Russellian view a sentence with a nonreferring definite description would be false but meaningful.

To return to proper names for a moment, we might argue that proper names semantically bear informative content, that is, semantically imply the existence of something with certain properties, just as 'that baboon' does. The name 'Charlottetown', for example, carries with it the implication that what is named is a city or town or something like that, rather than, say, a day of the week or a person. The name 'Fred' implies that the bearer is a male human being, although this is only a probability: I once knew a female beagle named 'Fred'. 'Oklahoma City' implies that the bearer is a city in Oklahoma, although it is possible that this sort of implication may not hold. There is a Kansas City in Kansas, but across the Missouri River one finds another city called 'Kansas City' that is in Missouri, not in Kansas. Kripkeans should not (and do not when they are careful) deny that proper names can carry these descriptive implications.

What is important to see in these cases, however, is that these are not, strictly, features of the meaning of these terms. Because proper names carry no *semantic* implications about characteristics, violation of any of the normal associations between particular proper names and certain characteristics does not make the sentences in which they occur false or meaningless (although they may be misleading). Provided that the right sort of circumstances that make something have a proper name have occurred, anything can have any proper name, regardless of its characteristics. A female beagle can be named 'Fred' or even 'Oklahoma City'. But this marks a difference between proper names and indexicals: 'That baboon' (used literally) can never refer to an orangutan. (But can you proper-name your pet orangutan 'That Baboon'?)

Propositional Attitudes and Indexicals

Propositional attitudes raise problems for indexicals that are related to those they raise for proper names. Consider the following case. Suppose that Arnold sees someone in a mirror and sees that that person's pants are on fire; Arnold says:

(20.1)   He is in danger.

and the indexical refers to the person seen in the mirror. But suppose that, unknown to Arnold, the person he sees in the mirror is actually himself (he does not see enough of the reflection to identify it as a reflection of himself). Not yet feeling the heat, Arnold sincerely says:

(20.2)   I am not in danger.

'I' in this sentence is an indexical again referring to Arnold.

On a directly referential account of indexicals, sentences (20.1) and (20.2) are contradictory. 'I' in sentence (20.2) and 'He' in sentence (20.1) refer to exactly the same individual; and sentence (20.1) asserts of this individual that he is in danger, and sentence (20.2) asserts of the same individual that he is not in danger. You can see that this case raises problems analogous to those discussed in the last chapter, when Arnold sincerely asserted, 'Stinky is at the party' and 'Fred is not at the party'. Arnold is willing to assert or assent to sentence (20.1) but not to sentence (20.2) although sentence (20.2) results from a substitution of a coreferential term into sentence (20.1). Consider

(20.3)   Arnold believes that he is in danger.

Is this true? In a sense it is, because Arnold believes of a person that that person is in danger, and that person is himself. In this sense it is also true that Arnold believes that Fred is at the party, because he believes of some person that that person is at the party, and that person in fact is Fred (although he calls him 'Stinky'). If we accept the proposal, argued for in the last chapter, to treat attributions of intentional attitudes as containing referentially transparent contexts, then it would be plausible to say that sentence (20.3) is true.

On the other hand, we might want to insist that sentence (20.3) is not true; this way of seeing things treats attributions of propositional attitudes as containing referentially opaque contexts. This may seem to match our normal ways of speaking better. We might say that Arnold does not think that *he* is in danger. If he did, he might be expected to feel fear, to engage in self-protective behavior, etc.; but he does not. Arnold thinks that *someone else* is in danger.

To argue this way leads to the view that the demonstratives 'he', 'I', and others have a sense as well as a reference. When Arnold asserts

(20.4)   I believe that I am not in danger.

what he says is true, because the second 'I' in sentence (20.4) has, in addition to a reference, a sense—a mode of presentation of its reference. The referent of this 'I' is Arnold, but under that mode of presentation in which each of us is presented to him/herself. Arnold does not believe of himself under that mode of presentation that he is in danger. When Arnold says:

(20.5)   I believe that he is in danger.

what he says is true, despite the fact that 'he' refers to Arnold again, because the word 'he' refers to a different mode of presentation from 'I'. It refers to the mode of presentation under which contextually indicated males are presented to one. (It is usual but not necessary that 'he' refer to someone other than the speaker; the fact that this is not necessary is shown by the fact that, when sentence (20.5) is spoken by Arnold, 'he' refers to Arnold.)

The postulation of sense is more plausible in this sort of case than it was for proper names. One problem with the postulation of senses for proper names is that proper names seem to be subjective and infinitely variable: Each person might have a different mode of presentation of the name 'Aristotle', thinking of Aristotle in a different way from others. But it seems that each of us has the same mode of presentation when we utter 'I': It presents an individual as one's *self*. Call this particular mode of presentation *self-presentation*. Normal uses of 'Aristotle', whatever mode of presentation the users have in mind, refer to the same thing: Aristotle. But each token of 'I', when spoken by a different person, has a different reference. Similarly, 'that' has a multitude of different references, as does 'today'.

The Content of Psychological States

Recall from the last chapter the suggestion that we consider the *content* of psychological states to be given by the objects in the world to which they are connected. If Arnold believes that Stinky is in the room, this means that he is in a particular sort of psychological relation to Stinky (=Fred). Thus he believes that Fred is in the room. We can take it that he also believes that Fred is not in the room; this means that Arnold is in another sort of psychological relation to Stinky (=Fred). Thus he has two beliefs about Fred: that he is and that he is not in the room. This was part of the attempt to do without senses in attributions of propositional attitudes.

Similarly, here we might want to say that Arnold's two beliefs (which he expresses by saying "I am not in danger" and "He is in danger") have the same content insofar as they both are psychological relations to himself. Thus we can say that Arnold has two beliefs about Arnold: that Arnold is and that he is not in danger. Again, logical incompatibility of sentences that express the content of these beliefs does not result in psychological incompatibility.

The reason why the view that the content of beliefs is given by their objects looks more implausible here is that this does not look like the right way to sort out beliefs. To see this, imagine the following situation: There are three people, Sally, Martha, and Sheila. Each expresses her own beliefs sincerely in the following sentences:

> Sally: "I am in danger."
> Martha: "I am in danger."
> Sheila: "Sally is in danger."

To see how we should sort out beliefs into *types*, answer the following question: Does Sally have the same kind of belief as Martha or as Sheila? Sally's belief is the same as Martha's insofar as each of them believes of a person presented in the mode of self-presentation that that person is in danger. Sally's belief is the same as Sheila's insofar as each of them believes of Sally that Sally is in danger (but under different modes of presentation).

I suspect that you are tempted to say that Sally has the same kind of belief as Martha. One motivation for this is that we can expect Sally and Martha to react to their beliefs in the same sort of ways: fear, self-protection, etc. We believe in rough-and-ready psychological laws: People with a certain kind of belief will react in general in certain ways. The kinds of things that are related in these laws of psychology are those that encourage the idea that Sally's belief is the same kind of belief as Martha's. If they are the same kind of belief and if beliefs are sorted out into kinds by similarities of content, then their content is given by mode of presentation, not by reference. Insofar as we attribute a belief of a certain sort to others by specifying its content, the meaning of the indexical inside the belief attribution must be its sense, not its reference.

On the other hand, we can take a different point of view: that Sally and Sheila have the same sort of belief. Both Sally and Martha can be expected to engage in *self-protection*, but is Sally's behavior really the same sort of behavior as Martha's? Suppose that Sally, Martha, and Sheila all care deeply about each other (and each about her own self) and want to protect anyone they care about deeply from danger.

Given these psychological dispositions plus the beliefs described, we predict that those beliefs will result in

> Sally acts to protect Sally.
> Martha acts to protect Martha.
> Sheila acts to protect Sally.

Put *this* way, Sally's behavior is *not* the same as Martha's; it is the same as Sheila's. This kind of sorting, relying on the external objects of the mental states for sorting them, encourages the transparent view of the attribution of psychological states. According to this view the semantics of indexicals would share with proper names the feature that their meaning is given by their reference, not by their sense.

But how, then, can we explain the fact that tokens of the same indexical have different referents?

'Aristotle', in the direct reference view, gets its meaning by its relation to Aristotle. Tokens of 'I', on the other hand, refer to a wide variety of people, so that word type cannot get its meaning by any simple universal connection to a particular individual. Nevertheless, perhaps we can say that the meaning of 'I' is its referent in a more complicated way: Its referent depends on who speaks it. In the mouth of Fred, 'I' refers to Fred. 'I' is thus a kind of function: Given different speakers, 'I' yields different referents. 'I' is thus a function that takes the speaker as argument and yields an object (that person) as value: It is an $o \rightarrow o$ function. Similarly, given different times of utterance, 'now' yields different times as referent; and different tokens of 'here' yield different places as referent, depending on where they are spoken. This should, however, be sharply distinguished from a descriptivist or sense view of the semantics of such indexicals: 'I' is not semantically equivalent to a definite description, such as 'the current speaker', nor is 'today' semantically equivalent to 'the day on which this sentence is uttered'.

Much more can be said about this complex matter, but I leave it here.

Suggested Reading

Kaplan, David. 1978. "Dthat," in *Syntax and Semantics*, Peter Cole, ed. New York: Academic Press, vol. 9, 221–243.
  Also reprinted in [5].

21

General Terms

Descriptivism about General Terms

Let us turn now to general nouns, which would appear to be primary candidates for a descriptivist analysis. Surprisingly, some philosophers think that they can also be rigid designators.

Consider the general noun 'elephant' in the sentence 'Dumbo is an elephant'. What is meant by this? When we say it, we are identifying Dumbo by a proper name, and it seems that we are saying that he is a member of that group of things in the world that have a certain set of characteristics. 'Elephant' applies to anything that happens to have these characteristics; but what are these characteristics? Presumably, they are what we use to identify things as elephants: being a large gray animal; having a thick, almost hairless skin; having a long, flexible, prehensile trunk; and having upper incisors forming long curved tusks. This list of characteristics, or something similar to it, is at any rate what dictionaries give us as the "definition" of 'elephant'. (As we have seen, however, dictionary definitions sometimes do not give characteristics *semantically* equivalent to the word defined. Recall the discussion of 'yellow' in chapter 7.) If 'elephant' is descriptional in terms of these characteristics, then ascribing 'elephant' to anything must be exactly semantically equivalent to saying that the thing has these characteristics. To know the meaning of the word 'elephant', then, we must know what characteristics are definitionally true of elephants. This is a descriptivist analysis of the semantics of the general term 'elephant'.

We have already discussed one problem with this analysis in connection with the descriptivist analysis of proper names: that particular elephants need not have *all* the characteristics. Suppose that an animal turns up having all the characteristics except that it has no tusks. We probably would not hesitate to call it an elephant anyway. One can amputate the tusks of an elephant or paint the animal purple and still have an elephant; perhaps we should change the list of characteristics to say that each characteristic must be one the animal would have unless it were changed artificially, or something similar. But there is a good deal of natural, genetic diversity in species, and the birth of a tuskless or purple elephant is possible; tuskless-ness or purpleness, however, would not disqualify the animal from elephanthood.

One way to solve this problem is the same as the "cluster" suggestion for saving the descriptivist theory of proper names: Assume that the list of defining characteristics associated with the term is a cluster of more or less relevant characteristics, and anything that is a close enough fit to this cluster therefore counts as an object to which that term applies.

But this will not do. Suppose that we discover on Mars a sort of animal that has *all* the characteristics but is not even distantly related to what we now count as elephants and cannot interbreed with them. These (it is argued) would be elephant look-alikes, but not elephants. This has not happened, of course, but if the descriptivist theory is correct and if the characteristics (or some large enough subset of them) are *definitional* of 'elephant', then the existence of some nonelephant that has all the characteristics is *impossible*; it is analytic, necessary, and knowable a priori that anything that is a perfect fit to the characteristics is an elephant.

Well, then, is ability to interbreed with elephants the defining char-acteristic? The problem with this suggestion is that it is circular. We have to identify something as an elephant *first* in order to identify anything else as an elephant by seeing whether that other thing can interbreed with the first. We cannot use this test for *all* elephants.

Philosophers who argue for a nondescriptivist analysis of certain general terms agree that there are certain properties we look for in order to assign the term 'elephant'; they also admit that there are properties we look for in order to apply a proper name. These proper-ties include those in the given "definition": being a large gray animal, etc. But the difference between the two positions is that the descrip-tivist takes it that such general terms refer in other possible worlds to whatever has such properties. Those who think that certain general terms refer rigidly think that they refer to a set of things in this and in certain other possible worlds, but *not* by virtue of having these properties.

Accidental and Essential Properties

An argument against a descriptivist analysis of 'elephant' in terms of *certain* properties, for example, having a trunk, is clear. It is possible that an elephant may not have a trunk. That is, in some possible worlds elephants do not have trunks. Thus having a trunk is not a necessary property of elephants. Similarly, elephants need not be large or gray, etc. Traditionally, a property that some set of things in fact has but does not have necessarily is called an *accidental property* of things in that set. (This philosophers' term has little to do with the ordinary use of 'accidental'.) Thus having a trunk is an accidental property of elephants; there is another possible world in which members of the set of elephants do not have trunks.

But we can presumably, also think of certain properties such that not only do all members of the actual set have that property but also each member of that set in every possible world (in which that set is not empty) has that property. This sort of property is called an *essential property* of things in that set. Thus suppose that there is no possible world in which elephants are not mammals. That is, being a mammal is an essential property of elephants. Of course, having this property is not sufficient to pick out elephants; there are other sets of things that also have this property (for example, baboons).

Suppose that there is some (perhaps complicated) property that is essential to being an elephant and that all *and only* elephants have this property. That is, in every possible world all elephants have this property, and only elephants have it. Let's call this property, the essence of elephanthood, *property E*. It appears that none of the properties that dictionaries usually list for 'elephant' is property E, and neither is property E a complicated cluster of those properties. What, then, could property E be? There is some controversy about this among biologists (not only for 'elephant' but for species names in general). Perhaps it has something to do with genetics: It is essential to being an elephant that something have a particular genetic structure. Or perhaps it has something to do with evolution: The lineage of an animal has to be traceable back to a certain sort of ancestor. Or perhaps it is not a general property at all; maybe being an elephant is essentially being closely enough related to some particular paradigm elephant that we point out.

Whether or not there is some essential property of elephanthood, the important point the nondescriptivist wants to make is that property E need not have anything to do with the semantics of the word 'elephant'. This is shown by the fact that we can all use the word 'elephant', understanding its meaning quite well, in blissful ignorance of what (if anything) the essential property of elephanthood is.

To see this, let's examine a general term for a set of things for which we *have* discovered the essential property: 'water'. (Strictly, there is a difference between 'elephant', a *general* term, and 'water', a *mass* term. Note that the set of elephants consists of elephants but that the set of water does not consist of "waters"; we do not speak of "a water" and do not count "waters". We can, however, ignore this difference.) We know that the essential property of being water is being made of H_2O, but before 1750 nobody knew this; they went around identifying things as 'water' the way most of us still do: by seeing if it is wet, colorless, tasteless, etc.

Should we conclude, then, that most of us now and nobody before 1750 understands the meaning of 'water'? This would be absurd. (By similar reasoning, we would have to conclude that nobody or almost nobody *now* understands the word 'elephant'.) The proper conclusion is that the meaning of the word 'water'—what we understand when we understand the meaning of that word—is not connected to the essential property of waterhood.

Everybody before 1750 and most of us now use certain accidental characteristics to identify something as 'water'. Does it follow that the meaning of the word 'water'—what we understand when we understand the meaning of that word—is connected to a cluster of these accidental properties? But this will not do either, because something could pass all these tests, that is, could have most or even all the characteristics in this cluster of accidental properties, and yet not be water (although almost everybody would think that it is). Imagine that a newly discovered underground lake is filled with wet colorless tasteless stuff and that everybody calls it 'water'. If later chemical analysis showed that this stuff is not H_2O but has some different chemical constituency, then it would turn out that everyone was wrong: It is not water, despite having *all* those characteristics we normally use (and always used before 1750) to identify something as 'water'. Therefore the meaning of that word cannot be identified with the set of accidental properties we normally use to pick such stuff out.

We can combine these two conclusions as follows: To say that something is water is to say neither that it is something that has the chemical constituency H_2O (that is, the essential property of water) nor that it is something that has all (or many) of the accidental properties (wet, colorless, tasteless, etc.).

What follows is that no descriptivist account of the meaning of this general term is correct, that is, that the attribution of this general term is not semantically equivalent to the attribution of any description.

Well, then, what *do* we mean by 'water'?

General Terms and Proper Names

A partial parallel with proper names should be clear. Here, the non-descriptivist would argue that, even though we routinely identify something as the bearer of a proper name by noticing that that thing has certain characteristics, calling something by a proper name is not equivalent to ascribing those characteristics to it. (We can even imagine that there is an essential property of being a particular individual, for example, property F, such that it is necessary that, if anything has that property, it is quantitatively identical with Fred. This sort of property is called an *individual essence*.)

But this is only a partial parallel. For a proper name that names only one thing, there is an alternative story of why that name names that individual: It is directly connected to it. But for general terms, this story will not work. General terms apply to an open-ended set of things, some of which we have never had any contact with. Even though we might (implausibly for most general terms) imagine that some particular group of things was "baptized" with their general name at some point, when the "baptizers" had some sort of direct contact with them, this does not explain why that general name applies to many other things with which the "baptizers" had no contact.

Suppose that a committee of zoologists discovers a new species of bird and that they decide to call it Martin's nuthatch. What makes it the case that other birds, with which the zoologists have had no contact, are also called this?

It is not difficult to imagine circumstances that attach a proper name to an individual; certain procedures count as doing this when they associate the name with that particular individual in such a way as to create a convention for such future associations. But the account of why a general term applies to a set of things must be more complicated, for a set of things is, in general, not present as a whole. We can surely imagine that the zoologists named some birds Martin's nuthatch that were altogether unknown to them at the time of naming, still undiscovered in the wild. Other Martin's nuthatches did not exist yet at the time of naming; they were yet to be born. Presumably there could even be merely possible but not actual Martin's nuthatches, ones that exist in some possible world but not in the actual world. Consider an egg laid by a Martin's nuthatch that happened to be unfertilized. Had it been fertilized and had it hatched, there would have been another Martin's nuthatch in the actual world. *That* Martin's nuthatch exists only possibly, not actually; and the zoologists' ceremony names that one also.

How can the zoologists name *all* Martin's nuthatches? Well, presumably, they have some sort of connection with one or more actual birds (although those birds need not have been right in front of the zoologists at the time); they utter the words, "Martin's nuthatch," having the power to create conventions for the future use of that general term, indicating somehow (perhaps by pointing or using an indexical term) the sample birds. This would clearly do as a way of naming one or several particular birds, but how can it serve to give a general name to an open-ended set of past and future, observed and unobserved, actual and possible, birds?

The descriptivist view explains how the zoologist's ceremony would name such a diverse and open-ended set. On the descriptivist view, all the zoologists need to do is define the new term 'Martin's nuthatch' by some general properties; anything that fits these general properties would thenceforth be called by that name. Perhaps they need not even state these properties; they can merely point to the sample bird or birds and stipulate that anything *sufficiently* similar to these birds, anything that shares enough of their noticed or unnoticed characteristics, will also be called a Martin's nuthatch. But the direct reference theory denies that this general name is to be understood as equivalent to any collection of properties, so this account is not open to them. The direct reference theorist, then, owes us an explanation of why the zoologists' ceremony makes it the case that birds outside the sample are also given that name.

Of course, most general terms are not given their meaning by such an official ceremony. No official ceremony established the meaning of the word 'elephant'. Presumably most general terms achieve meaning gradually on the basis of general use in a linguistic community and usually evolve from earlier uses. But this does not solve the direct reference theorist's problem: How is it that even communal use of a general term to refer to particular things establishes an open-ended set of other things to which that general term really does apply?

Natural Kinds

This is the answer supplied by direct reference theorists: The semantics of general terms is such that general terms apply not only to those individuals who are thus designated during the establishment of that term, but to anything else *of the same kind*. We thus use 'elephant' correctly whenever we attribute it to animals that are of the same kind as the ones to which that word has (by and large) previously been applied. Thus, according to the direct reference theory, saying that something is an elephant is roughly equivalent to saying that it is of the same kind as a paradigm sample of things, *not* that it shares any particular characteristics with that sample.

Of course, we can verbally classify things in any way we please and into any sort of arbitrary classification. But only *some* classifications lump things into their *real* kinds. A real, as opposed to merely arbitrary, classification of things is called a *natural kind*.

Clearly, the direct reference theorist cannot explain the notion of being of the same natural kind by means of shared characteristics. There are two ways, in general, that we can understand the notion that two things are of the same natural kind.

First, some philosophers think that there is a real fact of the matter, independent of the way we decide to talk or the way we think, that certain individuals all belong to the same kind of thing. On this view what kind of thing an individual is is a fact of nature. Nature comes split up into kinds of things that it is up to us to discover. Philosophers who believe that natural kinds are objective external facts of nature are sometimes called *realists*; those who do not believe this are called *nominalists* (although these words have a number of different uses). This split has been important throughout the history of philosophy and is important in many different philosophical areas. In the philosophy of science, for example, realists argue that one difference between real scientific laws and just "accidental" regularities is that scientific laws divide things according to the way nature divides them.

According to realists, general terms are established in use by reference to particular individuals but continue to refer (if at all) to any other individuals that are in fact of the same natural kind as the particular individuals.

Nominalists view natural kinds as human creations: They are the ways that we would divide things to best suit our practical and theoretical needs. Nominalists think that the world does not come objectively split into sorts of things but that humans sort things into kinds that they invent. On the nominalist view we *decide* that Dumbo and the other elephants belong to one set of things and that Clarence and the other camels to another, because this categorization fits our interests in understanding, predicting, and controlling the world. Our choices about kinds may or may not serve our needs, but they are never right or wrong in the sense that they match or fail to match the way things are really divided. Thus natural kinds are the ways that the most basic and successful science will divide things. Of course, this depends partly on the way things are, but it also depends on what our practical and theoretical needs are. What counts as the best theory of nature will be partially determined in the nominalist view by our needs and preferences.

In both the realist and the nominalist views, it is possible that everyone is wrong about using some general term. For example, we can imagine that whales used to be classified under the general term 'fish'. This was a mistake because whales belong to the same natural kind as baboons and buffalo, not to that of guppies and goldfish. Science originally misclassified them. Their *real* classification is the group that nature put them in, according to realists; it is the group (what we take now to be) ideal science puts them in, according to nominalists.

Unnatural Kinds

Neither the realist nor the nominalist view holds that just any kind is a natural kind: Certain classifications are merely arbitrary. 'Money' does not name a natural kind, nor does 'felon', 'king', 'bachelor', or 'brother'. The set of things exactly 50 miles from the Eiffel Tower is a kind of thing but not a natural kind. On the realist account this is a consequence of the fact that this sorting out of things does not cut them up according to their real divisions. On the nominalist view this classification would not figure in the most useful basic natural science. Perhaps 'grue' does not name a natural kind.

Consider the general term 'towerling', which I have just made up. Anything is a towerling just in case it is exactly 50 miles from the Eiffel Tower. Suppose that you wanted to learn what 'towerling' means. I could show you several things (Pierre's house, Jean-Paul's car, etc.) that are towerlings, and you might get the idea. But it is clear that the correct application of 'towerling' is not correctly explained the same way as the direct reference theorist has proposed for natural kind terms. 'Elephant', a natural kind term, is applied to whatever is of the same natural kind as some sample paradigm individuals; but this will not work for 'towerling' because towerlings are not a natural kind.

Nevertheless, 'towerling' is a general term. The way we understand 'towerling' is not by learning to use it for anything of the same natural kind as a sample; it is rather by finding out that it is equivalent to *anything that is 50 miles from the Eiffel Tower*. This is the essential property of towerlinghood, and 'towerling' *is* definable in terms of this property. The descriptivist analysis of kind terms *does* work for 'towerling', as it does for other general terms that name nonnatural kinds.

What we have, then, is two kinds of general term: those that apply to natural kinds and those that can be defined in terms of descriptions. By analogy with the distinction already made between proper names and definite descriptions, we can say that the first sort of general term is a *rigid designator*; it names the same natural kind of thing in all possible worlds. The second kind of general term is a flaccid designator; the things it applies to are not all of the same kind, even (in this case) in the actual world.

Now consider these two general terms: 'platinum' and 'the most valuable metal'. First of all, the terms are (let's assume, at least) *coextensive* in the actual world; that is, they apply to exactly the same set of things in the actual world (because, we assume, platinum is the most valuable metal in the actual world). 'Platinum', however, is a rigid designator. Nothing could be platinum unless it were of the same natural kind as those actual pieces of platinum in the actual world. But 'the most valuable metal' is a flaccid designator; it is possible (although not actual) that some other kind of metal, say, iridium, is the most valuable metal. In the actual world, then, 'the most valuable metal' happens to apply to a natural kind, namely, platinum; but 'the most valuable metal' applies to other sorts of stuff in other possible worlds; so it is a flaccid designator.

It is no accident that we often use general descriptions, such as 'the most valuable metal' or 'things exactly 50 miles from the Eiffel Tower', to refer to nonnatural kinds, because the only way we can refer to all the objects that belong in such a kind is flaccidly, by giving a description. When general terms for nonnatural kinds do not mention the defining characteristics, we nevertheless can give such a definition. But knowing definitive characteristics is not necessary for knowing the meaning of natural kind general terms, and even when we know what the essential characteristics are, according to the direct reference view these are not semantically equivalent to the general term.

Suggested Readings

Hull, David, 1978. "A matter of individuality." *Philosophy of Science* 45:335–360.
  The problem of the meaning of species terms in biology.
Putnam, Hilary. 1970. "Is semantics possible?" in *Belief and Metaphysics*, H. E. Keifer and M. K. Munitz, eds. Albany: State University of New York Press, 50–63.
  Also available in [5, 10].
Putnam, Hilary. 1973. "Meaning and reference." *Journal of Philosophy* 70:699–711.
  Also available in [10].
Salmon, Nathan U. 1981. *Reference and Essence*. Princeton: Princeton University Press, ch. 2.
  A good general survey of views on the semantics of general terms.

22

Truth and Meaning

Meanings as Truth Conditions

Chapters 11 through 21 constitute the bare beginnings of a *referential* or *truth-conditional semantics*. The object of such an enterprise is to provide an account of the meanings of each sentence by telling, in essence, what the truth conditions of that sentence are. We began by relying on the notions of a *name*, which refers to an object in the world, and of a *predicate*, which is a function that has a truth value as value given an object as argument. Basically, one knows what predicates mean when one knows how they relate objects to truth values; and one knows what names mean when one knows what objects they name. Given that you know who 'Fred' names and how 'is bald' relates objects to truth values, you know the truth conditions for 'Fred is bald': It is true if Fred is in fact related to True by 'is bald', that is, if Fred is bald.

The notion that meaning can be given by a theory of truth conditions of sentences in a language has been discussed and defended recently by Donald Davidson, adapting somewhat suggestions by an earlier philosopher, Alfred Tarski. Here is what a truth-conditional theory of the meaning of a language, according to the Davidson-Tarski view, looks like.

For each sentence in the language to be analyzed (call it the *object language*), the theory tells us under what conditions that sentence is true; that is, it gives the *truth conditions* for each sentence in the object language. If the object language is French, for example, the theory would tell us the truth conditions for the French sentence 'La neige est blanche'; that sentence is true just in case snow is white. The theory thus contains a list of sentences, each of which gives the truth conditions for a sentence in French. These sentences in the theory are called *T sentences*. Of course, it is impossible to construct a complete list of T sentences for any natural language consisting of an infinity of sentence types, but we can at least think about such a hypothetical infinite list. Such a list for the French language would contain for *every* possible sentence in French such T sentences as

'La neige est blanche' is true iff snow is white.
'Les elephants ont des trompes' is true iff elephants have trunks.
'Les oeufs sont toxiques' is true iff eggs are poisonous.

Iff is a philosopher's abbreviation for "if and only if." For any two sentences p and q, $\ulcorner p$ if and only if $q \urcorner$ means the same as $\ulcorner$ if p, then q, and if q, then $p \urcorner$. This is equivalent to saying that either both $\ulcorner p \urcorner$ and $\ulcorner q \urcorner$ are true or both $\ulcorner p \urcorner$ and $\ulcorner q \urcorner$ are false. In order to see the force of this sort of approach to sentence meaning, we must understand exactly how 'iff' works. 'Iff' does not imply any connection between the sentences it connects. Normally, in English if we say, "The picnic is off if and only if it is raining", we imply some sort of connection between the two facts; but in the logician's hands, this connective does not imply this. For example, 'Snow is white iff grass is green' is true because each of the sentences connected by the 'iff' is true, despite the lack of connection between the fact about snow and the fact about grass. Similarly, 'Elephants fly iff the capital of Bolivia is Cleveland' is true (because both component sentences connected by 'iff' are false), and 'Lemons are yellow iff the Empire State Building is made of marshmallow' is false (because one component sentence is true and the other is false).

Those objects surrounding the sentences are called *corner quotes*. The reason single quotes cannot strictly be used here is that a particular sentence with p and q in it is not being mentioned. Rather, what we are referring to is any verbal expression *of this form*; p and q are variables; they stand in the place of any two verbal expressions. Corner quotes may be read as "any expression of the form _____" or as "any expression obtained by substituting appropriate bits of language for each variable in _____."

Tarski argued that the list of T sentences constitutes a definition for 'true' (or perhaps for 'true in the object language'); this is disputed by some philosophers but need not concern us here. What Davidson argues is that this list constitutes a complete description of the meaning of the object language. What we would have here, then, if Davidson is correct, is an explanation of meaning in terms of truth.

This position is surprising and clearly needs defense and probably some fixing. Imagine, again, that you are trying to discover what the natives mean when they are speaking Tribish. Suppose that the first thing you did was to make a list of Tribish sentences and sort them out into True and False, not yet having the faintest idea of what they mean. (How could you do this? Never mind for the moment.) Suppose that you constructed T sentences for each Tribish sentence in your list by associating just any truth condition that happens to be true with each true Tribish sentence and just any truth condition that happens to be false with each false one. Part of your list giving T sentences for the true Tribish sentences might look similar to this:

'Gavagai mergle' is true iff snow is white.
'Mairzy dotes' is true iff grass is green.
'Needle nerdle noo' is true iff Moose Jaw is in Saskatchewan.
'Igpay atinlay' is true iff snow is white.

And for the false Tribish sentences:

'Snerdly bullwinkle' is true iff peachtrees bloom in Toronto in January.
'Sala gadoola midga gaboola' is true iff earthworms sneeze.

Now we have a list that gives us what (our preliminary version of) Davidson's position requires. We imagined that true truth conditions ('Snow is white', 'Grass is green', etc.) were assigned to each truth in Tribish entirely *at random*, and, similarly, false truth conditions were assigned to each false Tribish sentence. Clearly, you could construct a list knowing nothing whatever about the meaning of any Tribish sentence; all you would need to know is the truth value of each Tribish sentence, that is, whether each is true or false. (One does not need to know what a sentence means in order to know that it is true. If an immensely wise and trustworthy person says something in a language you do not understand, you still are justified in thinking that it is true. You know that, whatever it means, it is true.) If a list of true T sentences for Tribish constitutes an account of what every Tribish sentence means, then your list should do this.

But clearly it does not, because truth conditions were assigned randomly. One might as well have assigned any true truth condition to any true Tribish sentence (and false to false) so far as this weak criterion is concerned; one could even have assigned a single true truth condition (for example, that snow is white) to every true Tribish sentence, and a single false one (for example, that snow is purple) to every false Tribish sentence. The problem is that this is too easy and clearly tells us almost nothing about what Tribish sentences mean. Davidson's real theory has an additional complexity designed to save it from this absurd consequence.

An Axiomatic Theory

To see why Davidson's real theory does not result in this absurdity, consider first the fact that (most or all?) real natural languages contain an infinite number of sentences. Obviously, then, a complete list of T sentences for such languages cannot be given. This is a real difficulty if we think that what is supposed to be provided by a theory of meaning of sentences in an object language is what one is supposed to know when one knows what the sentences in that language mean; never mind that we would run out of time and paper when we try to write down an infinite list: How could we know such an infinite list? The answer (as outlined in chapter 1) is that what we know is a finite list of words and ways of combining them, such that we can figure out the meanings of an infinite number of sentences combining them. In other words, what we know is in effect an *axiomatic theory* with a finite number of axioms, which potentially yield as *theorems* every one of the T sentences in a language. An axiomatic theory is a theory with some finite number of basic principles plus a way of using these principles to yield other truths (theorems). High-school Euclidean geometry provides an excellent example of an axiomatic theory.

What does such a theory look like? The details of what our actual theories are like are not at all clear, but it seems reasonable to think that a theory about French might be constituted by, among other things, axioms about reference, for example,

> 'Jean Sebastien Bach' refers to Johann Sebastian Bach.
> 'Ronald Reagan' refers to Ronald Reagan.

and by satisfaction axioms about predicates, for example,

> 'Chauve' is satisfied by bald things.
> 'Stupide' is satisfied by stupid things.

and by connection axioms that together with other axioms can produce T sentences, for example,

> $\ulcorner a$ est $b \urcorner$ is true iff what $\ulcorner a \urcorner$ refers to satisfies $\ulcorner b \urcorner$.

This theory will yield as theorems such T sentences for French as

> 'Jean Sebastien Bach est chauve' is true iff Johann Sebastian Bach is bald.
> 'Jean Sebastien Bach est stupide' is true iff Johann Sebastian Bach is stupid.
> 'Ronald Reagan est chauve' is true iff Ronald Reagan is bald.

Of course, what is presented here is just the barest beginning of a theory for French sentences. Other axioms of these sorts and of other sorts as well are obviously necessary. I do not go any further in trying to see what sorts of things go into such a theory. The point is that such a theory is capable of producing T sentences for all the sentences in a language. And, it is important to note that Davidson's hope was that the provision of such a theory for any object language would not fall prey to the difficulty noted, the possibility of random distribution of just any truth conditions with any true sentence in the object language and just any false truth condition with any false sentence in the object language.

Here is why this seems to be a legitimate hope. Suppose that we begin by randomly associating a bunch of truth conditions with Tribish sentences, matching their truth values, and suppose that we just happen to come up with the T sentences

'Gavagai goo mergle' is true iff snow is falling.
'Mairzy goo dotes' is true iff grass is green.

Perhaps our axiomatic theory, constructed to account for these T sentences, thus contains the axioms

'Gavagai' refers to snow.
'Mairzy' refers to grass.
'Mergle' is satisfied by falling things.
'Dotes' is satisfied by green things.
$\ulcorner a$ goo $b \urcorner$ is true iff what $\ulcorner a \urcorner$ refers to satisfies $\ulcorner b \urcorner$.

So far so good. But suppose that this theory is mistaken. This is surely probable, given the random associations in the T sentences. Suppose that 'mergle' really applies to white things. The theory has as a theorem

'Mairzy goo mergle' is true iff grass is falling.

and this can be tested: See if the natives say this (or agree with it) or deny it when grass is falling; drop some grass on them from a roof. If they regularly deny "Mairzy goo mergle" on these occasions, then our theory must be wrong somewhere (it is not definite where). Now suppose that they say 'Mairzy goo mergle' when grass has turned white (from dehydration). This confirms, to some extent, a change in the 'mergle' axiom in our theory to

'Mergle' is satisfied by white things.

although it is important to see that all sorts of other changes would also make our theory consistent with this new evidence, for example, changing the 'mergle' axiom to

'Mergle' is satisfied by dehydrated things.

and/or by changing the 'mairzy' axiom and/or the 'goo' axiom. The hope is that accumulation of more and more evidence will determine a single "right" theory.

Obviously, our theory can be mistaken and still account for any finite collection of evidence. Some philosophers, however, argue against Davidson that alternative, incompatible theories might exist that could even account for an infinite amount of evidence. That is, we could have two theories such that both provide axiomatic ways for generating correct T sentences for *all* sentences in the object language.

If this argument is correct, what should we say about Davidson's theory? Some plausible responses become evident when we have compared Davidson's theory with the Quinian considerations raised in connection with radical translation.

Davidson and Quine

Davidson's view resembles Quine's in several ways. Both view meaning in the context of theory production for natural languages. Quine's view, however, appears to allow for a sort of evidence for suggesting and testing such theories that Davidson's (at least in the simple form given here) appears to rule out. Recall that for Quine sentences uttered in conjunction with immediate environmental stimulation (about which we postulate *stimulus meaning*) are paramount. Thus we are justified in thinking that sentences containing 'gavagai' might have something to do with rabbits because they are often uttered when a rabbit is in front of the speaker and when we might expect that the speaker is perceiving the rabbit. Davidson's views (as stated here) are thinner. We are to construct our theory of an object language merely on the basis of what is said in that language (and, given the principle of charity, what by and large can thus be expected to be true or false in that language) and on the basis of what is in fact true or false. Thus Quine's approach suggests an additional way of deciding between what, given Davidson's views, might be incompatible theories of the object language: One or the other theory might be more compatible with what we would expect the speakers to be perceiving when they utter particular sentences. Thus suppose that one of these incompatible theories includes the axiom

'Gavagai' refers to snow.

and the other

'Gavagai' refers to rabbits.

and that the latter may turn out to be better simply because sentences including 'gavagai' tend to be uttered in the presence of rabbits but not in the presence of snow.

Because the Quinian approach appears to provide an additional test for adequacy for meaning theories and one we believe would help choose the "right" theory, Quine's approach may be preferable—it may sometimes solve this problem. But it must be stressed that, even in Quine's view, theory is underdetermined by evidence, thus Quine's insistence on the indeterminacy of translation.

A Theory of One's Own Language

Recall that Quine's arguments about radical translation were intended to apply to the understanding of not only a completely strange foreign language but also languages we are already somewhat familiar with, even our own. Davidson's view shares this feature. Thus for Davidson our understanding of the sentences of *our own* language consists in our forming a theory that yields T sentences. A sample of a T sentence for English that any adequate theory you have of your own language must yield as a theorem is

'Snow is white' is true iff snow is white.

Pointing this out causes some philosophers (especially those with a superficial understanding of the Davidson and Tarski views) to break into giggles. It seems to them that a T sentence such as the one just given says only that a sentence is true exactly when it is true. Everyone already knew *that*; a theory that yields such empty and obvious truisms can hardly be a description of the substantial knowledge we have when we know a language.

But this sort of criticism is unjustified. Each T sentence really does reveal something about our language; T sentences actually relate significant facts about what our sentences mean, not just empty and obvious truisms. They do not simply say that something is true just when it is true; what they do is to give the meaning of a sentence by telling us under what conditions it is true. Of course, in T sentences such as the one given, we refer to the conditions that make a *mentioned* sentence true, *using* exactly the words in that sentence. The problem here is that the object language happens to be the same language in which we state the T sentence (we call the language in which we state the T sentence the *metalanguage*). This means, of course, that nobody who wants any information about the sentence in the object language could get any information from that T sentence; but this is a difficulty that is entirely expected: If someone does not understand a language, it is no surprise that he will not get any information from an explanation in that language. Nevertheless, some T sentences whose object language and metalanguage are both English can give information to English speakers; for example:

'A harmattan is blowing' is true iff a dry, dusty wind that blows from the Sahara and along the northwest coast of Africa is blowing.

This is a correct T sentence that follows from axioms of English that include

'Harmattan' refers to dry, dusty winds that. . . .

Of course, these are different from the axioms and T sentences that repeat the same words in the object language and in the metalanguage. To have a complete theory whose object language and metalanguage are both English, we should have either "truistic" axioms, such as

'Snow' refers to snow.

or axioms that take us eventually in circles. (The same is true of any unilingual dictionary.)

In any event it is not foolish to think that our knowledge of the meanings of English sentences consists in our knowing an axiomatic theory that includes such axioms as

'Snow' refers to snow.

and that yields such T sentences as

'Snow is white' is true iff snow is white.

because our knowledge of these axioms does not consist of our internal "possession" in some sense of verbal axioms and theorems stated in the metalanguage English. If all our knowledge were possession of sentences written in our native language, then we would not have informative knowledge of this sort.

One alternative is the possibility that our knowledge in general is not "inside us" in language at all (although, of course, our knowledge about our native language as object language must somehow include the internalization of that object language). This seems quite reasonable: Pointing out that one thing that speakers of English all know is that 'snow' refers to snow hardly seems absurd. What is absurd is that one can teach others that this is the case by saying to them,

" 'Snow' refers to snow" or that our knowledge of English includes exactly this sentence "written" inside our minds.

Another alternative I have examined at length is that knowledge is "written" in an internal language, namely, innate Mentalese. Thus the metalanguage in which we internally "state" the axioms and derive T sentences about English is Mentalese (see chapter 3), and such axioms and theorems would not have the empty quality they show when the metalanguage and object language are the same.

In conclusion, you should note that the theory that attempts to explain the meanings of sentences by their truth conditions, relying on reference and satisfaction of predicates, will work only to the extent that language is extensional.

Suggested Readings

Davidson, Donald. 1967. "Truth and meaning." *Synthese* 17(3):304–323.
  Reprinted in [5, 9].

Davidson, Donald. 1976. Reply to Foster," in *Truth and Meaning,* Gareth Evans and John McDowell, eds. Oxford: Clarendon Press, 33–41.

Foster, J. A. 1976. "Meaning and truth theory," in *Truth and Meaning,* Gareth Evans and John McDowell, eds. Oxford: Clarendon Press, 1–32.
  Objections to Davidson's views.

Loar, Brian. 1976. "Two theories of meaning," in *Truth and Meaning,* Gareth Evans and John McDowell, eds. Oxford: Clarendon Press, 138–161.
  Objections to Davidson's views.

Tarski, Alfred. 1944. "The semantic conception of truth and the foundations of semantics." *Philosophy and Phenomenological Research* 4:341–374.
  Although somewhat technical and presupposing a good deal of background in logic, this article presents a fairly comprehensible account of Tarski's ideas. Reprinted in [4, 5, 7].

23

The Boundaries of Meaning

Implicature

So far, we have considered language used and understood *literally*. To take everything said or written only in a literal sense is, however, to miss a good deal. How language functions in nonliteral ways is a big subject, one that has been studied at length by those who are interested in rhetoric and literature and to some extent by philosophers of language. In this concluding chapter I take a brief look at this subject.

Grice provides the following example:

> Suppose that A and B are talking about a mutual friend, C, who is now working in a bank. A asks B how C is getting on in his job, and B replies, "Oh quite well, I think; he likes his colleagues, and he hasn't been to prison yet." (Grice 1975, p. 43)

Grice distinguishes what B *said* in the last part of his sentence, which is simply that C has not been to prison yet, from what B *implied*, *suggested*, or *meant*, which might be that C is the sort of person likely to yield to the temptation provided by his occupation, that C's colleagues are really very unpleasant and treacherous people, or something else. These things go somewhat beyond the narrow and literal sort of meaning that we have been examining (what has been *said*); Grice gives this sort of meaning the name *implicature*.

Sometimes, Grice argues, "the conventional meaning of the words used will determine what is implicated, besides . . . what is said" (Grice 1975, p. 44). His example of this is:

> If I say (smugly), "He is an Englishman; he is, therefore, brave," I have certainly committed myself, by virtue of the meaning of my words, to its being the case that his being brave is a consequence of (follows from) his being an Englishman. But while I have said that he is an Englishman, and said that he is brave, I do not want to say that I have *said* . . . that it follows from

his being an Englishman that he is brave, though I have certainly indicated, and so implicated, that this is so. (Grice 1975, pp. 44–45)

Why is this supposed to be an implicature, rather than something that is literally said? The speaker does not say "His being brave is a consequence of his being an Englishman," but the word 'therefore' in what the speaker says shows nevertheless that he takes this to be the case. Compare (the overused example) 'Jones has stopped beating his wife'. This sentence does not say that Jones used to beat his wife, but in order that it be said appropriately, the speaker must surely believe that Jones used to beat his wife.

Grice thinks that this example differs from the first in that in the first the conventional meaning of the words alone does not determine what is implicated. Is it that C can be tempted to dishonesty or that C's colleagues are treacherous or something else? This can be determined (if at all) only from the context of utterance of this token, from the direction of the rest of the conversation of which this is a part. Thus Grice calls this variety of implicature *conversational implicature*.

The main body of Grice's article is devoted to a catalogue and explanation of what he takes to be the general principles of implicature. These turn out to be interesting and complex, but I do not go into them here. My concern is whether such a catalogue is really part of an explanation of meaning at all.

Metaphor

To get at this question, I concentrate on one of the great number of types of implicature Grice discusses, *metaphor*, which is defined as the

> application of name or descriptive term of phrase to an object or action to which it is not literally applicable (e.g., *a glaring error, food for thought, leave no stone unturned*. (*The Concise Oxford Dictionary*)

Grice explains the way metaphors work as follows:

> Examples like "You are the cream in my coffee" characteristically involve categorial falsity . . . ; so it cannot be *that* that such a speaker is trying to get across. The most likely supposition is that the speaker is attributing to his audience some feature or features in respect of which the audience resembles (more or less fancifully) the mentioned substance. (Grice 1975, p. 53)

Categorial falsity is putting something into the wrong category of things.

Thus we could turn any metaphor into a literal truth by inserting 'resembles' or 'is similar to' or something like that. Thus, when someone says 'Seymour is a pig,'' but Seymour is clearly to everyone a human, what is implicated is that Seymour is *like* a pig. In short, what a metaphor implicates, a simile says. (A simile is a ''reference to thing or person with explicit comparison to it of what is being discussed . . . *(the kingdom of heaven is like to a grain of mustard seed)*'' *(The Concise Oxford Dictionary)*.)

The view that metaphors implicate likenesses, however, is clearly not good enough as a detailed theory of metaphor. As Searle points out, everything is in some way or another like anything else, but only some metaphors work. 'This book is a trombone' has no clear metaphorical meaning, although it is clear that this book is like a trombone in several ways: Both can be picked up with one hand, both are smaller than a house, and so on. Why is it that metaphors suggest certain comparisons but not others? Nobody would take it, for example, that 'Seymour is a pig' is a metaphor suggesting that Seymour is like a pig in that both are warm-blooded mammals. Searle attempts to provide the principles for interpreting metaphors in general; I do not think he has succeeded. For example, one of his principles for finding out which comparisons are implicated is that ''it is a fact about our sensibility, whether culturally or naturally determined, that we just do perceive a connection'' between the object and that with which it is being compared (Searle 1979). I do not go into this matter any further, but note that there is something to be explained here.

The problem is compounded when we consider what might be called *open metaphors*. Some (closed) metaphors are comparatively specific in suggesting points of similarity between the objects they compare; for example, 'Igor is a gorilla' suggests fairly clearly that Igor is like a gorilla in being short, muscular, fierce, vicious, brutish, and thuglike. (This example illustrates a problem in explaining how metaphors work. We all know by now that real gorillas are usually quite gentle.) But compare Shakespeare's 'Juliet is the sun'. What sort of sun characteristics does Romeo here implicate Juliet has? Some probable answers perhaps include that Juliet, like the sun, is a source of vitality and warmth; perhaps also that her arrival, like the sun's, is the time when he (metaphorically?) awakens; perhaps also that in her (metaphorical) ''light'' he can (metaphorically) ''see'' what he could not otherwise. Sometimes it is difficult to decide whether or not a similarity is implicated, and it might be impossible to list *all* the similarities that might be discovered in this rich metaphor.

It is clear, however, that some similarities are *not* implicated: Romeo is not, for example, implicating that Juliet is a huge hot ball of gas. We know this because we have read the rest of the play; this metaphor, 'Juliet is the sun', is a matter of *conversational implicature*, in which the place of the metaphor in what surrounds it gives information (in ways that are hard to describe) about how to take it.

Having taken a brief look at the complexities of metaphorical "meaning," we are in position to face the problem of whether this is in fact a matter of meaning proper.

Davidson writes:

> The central mistake against which I shall be inveighing is the idea that a metaphor has, in addition to its literal sense or meaning, another sense or meaning. . . . I depend on the distinction between what words mean and what they are used to do. I think metaphor belongs exclusively to the domain of use. . . . Literal meaning and literal truth-conditions can be assigned to words and sentences apart from particular contexts of use. (Davidson 1978, p. 30–31)

One of Davidson's objections to the notion that there is a metaphorical meaning to words can be seen when we compare open and closed metaphors. A metaphor is closed to the extent that a clear and limited set of comparisons are, as a rule and regardless of context, implicated. Certain usages of what once might have been open metaphors by now have become so standard, so closed, that it is perfectly clear what characteristics they impute to their subject. For example, if I say about Seymour that he is a pig, it is perfectly clear what sort of characteristics I am attributing to him. Thus the meaning of 'pig' in 'Seymour is a pig' is conventionally fixed; there is no trouble in attributing a meaning to the word or in formulating exactly what the word means. The trouble here is that, insofar as the meaning is fixed, to that extent the usage ceases to be a metaphor. A dictionary offers as one sense of 'pig': "Greedy, dirty, sulky, obstinate, or annoying person" (*Concise Oxford Dictionary*). This has become a fixed meaning of the word, and therefore 'Seymour is a pig' turns out not to be a metaphor at all but rather a literal assertion (given one of the meanings of 'pig'). We can imagine, however, that this sort of use of 'pig' was once metaphorical; as its meaning became fixed, however, it stopped being a metaphor. Clearly, many meanings of words that we now take as quite literal started their lives as metaphors: Speaking of the mouth of a bottle, for example, was probably once metaphorical talk, but now this is a *dead metaphor*—just literal talk. To put the point briefly: If there really are semantic rules that fix exactly what characteristics are imputed by a particular predication, then that predication is not a metaphor at all.

Real metaphors, then, are open ones, ones in which there is no conventional semantic rule that specifies which characteristics are imputed to the object. But if there is no such rule, we cannot speak of a special *metaphorical meaning* of a word. Of course, producers of metaphors often have certain characteristics in mind when they produce open metaphors, and they often succeed in communicating these characteristics to the hearers; but this sort of association is what I have been insisting is mere *speaker's* meaning, not *sentence* meaning, and is not relevant to semantics.

Recall Grice's distinction between conventional implicature and conversational implicature. Conventional implicature relies only on the conventional meanings of the words uttered, whereas conversation implicature depends on the context of utterance. Grice classifies metaphor as a species of conversational implicature; this suggests that he agrees with Davidson, that what comparisons are implicated by a metaphor is not a matter of conventional (sentence) meaning but merely a matter of particular use. Thus there is no finding out exactly what comparisons a live metaphor implicates by consulting merely the semantic conventional meanings of the words; we need to consider in addition the probable intentions of the speaker, and we find out about these by inferring from the context of talk, from the drift of the rest of the conversation.

And Searle agrees:

> Many writers on the subject try to locate the metaphorical element of a metaphorical utterance in the sentence of expressions uttered. They think that there are two kinds of sentence meaning, literal and metaphorical. However, sentences and words have only the meanings that they have. Strictly speaking, whenever we talk about the metaphorical meaning of a word, expression, or sentence, we are talking about what a speaker might utter it to mean, in a way that departs from what the word, expression, or sentence actually means. We are, therefore, talking about possible speaker's intentions. (Searle 1979)

With so much agreement here, it might seem best simply to leave this issue alone! I however, raise a couple of questions about the common position here and consider some points of disagreement between Davidson and Searle.

When Is Something Part of Meaning?

Although both Searle and Davidson insist that meaning is a matter of truth conditions, they disagree nevertheless. In the given quote Davidson says, "Literal meaning and literal truth-conditions can be assigned to words and sentences apart from particular contexts of use." But Searle argues that literal sentence tokens determine a set of truth conditions relative to the context of utterance and to a set of assumptions. There are many different kinds of examples of this; an easy one is provided by indexicals. The truth conditions for 'Today is Friday' depend not only on the meanings of those words but also on the day of the week on which it is uttered. Another sort of example is provided by words such as 'tall'; a person can be described as tall even though she is shorter than a giraffe that could correctly be called 'short'. Thus the truth conditions for 'tall' depend not only on the meaning of the word but on the kind of thing that is being described, on the context of the utterance of a token. Nevertheless, Searle insists that the truth conditions for bits of language—their sentence meaning—is a conventional matter. Compare this to Grice, who appears to share Davidson's position that, insofar as the meaning of what is said depends on context, it is not a conventional matter.

Of course, Davidson is aware that convention sometimes provides only a function from context to reference or to truth conditions of a predicate. Where, then, does the disagreement lie? Perhaps we have here only a verbal disagreement about what should be called 'meaning'. Davidson and Searle (and Grice) all agree that the particular reference of 'today' depends on the day of utterance and that that convention supplies only the function that determines what the reference in 'today' is, given as argument a particular day of utterance.

But then it is hard to see where we would draw the line between what is provided by the semantics of a language and what is provided by other regularities; and it is hard to see why the open-ended implicatures of a particular token of metaphor should not be seen as a feature of meaning. After all, they are a function of the conventions for literal meaning of the word plus the conventions for creating and understanding metaphors. To some extent there are general rules for creating and understanding metaphors; why not count them as semantic rules as well? The chief reason that Davidson, Grice, and Searle seem to have for ruling them out is that the word types alone do not determine the metaphorical meaning: One needs to consider context as well. But this is true even of literal language.

Although Searle and Davidson agree that the truth conditions and reference functions of language are a matter of semantics, they disagree about whether use potential is semantic. As we saw in chapter 9, Searle thinks that meaning and use are essentially connected; in his view meaning is (in a nutshell) conventional use potential. He disagrees, then, with Davidson, who wants to draw the boundaries of meaning much more narrowly to explain the meaning of a sentence type entirely with regard to matters of reference and truth; for Davidson what can be done with a sentence is another matter altogether.

Searle does, however, recognize the difference between speaker's meaning (what a particular speaker intends to use a bit of language for) and sentence meaning (the conventional use potential that is an objective fact of the language). He argues that metaphorical "meanings" are speaker's meanings, not real (sentence) meanings. He thus agrees with Davidson that there are only literal meanings: Metaphorical "meanings" are not meanings.

Perhaps this is an inconsistency in Searle's view. After all, he devotes most of the article we have been discussing to attempting to describe the conventional rules whereby apt metaphors are constructed, used, and understood. He must think, then, that metaphorical uses of language are hardly idiosyncratic, hardly matters of accidents of individual intention. If there are such general principles for metaphors, then these would seem to be just as much meaning rules of language as rules for promising or warning.

Davidson, however, argues against metaphorical meaning from a more self-consistent position. Because no use conventions are semantic and because the rules for metaphor are use conventions, metaphor rules are not rules of meaning.

Who is right? In a sense this question might be seen as another of the familiar empty sort: It does not matter, really, whether we decide to use the word 'meaning' to include conventional use potential or to restrict it to matters of reference and truth. But perhaps Searle's position on this might seem a bit more plausible. Learning what the contents of a language mean is, after all, more than learning reference and truth. In addition, it involves learning the conventional *uses* of language: asking questions, warning, promising, informing, etc. It seems, then, a bit more intuitive to include the facts about the conventional use potential of language among the facts of meaning.

In this book I have introduced the two main traditions in contemporary philosophy of language: the Searlian investigation into linguistic use conventions and the Davidsonian approach, which concentrates on reference and truth. Although philosophers disagree about which is more central to understanding meaning, they must admit that both approaches have discovered a good deal about the general nature of language and that significant controversies to be settled and discoveries to be made remain in each area. Much more has been said about everything treated in this book. Suggestions for further reading follow almost every chapter. These readings have been chosen so that, having read this book, you will have the background necessary to cope with them; they take you far beyond this introduction, where I hope you will go.

Suggested Readings

Black, Max. 1962. "Metaphor," in his *Models and Metaphors*. Ithaca: Cornell University Press, 25–47.

Davidson, Donald. 1978. "What metaphors mean," in *On Metaphor*, Sheldon Sacks, ed. Chicago: University of Chicago Press, 29–45.
Reprinted in [5].

Grice, H. P. 1975. "Logic and conversation," in *Syntax and Semantics*, Peter Cole and Jerry L. Morgan, eds. New York: Academic Press, vol. 3, 41–58.
Conversational implicature. Reprinted in [5].

Searle, John, 1979. "Metaphor," in *Metaphor and Thought*, Andrew Ortony, ed. Cambridge: Cambridge University Press, 92–123.
Reprinted in [5].

Anthologies Cited

1. Davidson, Donald, and Gilbert Harmon, eds. 1972. *Semantics of Natural Language*. Boston: Reidel.
2. Feigl, Herbert, and Wilfrid Sellars, eds. 1949. *Readings in Philosophical Analysis*. East Norwalk: Appleton-Century-Crofts.
3. Lehrer, Adrienne, and Keith Lehrer, eds. 1970. *Theory of Meaning*. Englewood Cliffs: Prentice-Hall.
4. Linsky, Leonard, ed. 1952. *Semantics and the Philosophy of Language*. Champaign: University of Illinois Press.
5. Martinich, A. P., ed. 1985. *The Philosophy of Language*. Oxford: Oxford University Press.
6. Nagel, Ernest, and Richard B. Brandt, eds. 1965. *Meaning and Knowledge*. New York: Harcourt, Brace & World.
7. Olshewsky, Thomas M., ed. 1969. *Problems in the Philosophy of Language*. New York: Holt, Rinehart & Winston.
8. Parkinson, G. H. R., ed. 1968. *The Theory of Meaning*. Oxford: Oxford University Press.
9. Rosenberg, Jay F., and Charles Travis, eds. 1971. *Readings in the Philosophy of Language*. Englewood Cliffs: Prentice-Hall.
10. Schwartz, Stephen P., ed. 1977. *Naming, Necessity, and Natural Kinds*. Ithaca: Cornell University Press.
11. Searle, J. R., ed. 1971. *The Philosophy of Language*. Oxford: Oxford University Press.

Index